Defining Environmental Justice

Defining Environmental Justice

Theories, Movements, and Nature

David Schlosberg

OXFORD
UNIVERSITY PRESS

OXFORD
UNIVERSITY PRESS

Great Clarendon Street, Oxford ox2 6DP

Oxford University Press is a department of the University of Oxford.
It furthers the University's objective of excellence in research, scholarship,
and education by publishing worldwide in

Oxford New York

Auckland Cape Town Dar es Salaam Hong Kong Karachi
Kuala Lumpur Madrid Melbourne Mexico City Nairobi
New Delhi Shanghai Taipei Toronto

With offices in

Argentina Austria Brazil Chile Czech Republic France Greece
Guatemala Hungary Italy Japan Poland Portugal Singapore
South Korea Switzerland Thailand Turkey Ukraine Vietnam

Oxford is a registered trademark of Oxford University Press
in the UK and in certain other countries

Published in the United States
by Oxford University Press Inc., New York

British Library Cataloguing in Publication Data
Data available

Library of Congress Cataloging in Publication Data
Data available

Typeset by SPI Publisher Services, Pondicherry, India
Printed by the MPG Books Group in the UK

978–0–19–928629–4 (Hbk.)
978–0–19–956248–0 (Pbk.)

1 3 5 7 9 10 8 6 4 2

For my family, Sheila, Mira, and Valerie

Preface

'How can you write a book on environmental justice without defining what you mean by justice?' That was the question, asked after I finished my first book on the US environmental justice movement, which turned into a challenge that has had me thinking and writing about this topic for the past seven years. Initially, my response was that it was easy to write such a book. My focus in that first work was on the innovative political structure and demands of the environmental justice movement, not about justice per se; additionally, I did not see it as proper to offer my own definition—that should come from the movement itself. But, of course, how one defines the 'justice' of environmental justice was an important question, and one that just would not leave me alone. And as I started to examine the issues in depth, the question of defining environmental justice brought me to related questions. How *do* movements for environmental justice define the concept of justice? Do different groups define the concept in varied ways? Have movement groups articulated notions of justice that go beyond traditional distributive conceptions, as many political theorists have in the past two decades? Is there a major difference between the definition of environmental justice (justice on environmental issues among the human population), and ecological justice (justice between humans and the rest of the natural world)? Can we have multiple notions of justice in various groups connected to the same movement? Can the language used in environmental justice movements also be applied to conceptions of ecological justice? And how can justice not only be conceived, but also implemented?

So, one good question led to many more, and my hope is that, with this work, I have begun to provide a few answers. In some ways the goals are simple. One of my tasks was to explore how movements that organize around environmental justice define the term themselves. In what follows, I argue that movements do not have a single definition of justice; in fact, they articulate many, just as justice theorists have been doing.

Justice is about distribution, but it is also about individual and community recognition, participation, and functioning. Groups emphasize different notions of justice, on different issues, in various contexts; there is a flexible, heterogeneous, and plural discourse of justice. My point here is not to argue that theorists should blindly adopt notions of justice simply because activists define it a certain way; but I do think that academics have to listen to such movements and learn from them—and, yes, maybe even incorporate movement definitions into an academic approach.

The other major task here goes beyond the articulations of most of the groups that use environmental justice as an organizing theme, and into the question of how we do justice not just within the human species on environmental issues, but across the species divide as well. Here I explore whether it is possible to use this expanded set of justice discourses—on distribution, but also on recognition, participation, and functioning— when discussing relationships of justice between the human and non-human realms. My argument is that in both environmental and ecological justice, we can use a similar set of concepts, tools, and languages; indeed, the same conceptions can be applied to both environmental and ecological matters. Realizing this may help us get beyond the divide between environmental and ecological justice, and into a practice of recognition, expanding decision-making, and providing the capacities necessary for individual and community functioning to human and nonhuman alike.

I have benefited from the opportunity to give a number of public talks that eventually became part of this book in numerous venues, including Keele University (twice), the London School of Economics and Political Science, University of Colorado at Colorado Springs, the Intertribal Council of Arizona, Australian National University, Griffith University, and here at Northern Arizona University. I also appreciate the audiences at a number of conferences, starting with one on *Moral and Political Reasoning in Environmental Practice* organized by Andrew Light and Avner de-Shalit at Oxford in 1999, and continuing with presentations at the International Political Science Association meeting in Quebec in 2000, the European Consortium for Political Research Joint Sessions in Grenoble 2001 and Granada 2005, the ECPR general conference in Marburg in 2003, the American Political Science Association meeting in Washington 2005, and a conference on *Globalization and the Environmental Justice Movement* at the University of Arizona in 2004. The Western Political Science Association has a robust section on environmental political theory, and I have subjected my colleagues there to iterations of this research in both Long Beach, CA in 2002 and Oakland, CA in 2005.

I thank the audiences at all of these venues, including John Barry, Brian Baxter, Derek Bell, Peter Cannavo, Bill Chaloupka, Peter Christoff, Andy Dobson, Brian Doherty, Tim Doyle, John Dryzek, Robyn Eckersley, Adam Fagan, Graeme Hayes, Michael Howes, Patricia Keilbach, Breena Holland, Christian Hunold, Andrew Light, Ian Lowe, James Meadowcroft, John Meyer, Peter Newell, Jouni Paavola, Alex Plows, Chella Rajan, Chris Rootes, Paul Routledge, Adam Simpson, Kim Smith, Cassandra Star, and Kee Warner. Once again, my own bad memory and faulty recordkeeping have left many deserving commenters off of this list; to them I offer both thanks and apologies. I must also thank colleagues at my all-too-brief year at the London School of Economics—in particular John Charvet, Cecile Fabre, David Held, and Paul Kelly—and at my Fulbright-sponsored sabbatical at the Australian National University—John Dryzek, Simon Niemeyer, Kersty Hobson, Bob Goodin, and Val Plumwood—for various types of feedback, advice, and support. As always, I thank my students as well, for their reactions to the ideas from this book presented in the classroom.

One must always give thanks to the anonymous referees, though, for one reason or another, not all of them remain anonymous. Doug Torgerson deserves special thanks not only for his general advice, but also for pushing me (on more than one occasion) to engage with the work of John Rodman. And I am thoroughly indebted to Avner de-Shalit for the time and effort put into commenting on both my original proposal and the draft manuscript; his insights have been particularly helpful on a number of troublesome issues in the text. My editor at Oxford, Dominic Byatt, has offered me a great combination of support and patience, which is, as always, much appreciated. This is the standard point in a preface when the author graciously claims responsibility for all of the errors that remain in the text, but my 9-year-old daughter has been relentless in her insistence that I finish this book ('You're not done with that book YET?' 'When are you going to be finished with that BOOK?'), so I am inclined to share the blame for any remaining mistakes with her.

Northern Arizona University was generous enough to offer me summer research support to work one of the initial chapters of this book. The Australian–American Fulbright Association awarded me a sabbatical stay with the Social and Political Theory Program at ANU—a phenomenal experience for which I am very appreciative. In particular, I offer hearty thanks to Mark Darby of the Fulbright Association for his support (and great beach suggestions). The research referred to in Chapter 8 regarding electronic participation in environmental decision-making was funded by the National Science Foundation's now defunct program on the Social Dimensions of Engineering, Science, and Technology (SES-0322662); needless to say, my conclusions and recommendations do not necessarily reflect the position of the NSF.

None of the help of colleagues and friends noted above really would have mattered, or helped me to complete this project, if it were not for the support of my family—my wife Sheila, and my two girls Mira and (the above-mentioned) Valerie. Of course I thank them for putting up with lost weekends and late nights at the office, but much more importantly I thank them for rejuvenating me, teaching me, and for filling my life with love, laughter, learning, beauty, and adventure. My desire for justice is not simply academic; it may sound cliché, but it is true: my girls drive and inspire me to be a better person, dad, partner, and citizen of the earth. For that, I dedicate this book to them.

Acknowledgments

I have previously published a number of articles and chapters that have been thoroughly reworked for various parts of this book. My first attempt at examining the definition of justice in the US environmental justice movement was published as 'The Justice of Environmental Justice: Reconciling Equity, Recognition, and Participation in a Political Movement', in A. Light and A. de-Shalit (eds.), *Moral and Political Reasoning in Environmental Practice*. Cambridge, MA: MIT Press, 2003. I began the examination of environmental justice in global environmental movements in 'Reconceiving Environmental Justice: Global Movements and Political Theories.' *Environmental Politics* 13(3): 517–40 (2004) [also published in J. Paavola and I. Lowe (eds.), *Environmental Values in the Globalizing World: Nature, Justice and Governance*. London: Routledge (2005)]. A chapter on 'Environmental and Ecological Justice: Theory and Practice in the U.S.', in R. Eckersley and J. Barry (eds.), *The State and the Global Ecological Crisis*. Cambridge, MA: MIT Press, 2005 was an earlier attempt to explore the role of the state in responding to environmental justice claims. Finally, some of the material in Chapters 7 and 8, on pluralism and engagement, first appeared in a piece on 'The Pluralist Imagination', in J. Dryzek, A. Philips, and B. Honig (eds.), *Oxford Handbook of Political Theory*. Oxford: Oxford University Press, 2006.

Contents

Part I

Justice in Theory and Practice

1

Defining Environmental Justice

What, exactly, is the 'justice' of environmental justice? What do activists and movements mean when they employ the term? And what is the relationship between environmental justice, which addresses environmental risks within human communities, and ecological justice, focused on the relationship between those human communities and the rest of the natural world? Do those who speak of environmental justice, and those who call for ecological justice, understand the concept of 'justice' in similar ways? Those are my central questions, and the basic task of this book is to explore what is meant by justice in discussions of both environmental and ecological justice.

Activists and academics within the environmental justice movement in the USA and globally have been discussing the meaning of justice for two decades. Likewise, theorists concerned with doing justice to nature have put forth numerous accounts of ecological justice. I certainly do not claim to be the first down this trail. But as someone who has studied both the movements and theories, I have found these discussions inadequate and somewhat frustrating—there has always seemed to be something missing in them. Actually, I see two major gaps that need to be addressed.

First, while the justice literature in political theory has expanded over the past few decades, the innovations there have rarely been applied to the environmental justice movement. For years, justice studies were defined by, and proceeded from, the theories of John Rawls. They focused on a conception of justice defined solely as the distribution of goods in a society, and the best principles by which to distribute those goods. I have no criticism of justice conceived in distributional terms like this; not only does such an approach make sense theoretically, but, importantly, many social movements also defined justice in terms of what their constituents got—and did not get—in a given society. As I describe, many of the

3

defining arguments of the environmental justice movement, for example, were all about distributional patterns that were violations of any number of distributive principles of justice.

The problem that I see is *not* that distributive theories of justice cannot be applied to environmental justice. Rather, the issue is that justice theory has developed a number of additional ways of understanding the processes of justice and injustice—and these developments have rarely appeared in the literature on the environmental justice movement. Authors such as Iris Young, Nancy Fraser, and Axel Honneth argue that while justice must be concerned with classic issues of distribution, it must also address the processes that *construct* maldistribution; they focus on individual and social recognition as key elements of attaining justice. Central here is not only the psychological component of recognition, but also the status of those less well-off in distributional schemes. In addition, Amartya Sen and Martha Nussbaum have developed a theory of justice that focuses on the capacities necessary for individuals to fully function in their chosen lives. The focus is not just on the distribution of goods, but also more particularly on how those goods are transformed into the flourishing of individuals and communities. The approach gives ethical significance to this functioning and flourishing, and finds harm—injustice in fact—in the limiting of them. Capabilities theory examines what is needed to transform primary goods (if they are available) into a fully functioning life—and what it is that interrupts that process. In addition, contemporary theories of justice also often have a component of procedural or participatory justice. For Fraser, participation is the third leg of a triad that also includes distribution and recognition; for both Sen and Nussbaum, participation is a key political capability, necessary for individuals to ensure functioning. In essence, many contemporary theories of justice refer to a standpoint that is broader than just how things are distributed. This standpoint includes our intuitions and theories about recognition, participation, and the way people function—they also relate as much to *groups* as to individuals.

Yet for all of these developments in justice theory, very little has been applied to the environmental justice movement. Most discussions of environmental justice focus on maldistribution—the fact that poor communities, indigenous communities, and communities of color get fewer environmental goods, more environmental bads, and less environmental protection. Some examiners of the movement and the concept of environmental justice have emphasized the importance of procedural justice and participation (Lake 1996; Shrader-Frechette 2002). And a number have focused on issues of recognition, while not directly referring to the theoretical literature; these examine the cultural and racial barriers to individuals and communities getting a just distribution (see, e.g. Pulido 1996 and most of Bullard's work). However, there has been no thorough and comprehensive exploration of environmental justice movements with the goal of examining the conceptions and discourses of justice that they use. The argument here is that movements use a wide range of conceptions of justice, and we can find arguments in those movements for distribution, recognition, participation, and capabilities. The environmental justice movement supplies ample evidence that all of these conceptions of justice are used in practice, and that, in fact, a comprehensive understanding of the way that movements define the 'justice' of environmental justice must include all of these discourses.

It should be no surprise that such diverse definitions exist within groups and movements that organize around a conception of environmental justice. Many recent theorists of justice—Young, Fraser, Sen, and Nussbaum, for example—explicitly note the influence of social movements on their own definitions. I argue, however, that movements add more to the justice discourse than many of these theorists account for, and there are two points in particular that justice theorists should pay attention to. For one, groups and movements often employ multiple conceptions of justice simultaneously, and accept both the ambiguity and the plurality that come with such a heterogeneous discourse. Second, and crucially, movements also apply conceptions of justice not only to individuals, but to groups and communities as well. Here, movements have no problem stepping beyond the almost unanimous consensus of justice theorists that definitions of justice apply to individuals alone. Environmental justice movements explore, represent, and demand justice—fair distribution, recognition, capabilities, and functioning—for communities as well as individuals. These movements are most often broad, plural, and inclusive; likewise, their definitions and discourses of justice range from those based on individual distributive complaints to those based on the survival of community functioning.

So the distance—and relationship—between justice theory and environmental justice movements is the first gap I hope to span in this book. I use the first to explore the latter, and use the latter to expand upon the first. My hope is to bring empirical evidence and activist definitions to the attention of theorists of justice for their serious consideration, and to offer activists and movements a theoretical overview of the positions and demands they express.

The second gap that I explore in this book is the disconnect between environmental justice on the one hand and ecological justice on the other. The vast majority of work on environmental justice does not concern itself with the natural world outside human impacts, and most work on ecological justice does not pay attention to issues raised by movements for environmental justice. There are, certainly, exceptions. Dobson's work (1998, 1999) and Low and Gleeson (1998) attempt to bridge environmental and ecological justice, and there are interesting collections that broach the topic (e.g. Cooper and Palmer 1995). But the fact is that most of the literature on environmental justice exists independently from the literature on ecological justice—most environmental justice work (e.g. Cole and Foster 2001; Bullard 2005) does not address doing justice to nature, while most ecological justice writing (Baxter 2005; Wenz 1988) focuses on just that. I want to explore the important differences between environmental and ecological justice, but also speak to the potential of using the same language(s) of justice in addressing both sorts of issues and relationships. I pay particular attention to movement groups that bridge this gap in their literature and actions, such as indigenous environmental groups and movements for food security and climate justice. My central question is whether we can apply the same conceptions of justice, and the same broad discourse of justice, to both sets of issues—environmental risks in human populations and the relationship between human communities and nonhuman nature. One major claim of the book is that we can draw parallels between the application of notions of justice as distribution, recognition, capability, and participation in both the human and nonhuman realms. I argue that a broad set of theoretical concerns, notions, and tools can be applied to both environmental and ecological justice.

The point of this second task is really twofold. First, as noted above, it simply seems important to examine the potential of the same theoretical discourses of justice as they apply to different issues in environmental politics. Academics and activists alike should not be talking past one another on a political discourse as salient and encompassing as justice. But, related, I am also interested in the possibility of illuminating a broad discourse of environmental and ecological justice that can frame arguments in ways that advocates for both can relate to. I fully agree with what Taylor (2000: 562) concluded in her examination of the framing of the concept of environmental justice in the USA. Taylor claims that the concept of environmental justice bridged a number of issues, and linked numerous problems in one frame. As such, it was effective because it did not attempt to create a new discourse from scratch, but instead incorporated highly salient issues into a broader frame that many could identify with. In being a broad, plural, and inclusive discourse, environmental justice as an organizing frame was quite successful. What I am suggesting is that we extend that framework even further, to include the conception of ecological justice as well.

If both environmental and ecological justice concerns can be addressed using the broad language of distribution, recognition, capabilities, and procedural justice, then a larger frame can be established that could link both sets of concerns. The model here, in a way, is Rachel Carson's *Silent Spring* (1962); there, Carson was able to bring together these two previously disconnected environmental concerns—that for the natural world and the animals that inhabit it, and the concern for human health and industrial impacts on individuals and communities. Carson helped to inspire a larger and more diverse environmental movement by illustrating the connections between the issues, and so broadening the discourse beyond one or the other concern. I certainly do not claim to approach the talent or eloquence of Carson; my point is only that I am inspired by her accomplishment of expanding an inclusive conception of the 'environment'. I see the same sort of potential to bring together environmental and ecological justice into a larger, broader, more encompassing discourse.

Now this approach goes against the arguments of other recent academic examiners of environmental justice. Dobson (1998, 2003) saw little overlap between the social justice community and those arguing for environmental sustainability. Dobson, however, only looked at notions of distributive justice in coming to his conclusion; if justice were to be defined much more broadly, then both environmental and ecological justice communities might share a common, expansive, discourse of justice. More problematically, Getches and Pellow (2002) insist on *restricting* the operational definition of environmental justice, and limiting the types of communities that could make environmental justice claims. While they claim pragmatic reasoning here—keeping the movement agenda manageable—their advice goes against the practice of the movement and against a thorough understanding of what the justice of environmental justice is. Such an approach limits the ability of actors to make connections with other movements and concerns. Similarly, Pellow and Brulle (2005: 16) insist that environmental justice activists 'must bound and limit the purview of their concerns. If instead they seek to explain every problem at the intersection of development and social inequality in terms of environmental injustice, surely their movement will lose its explanatory (and mobilizing) power.'

On the contrary, the following work makes exactly the opposite argument. The proposition here is that a more thorough definition of justice—one that encompasses the expressed concerns of environmental justice groups, the conception of justice to the nonhuman world, and the recent contributions of justice theory—can offer a broadly accessible, plural, and workable frame. I am not arguing for a single, all-inclusive, holistic theory of environmental and ecological justice; rather, the point is to expand the discourse of justice, and legitimize the use of a variety of tools and notions as they apply to various cases. Issues of inequality, recognition, participation, and the larger question of the capabilities and functioning of individuals and communities—human and nonhuman—can come together in a broad and inclusive discourse that can strengthen the explanatory (and mobilizing) power of the movements that use the language of environmental and ecological justice.

I proceed in four parts. In Part I, in Chapter 2, I explore recent theories of justice, focusing on those that move beyond a sole focus on the traditional distributive paradigm. Particular attention is paid to various theories of recognition, and I defend recognition as a distinct element of justice against theorists who insist that it can be collapsed within a distributive framework. I also explore the capabilities approach of Sen and Nussbaum (including some of the differences between them), and argue how each of these elements of justice can be seen at both the individual and group level. Ultimately the argument is that a thorough understanding and approach to justice requires us to see the linkages between distribution, recognition, capabilities, and participation.

In Part II, I examine how movements for environmental justice define the concept of justice. Chapter 3 looks specifically at the environmental justice movement in the USA, and Chapter 4 examines global movements that use environmental justice as an organizing frame. There are some key differences in the way environmental justice is mobilized in the USA, as compared to global movements. Groups in the USA self-identify as 'environmental justice' organizations, while in a number of global environmental movements—on issues such as globalization, food security, indigenous rights, and climate justice—environmental justice is incorporated as one organizing principle or demand among many. Groups in the USA are also less likely than these global movements to make connections between environmental and ecological justice. In both the USA and global movements, however, groups use a wide variety of conceptions of justice;

justice is understood in multiple and interlinking ways, and is applied to both individuals and, importantly, to communities.

Part III turns to understandings of ecological justice—justice to the nonhuman part of the natural world. Chapter 5 is an overview, and critique, of many existing distributional theories of ecological justice. After a discussion of some of the key difficulties identified by liberal theorists in applying the concept of justice to the natural world, I examine a variety of theories that attempt to expand liberal and distributional notions of justice to future generations of humans and to nonhuman nature. Here, I also address the lack of attention in much of this literature to either movements or recent developments in justice theory. I discuss why most academic conceptions of ecological justice based in distribution are crucial, but yet incomplete and inadequate in their definitions and prescriptions. Chapter 6 turns to the potential of developing a theory of ecological justice that moves beyond a sole concern with the distributive paradigm. The central focus is on bringing conceptions of the recognition of nature, and of capabilities for the nonhuman world, into a broad and comprehensive understanding of ecological justice. The point is not to develop a singular holistic and universal theory of ecological justice, but rather to illustrate the potential of various discourses, concepts, and frames as they can be extended to individual animals, communities, and natural systems.

Part IV explores some of the implications of my findings. Chapter 7 addresses the difficult question of how to reconcile the multiple and multifaceted notions of justice that exist simultaneously in environmental and ecological justice. Rather than insisting on a singular, overarching, and static definition of justice, the point is that we really need a plurality of themes to apply to particular cases as the context requires. I argue for a pluralist approach that allows for unity among different concerns and movements while avoiding the uniformity that is so often debilitating in constructing broad discourses and movements. Finally, I conclude on a pragmatic note, with a chapter on how environmental and ecological justice can be applied in both state political practice and the public realm. This conclusion explores practices of ecological reflexivity and political engagement, and suggestions for democratic and institutional transformations, which can help us implement a broad and pluralist notion of environmental and ecological justice.

2

Distribution and Beyond: Conceptions of Justice in Contemporary Theory and Practice

How are we to begin our definition of environmental justice? I start with an overview of the conceptions that have been generated by political theorists over the past few decades. Admittedly, however, my approach is not representative of the literature in justice theory written in that time; to do so would be to focus about 95 percent of my efforts on conceptions of distributional justice. Rather, my discussion begins, only briefly, within that familiar realm. The point here is not to attempt a comprehensive or even basic overview of theories of just distribution; many others dedicated to the approach have done so quite well. More simply, my aim is to lay out the basic concerns of distributional justice, in order to contrast them with the concerns of those that attempt to either refocus, or expand upon, the distributive paradigm. In particular, the conception of recognition as an independent and significant component of justice is examined in some detail, with a focus not on *replacing* distribution, but instead on exploring the possibility of *combining* numerous concerns into a broad and multi-faceted approach to justice. I also examine the role of participation and procedural justice within a larger conception of justice. Finally, I turn to capabilities theory, which can be seen as a link between distributive, procedural, and recognition-based conceptions of justice.

One key problem with contemporary liberal theories of justice is that recognition, and its link to both distribution and to participation, is simply under theorized. In the thirty-five plus years since Rawls's opus *A Theory of Justice*, we have seen a micro-industry within political theory dedicated to justice as fairness, impartiality, models of distribution, and the like—but very, very little on what even Rawls admits is key to the distributional concern: respect and recognition. That recognition is an element of justice should be uncontroversial; that it has been so neglected should be admitted and addressed. One simple claim of this book is that justice, in political practice, is articulated and understood as a balance of numerous interlinked elements of distribution, recognition, participation, and capability. While later chapters explore this empirical reality in some detail, the premise here is, unfortunately, that the academic study of justice is not quite so balanced. The point, however, is not to dismiss distribution, or to call for a move *beyond* distribution; it is simply to put it in its place alongside other components of a comprehensive understanding of justice.

Justice as Distribution

In the past nearly four decades of the literature of political theory, justice has been defined almost exclusively as a question of equity in the distribution of social goods. Brian Barry (1999) insists that the concept of justice only applies where some distributive consideration comes into play; other issues are merely questions of right and wrong. Justice, in this reading, is fully contained within the set of rules that govern our distributional relationship. As Brighouse (2004: 2) claims in his recent survey of theories of justice, the 'fundamental question is this: how, and to what end, should a just society distribute the various benefits (resources, opportunities, and freedoms) it produces, and the burdens (costs, risks, and unfreedoms) required to maintain it?' The subject of justice, then, is the very basic structure of a society; it defines how we distribute various rights, goods, and liberties, and how we define and regulate social and economic equality and inequality.

John Rawls's classic *A Theory of Justice*, for example, defines justice as 'a standard whereby the distributive aspects of the basic structure of society are to be assessed'. Justice, then, defines 'the appropriate division of social advantages' (Rawls 1971: 9–10). Rawls's initial task, and his primary innovation, is the development a fair way of *developing* such principles of distribution. For Rawls, in order to develop a right theory of justice, we are to step into an imaginary 'original position', behind what he calls a veil of ignorance, to a place where we would not know our own strengths and weaknesses or our own place in the grand social scheme of things. Without knowing one's station in life, or where one would wind up after developing principles of justice from an impartial position, Rawls argues that we could develop a particularly fair notion of justice that everyone could agree with. With such an impartial position in mind, Rawls offers two basic, defensible, principles of justice: everyone would have the same political rights, and the distribution of economic and social inequality in a society should benefit everyone, including the least well-off. The whole point of Rawls's notion of 'justice as fairness' is justice as just distribution—or, more properly, the rules that govern a just distribution of social, political, and economic goods and bads.

Rawls represents the focal point and fount of liberal justice theory: fair distributions away from any substantive agreement on what we each believe as 'good'—pictures of the good life. Barry (1995, 2005) has taken the lead, following Rawls, on this notion of justice; his central argument reiterates that we should agree on the *rules* of distributive justice while remaining impartial to different notions of the good life individuals have. This line of justice theory represents an impartial, proceduralist approach, and is probably the most popular conception of justice in the academy. Such an approach differs from more substantive and consequentialist theories of distributive justice—for example, a utilitarian conception that focuses more on the specific outcomes of the distributive process, or substantive notions that flow from a particular idea of what a good society should look like. Other distributive theories in the past three decades focus more specifically on what is to be distributed (goods, rights), and what the principles governing those proposed distributions should be (e.g. need, desert, or entitlement). Overall, the point is that such variations on the distributive approach to justice have been the dominant discourse in justice theory over the past few decades.

Again, my task here is not to expound on the various theories of distributive justice; rather it is simply to note the focus on distribution in justice theory.[1] Rawls not only blazed the trail, but also left a series of new trailheads in his wake. In all of these approaches, the central conceptual framework of a theory of justice is focused on how and what gets distributed in the construction of a just society.

Justice as Recognition—Definitions

But such a focus has not been uniformly accepted, and some recent theorists have veered from this central path. Numerous challenges have been made to the traditional distributional way in which the concept of justice has been approached in the political theory literature. Beginning in 1990 with the publication of Iris Young's *Justice and the Politics of Difference*, and continuing most forcefully with the work of Nancy Fraser (1997, 1998, 2000, 2001), the distributional approach—or more specifically the sole emphasis on distribution without an examination of the *underlying* causes of maldistribution—has been challenged. For these theorists and others, one of the key inadequacies of theories of liberal justice is its singular focus on the development of, and debate around, ideal and fair processes for the distribution of goods and benefits. Moreover, these critiques of distributional theory are thoroughly influenced by the real world of political injustice, rather than the imagined realm of an original position. With the examination of real injustices as the focus, these critics argue that there is much more to injustice than maldistribution, especially when one begins to look at exactly who is left out of actual distributions.

Recognition is the central concern here, as both Young and Fraser—along with other theorists such as Honneth (1995, 2001) and Taylor (1994)—contend that a *lack* of recognition in the social and political realms, demonstrated by various forms of insults, degradation, and devaluation at both the individual and cultural level, inflicts damage to oppressed individuals and communities in the political and cultural realms. This is an injustice not only because it constrains people and does them harm, but also because it is the foundation for distributive injustice. Rawls and other liberal theorists focus on ideal schemes and processes of justice in liberal societies; both Young and Fraser explore one of the key *real* impediments to such schemes, and how they can be addressed through recognition.

Young (1990) made the earliest direct and forceful challenge to theories of justice based solely on issues of distribution, criticizing those theories for focusing overwhelmingly on schemes of distribution, while ignoring the social context in which unjust distributions exist. Simply put, Young insisted that distributional patterns happen for a reason, and the reality of domination and oppression must be taken as the starting point for any thorough and pragmatic theory of justice. Young argues that while theories of distributive justice offer models and procedures by which distribution may be improved, none of them thoroughly examines the social, cultural, symbolic, and institutional conditions underlying poor distributions in the first place. The critique is not simply one against the various models of distributive justice, but of the way distributive theories simply take goods as static, rather than due to the outcome of various social and institutional relations. The claim here is straightforward: 'While distributional issues are crucial to a satisfactory conclusion of justice, it is a mistake to reduce social justice to distribution' (p. 1). In moving toward justice, issues of distribution are essential but incomplete. Injustice is not solely based on inequitable distribution or, more to the point, there are key reasons why some people get more than others.

Young asks not only what distribution looks like, but also—crucially— what *determines* poor distributions. Part of the problem of injustice, and part of the reason for unjust distribution, is a lack of recognition of group difference. Distributional injustice, she argues, comes directly out of social structures, cultural beliefs, and institutional contexts. If distributional differences are constituted, in part, by social, cultural, economic, and political processes, any examination of justice needs to include discussions of the structures, practices, rules, norms, language, and symbols that mediate social relations (1990: 22). Young begins with the argument that 'where social group differences exist and some groups are privileged while others are oppressed, social justice requires explicitly acknowledging and attending to those group differences in order to undermine oppression' (p. 3). The central question regarding distributional justice is not, in the first instance, 'what is the best model for distribution', but instead 'how does the current maldistribution get produced?' For Young, distribution is not the only problem; a concept of justice needs to focus more on the elimination of institutionalized domination and oppression, particularly of those who represent difference and remain un-, mis-, or malrecognized.

Likewise, Nancy Fraser's project has been focused on demonstrating that justice requires attention to *both* distribution and recognition; justice is, at least, 'bivalent' in this sense. Maldistribution and misrecognition are distinct, separate forms and experiences of injustice, though they are often linked in practice. Fraser argues that culture is a legitimate and necessary terrain of struggle—a sight of justice in its own right, yet also deeply tied to economic inequality (2000: 109). For Fraser, misrecognition is tied to institutional subordination and inequity; her focus is on both the structural nature of the construction of subordinate and disrespected identities and communities, and on the maldistribution experienced by these subjects. As with Young, Fraser insists that we have to examine the 'why' of inequity, and how the social context of unjust distributions is a unique and necessary subject of justice theory; this is the key to both understand and remedy existing injustices. Examining the context of oppression—rather than simply either existing distributions, better distributions, or ideal procedures to procure just distributions—is central to Fraser's justice project. Whether, and how, individuals and communities are recognized is crucial.

In the political realm, Fraser calls for 'participatory parity' of all affected parties in the polity as the necessary procedure to alleviate both distributional and recognition-based forms of injustice. As Fraser argues, such a need for participation illustrates not just the need for a bivalent understanding of justice, but a trivalent one. The point, as I return to shortly, is that both injustices and their remedies are integrally linked.

In the social and cultural realm, the key to understanding recognitional injustice lies in understanding the social norms, language, and mores that mediate our relation between those who are denigrated and so less well-off in the scheme of justice. The argument is that mis- or malrecognition is a cultural and institutional form of injustice. This type of cultural injustice is 'rooted in patterns of representation, interpretation, and communication' (Fraser 1998: 7). In confronting the injustices of cultural domination, nonrecognition, and lack of respect, various movements focus on remedies based in cultural, symbolic, and, ultimately, institutional change. The point is to examine the range of social and cultural values and practices that impede the full recognition of a group as an accepted member of the moral and political community. There are both sociocultural and political elements to this type of recognition. In the social realm, Dean's notion (1996) of 'accountability' is very useful. In Dean's framework the focus is on the process of the construction of the 'status' of the misrecognized; she insists we uncover where accountability and responsibility lie for both the construction of problematic notions and the reconstruction of ones based in more authentic recognition. Here, the conception of justice occupies social and cultural space beyond the bounds of the state.

Psychology versus Status

Now, what one means by recognition is nearly as contested as the concept of distribution. While there are numerous approaches to the term, I want to focus on two key definitions and the discussions surrounding them. Charles Taylor (1994) and Axel Honneth (1992, 1995, 2001), key proponents of the concept of recognition as an element of justice, focus thoroughly on the individual psychological aspects of the need for recognition. The central idea for both authors is that self-worth comes from the recognition given by others. As Honneth argues, we rely on the recognition of others for our own human dignity and integrity, hence the need for reciprocal and intersubjective recognition. 'The language of everyday life is still invested with a knowledge—which we take for granted—that we owe our integrity, in a subliminal way, to the receipt of approval or recognition from other persons' (Honneth 1995: 188). Taylor insists that, 'misrecognition can inflict harm, can be a form of oppression, imprisoning someone in a false, distorted, and reduced mode of being' (1994: 25). In this sense, then, 'recognition is not just a courtesy we owe people. It is a vital human need' (p. 26).

Taylor's discussion of recognition is limited however, and so has not become as illustrative of this aspect of justice theory as has Honneth's. Taylor distinguishes between two kinds of recognition: (a) the equal dignity of all, and (b) the politics of difference, where everyone is recognized for their particular distinctiveness. '*Everyone* should be recognized for his or her unique identity.... With the politics of equal dignity, what is established is meant to be universally the same, an identical basket of rights and immunities; with the politics of difference, what we are asked to recognize is the unique identity of this individual or group, their distinctness from everyone else' (pp. 37–8). This latter form of recognition causes Taylor some distress. The 'demand for equal recognition extends beyond an acknowledgment of the equal value of all humans potentially, and comes to include the equal value of what they have made of this potential in fact. This creates a serious problem...' (p. 42). At this point, unfortunately, Taylor's discussion degenerates a bit, as he moves to criticize what he calls at various points 'incoherent', 'radical', 'subjectivist', 'half-baked', 'neo-Nietzschean' theories that support multiculturalism (pp. 66, 70). As a number of responses have pointed out, Taylor seems to want only some identities recognized. Recognition becomes especially difficult for him when it comes to the margins, innovation, newness, and any challenge to the universalizability of identity.[2]

Honneth's discussion is both a bit more complex and a bit more accepting of difference than Taylor's. For Honneth (1992: 190–1; 1995: 132–4), there are three key forms of disrespect: the violation of the body (here Honneth refers specifically to torture), the denial of rights, and the denigration of ways of life.[3] Each, Honneth insists, has an inherent psychological dimension. Recognition here is much broader than a simple tolerance; individuals must be fully free of physical threats, offered complete and equal political rights, and have their distinguishing cultural traditions free from various forms of disparagement. But Honneth remains firmly attached to the psychological interpretation and state of the individual. For example, physical injuries only become a moral injustice for Honneth if victims view them as intentionally disregarding their personal well-being (2001: 48). It is not just the inflicting of pain that is the injustice, but the *perception* of misrecognition on the part of the victim. All misrecognition then, even systemic social and cultural denigration and domination, is most importantly, for Honneth, a psychological condition.[4]

This psychological recognition, argue both Taylor and Honneth, is a crucial element of justice. As with Young, both Taylor and Honneth contend that a *lack* of recognition—demonstrated by various forms of insults, degradation, and devaluation at both the individual and cultural level—is an injustice not just because it constrains people or does them harm, but because it 'impairs these persons in their positive understanding of self—an understanding acquired by intersubjective means.' (Honneth 1992: 189). Taylor (1994: 25) asserts that

[t]he thesis is that our identity is partly shaped by recognition or its absence, often by the *mis*recognition of others, and so a person or group of people can suffer real damage, real distortion, if the people or society around them mirror back to them confining or demeaning or contemptible picture of themselves. Nonrecognition or misrecognition can inflict harm, can be a form of oppression, imprisoning someone in a false, distorted, and reduced mode of being.

Lack of recognition, then, is a harm—an injustice—as much as a lack of adequate distribution of various goods.

Fraser, on the other hand, argues that this approach to the politics of recognition is too psychologically based; she turns her attention to the social status of individuals and communities, and insists on a structural understanding of misrecognition more as an institutional practice than an individual experience. For Fraser, a focus on social relations, rather than psychology, helps us understand misrecognition as a 'status injury' (Fraser 1998: 25). Misrecognition is not freestanding or psychological, but an 'institutionalized relation of social subordination' (Fraser 2000: 113). It is this institutional status injury, not psychological damage, which is central to Fraser's theory of justice.

Fraser identifies three status-based, as opposed to psychological, definitions and processes of misrecognition. First is a general practice of cultural domination; second is a pattern of nonrecognition, which is the equivalent of being rendered invisible; and third is disrespect, or being routinely maligned or disparaged in stereotypic public and cultural representations (Fraser 1998: 7). Fraser is much more comfortable identifying and relying on these structural, social, and symbolic indicators of misrecognition or lack of respect, as they do not rely on the psychological interpretation or feeling of the victim. While Fraser's initial concern is with gender relationships, the status approach is a viable way to analyze a variety of structural injustices, including that of individuals and communities suffering environmental injustice. More broadly, I argue later, the status approach will be a useful way to examine the way that nonhuman nature is maligned and disrespected in human culture in all three ways outlined above.

There have been numerous arguments between Fraser and Young (reprinted in Willett 1998) and Fraser and Honneth (2003) regarding the definition and nature of recognition. The argument with Young centers mostly on the relative emphasis on recognition versus redistribution. With Honneth this question is argued as well, but the key difference is between the psychological versus structural nature of recognition. As is usually the case with academic dichotomies, there is validity in both sides. As I discuss below, one must take both recognition and redistribution seriously in any contemporary theory of justice, and Fraser certainly has made that argument. In the argument with Honneth, however, Fraser overstates her case in an attempt to move away from a victim-centered understanding of recognition.

Fraser argues that Honneth's politics of recognition is problematic because it is tied singly to self-realization; she argues that he does not recognize the key structural and institutional manifestations of misrecognition (Fraser 1998: 24). But Honneth is keenly interested in the importance of self-esteem in the political realm, and the fact that such self-esteem comes from recognition by others—not just from individuals, but also from culture and the state—leads to a very thorough critique of the effect of cultural and political institutions. Honneth's second notion of disrespect specifically 'refers to those forms of personal disrespect to which an individual is subjected by being structurally excluded from the possession of certain rights within a society' (Honneth 1995: 133). His third form of disrespect includes the cultural and institutional concurrence in the denial of self-esteem. Honneth argues that a focus on self-realization *and* the institutional limits to both self- and other-based recognition is at the core of existing social movement struggles. So while the *experience* of misrecognition is psychological, the *implications* of Honneth's notion of recognition go far beyond a simple call for internal self-realization, as Fraser asserts: a structural and institutional critique is an absolutely necessary part of the call for recognition.

Still, Fraser correctly argues that while it is simple to dichotomize the definition of recognition into the psychological versus the structural, we can see recognition on both dimensions simultaneously; misrecognition

19

may be both individually experienced and structurally constructed. For example, civil rights protesters who carried signs proclaiming, simply and poignantly, 'I Am a Man'—certainly a call for more than education or voting rights—conveyed the issues of both individual self-worth and institutional and cultural status. While it is true that there is a difference between understandings of recognition based in psychology and in status, the two are not mutually exclusive in either a theory of misrecognition or in suggestions for its alleviation. The key point remains that recognition is central to a theory and practice of justice, though there are differences in how to analyze its absence.

Distributive Critiques of Recognition

For all of this discussion of recognition as an element of justice in recent theoretical literature, the concept is not something readily accepted by many traditional distributive justice theorists. Most such theorists reading these words are probably already articulating their disagreements, as there has been quite a resistance to the argument for recognition as an element of justice. For reasons I do not fully understand, many liberal theorists see the discussion of recognition as an element of justice as a direct attack on the intellectual legacy of Rawls. Their response is usually that Rawls thought of it first, and incorporated the question of recognition into his distributive paradigm.

While many theorists readily admit that recognition, in particular self- and social respect, is crucial to a theory of justice, they argue that it is usually (and best) addressed within the distributive framework. Most often, then, recognition is rejected as a category mistake; simply put, recognition is not a *distinct* issue of justice. Most of these theorists simply want to include recognition as a precondition within the distributive sphere. But there is some confusion over the issue, however, in particular over whether recognition is an *assumption* and *precondition* of distribution, or whether it is a *good* to be distributed. Rawls himself insists that self-respect is both a precondition and a result of his two principles of justice (1993: 318–20).

One argument is that recognition and respect are *inherent preconditions* for distributive justice. Equality of persons, which is at the center of liberal theories of justice, starts with an assumption of equal *respect* for all citizens. Rawls calls self-respect a primary good (1971: 440), even, perhaps 'the main primary good' (p. 544, though that was dropped to the end of a list of five in 1993: 181). This precondition argument is straightforward; after all, one must be recognized and respected in order to be included behind the veil of ignorance in Rawls's original position, and one's station in life—whatever it may be—is also implicitly recognized. Interestingly, Rawls (1971: 440) refers to many of the same psychological needs that Honneth attaches to recognition. So it is clear that recognition and respect are crucial to Rawls and his theory of justice.

The same holds for many other liberal theorists. Walzer (1983: xii), for example, notes in his classic *Spheres of Justice* that recognition is central to the moral question of justice. But Walzer also simply assumes recognition as an *inherent* trait of just relations. Likewise, Miller (2003) seems quite sympathetic to the arguments for recognition and the respect that comes with it, but again argues, following Rawls, that respect and dignity are *preconditions* for distributive justice.[5] As recognition is included in the definition of distributive justice, Miller dismisses the key claim of recognition as a distinct category of justice. Miller, in summary, represents the position of many liberal theories of justice, where recognition is assumed, and subsumed, within the distributive sphere of justice. The upshot here is that some theorists of justice argue that recognition and respect are accounted for in theories of distributional justice.

The most basic critique of this assumption argument is that while it may work in theory, recognition is not simply assumed in the real world of injustice. In fact, as critical theorists, both Fraser and Honneth consciously take their prompts from the actions and demands of recent social movements. There, the battle for recognition is as large as the one for fair distribution. In other words, the assumption argument is problematic on pragmatic and empirical grounds. It may be a comfort to argue that recognition is included in one's *theory*, but what is to be done when that is not the case *in practice*? Theorists may argue that if various distributional ideals, or ideal processes, were implemented, then recognition would be inherent and assumed. If, for example, all communities were exposed to the same amount of environmental risk no matter their race, class, or sociocultural status, then those communities would not be demanding recognition, as that recognition would be a precondition of the just distribution.

The response to such a claim is that without recognition, such an ideal distribution *will never occur*. If existing maldistribution is related to misrecognition, then without recognition—and not just self-respect, but social and structural recognition—we will never have such ideal processes or outcomes. This is the case whether bad distribution results in a lack

21

of recognition or the lack of recognition leads to bad distribution (one of the issues in the Fraser–Honneth debate 2003). The claim made by distributional theorists that recognition is assumed offers no practical discussion of recognition, no link between a lack of recognition and existing distributional inequities, and no attention to the institutional structures and practices that mediate both recognition and distribution. Justice in theory may happen in isolation, neutrality, or behind a veil of ignorance, but that is simply not the case in practice. If the interest is about attaining *justice*, rather than attaining a sound *theory* of justice, recognition is central to the question and the resolution—and is not simply to be assumed. Again, the point here is that the assumptions of distributional justice simply do not stand in the empirical realm. This is the first, very pragmatic, reason for focusing on recognition as an element of justice.

Rawls and many liberal justice theorists also see respect and recognition as a *good* that can be distributed. While respect is an essential precondition to justice in the original position (Rawls 1971: 440), it is also one of the objects to be distributed in a just system. Yet Rawls never directly or explicitly discusses the distribution of respect as a good, only that it is related to the distribution of some material goods. So while it is clear that respect is crucial to Rawls and his theory of justice, he leaves us thinking about recognition in two different and contradictory ways— both of which continue to appear in the literature, and both of which are problematic.

It is tautological to argue, as Rawls does, that recognition is both inherent/presumed in a distributional system *and* something to be distributed by those systems. If it is a good that needs to be distributed, or redistributed, we cannot assume it to be so before such a distributive system is set up. If recognition does not exist in practice, then the status of those unrecognized as members of the community of justice must be addressed before any goods can be distributed to them. We cannot simply assume recognition as a precondition, or assert it can easily be distributed.

Miller directly addresses the question of recognition as a good, but to another problematic end. For Miller, recognition, which he defines as status, has both objective and subjective sides; this is not unlike the psychological and status definitions described above. But what this means for Miller is that the range of definitions of recognition is too wide, and so 'we may be reluctant to think of recognition as something whose allocation can be regulated by interpersonal principles of justice' (Miller 1999*a*: 10). Interestingly, Miller uses the difficulty of fully agreeing on what recognition is to dismiss it either as a good or, more broadly, as something distributive justice can allocate. But Miller does not fully engage in an examination of what recognition *can* mean within a theory of justice.

Young dismisses the conception of recognition as a good, and yet uses the logic of this rejection to argue for a more thorough engagement with what it means to include the concept in a theory of justice. For Young, recognition is just not a 'thing' to be distributed, but a relationship, a social norm embedded in social practice. Young finds discussions regarding equal distribution of 'opportunities' or even of 'rights' problematic. When we give groups previously denied the right to vote or the right of free speech those rights, they do not come at the 'expense' of others—they are not redistributed from one to another, as is income or other goods. Recognition is not limited, materially, in the way goods are. One of the key problems of the theory of distributive justice, argues Young, is that 'it does not recognize the limits to the application of a logic of distribution' (1990: 24).

In addition, while theories of distributive justice focus on the state as a neutral arbiter, a state cannot allocate recognition as it does other goods. Recognition cannot simply be distributed as, say, education or housing assistance. A state may set an *example* of recognizing a socially demeaned group and validate difference in the political realm (through voting, or marriage rights, for example), but recognition must happen as much in the social, cultural, and symbolic realms as in the institutional. The state may implement affirmative action, but social recognition for communities currently misrecognized and politically excluded is a broader issue. In other words, the concept of justice as recognition moves beyond a focus on the state alone for remedies, and brings justice theory squarely into the political space beyond the state.

This is not to say that states, for example, cannot distribute recognition in some respects. They can, for example, extend the franchise, implement affirmative action, or license gay marriage. I am not arguing that recognition can never be embodied as a good in some respects. But, as even Rawls argues, recognition is not *only* a good; it is also a precondition of membership in the political community. Recognition by the state is an example for others in the social sphere—where various types of misrecognition may continue. Recognition must be understood as a necessary aspect of political life—yet one that is neither assumed nor simply distributed by the state. We can strive for the ideal of the full recognition of all citizens, and for the state to distribute what it can of recognition and support such recognition in the social, cultural, and economic realms. But such an ideal will take demands and work—not simply theoretical assumptions and assertions.

A Misunderstanding and the Need for a Multifaceted Approach

Perhaps some of the animosity to the concept of recognition in the community of justice theorists is due to a misunderstanding of its proposed status in a broad theory of justice. More traditional liberal theorists may have been put off by Young calling the first chapter of her 1990 book 'Displacing the Distributive Paradigm'. Young and Fraser's early argument on the relative importance of distribution versus recognition may have added to the impression that the question was between distribution *or* recognition as the center of a theory of justice. Liberal theorists may also have been concerned that some theorists, such as Taylor, discuss recognition without substantive reference to distributional aspects of justice. Yet Young does not explicitly deny the importance of distributional theories of justice; rather, while 'distributional issues are crucial to a satisfactory conclusion of justice, it is a mistake to reduce social justice to distribution' (1990: 2). Fraser and Honneth as well have been very clear in their arguments that recognition is just one crucial element of justice, to be considered alongside distributional and participatory issues. A concern for recognition does *not* mean that we ignore distributional issues, but rather include them in a broader, inclusive understanding of justice.

The idea that recognition requires us to move *beyond* distribution, and *reject* a distributional approach to justice, simply does not appear in the recognition literature. Young, Fraser, and Honneth all insist that we have to look at the 'why' of inequity in order to both understand and remedy it. While more traditional justice theorists focus on ideal schemes and process of justice in liberal societies, recognition theorists have made clear that attention to the *real* impediments to such schemes must be addressed with attention to the existence or denial of recognition in both the political and sociocultural realms. Just as distributional theorists do not want their key concern subsumed in a theory of justice focused on recognition, recognition cannot simply be subsumed, or assumed, in a theory of distribution.

Unfortunately, it is not only traditional justice theorists who have insisted on a dichotomy between distribution and recognition by focusing on one or the other conception of justice. In addition, some on the academic left have lamented the move toward justice as recognition, especially as it has been developed in the 'identity politics' of social movements or the post-material critiques of the 'cultural' left. The whole point of Fraser's forays into the examination of these various justice claims is to show that they are not antithetical.

Fraser argues that this split between 'social' justice and cultural politics—justice as equity and justice as recognition—represents a false dichotomy. Fraser insists that '[j]ustice today requires *both* redistribution and recognition' (1997: 12). 'Justice requires both, as neither is sufficient' (1998: 5). Communities, or collectivities, are, in fact, bivalent—they are often differentiated as a collective by both economic structure and the status order of society. In this case, neither a politics of redistribution nor one solely of recognition will suffice to remedy injustice. 'In general, then, one should roundly reject the construction of redistribution and recognition as mutually exclusive alternatives. The goal should be, rather, to develop a two-pronged approach that can address the twofold need for both' (p. 23).

Likewise, Honneth also notes a relation between material equity and justice as recognition. Honneth recognizes the more utilitarian struggle over the equitable distribution of goods, including cultural goods, as a motivator for collective action. This is contrasted with a model of social conflict that has the denial of social or legal recognition at its core. But Honneth does not want to replace the theoretical model for the former with one for the latter: 'It is important to stress... that this second model of conflict, based on a theory of recognition, should not try to replace the first, utilitarian model but only extend it' (1995: 165). Like Fraser, Honneth argues that social movements encompass both notions of justice.[6]

Procedural Justice and the Necessity of a Linked Approach

But there is another dimension to the concept and practice of justice in addition to distribution and recognition; *procedural* justice in which justice is defined as fair and equitable institutional processes of a state. Some traditional justice theorists, such as Miller, use the assumptions of a procedural approach as another argument against recognition. Miller argues that respect and recognition are necessary preconditions to any theory of procedural justice. Here, once again, the claim is that if procedural justice—however defined—is attained, recognition is included and so is to be assumed. As with the preceding discussion, however, the concern of many theorists of recognition, as well as some who focus on procedure, is the *empirical* reality of procedural injustice.

This sort of interpretation of procedural justice misses the point of those like Fraser, Honneth, and Young, who insist on a thoroughly integrated understanding of justice. Importantly, these theorists, and others, are beginning to note that the relationship between justice as equity and justice as recognition is played out in the procedural realm, as both hinder the ability of individuals and communities to participate. The point is to focus on the direct link between a lack of respect and recognition and a decline in a person's membership and participation in the greater community, including the political and institutional order. If you are not recognized, you do not participate; if you do not participate, you are not recognized. In this respect, justice must focus on the political process as a way to address both the inequitable distribution of social goods and the conditions undermining social recognition. Democratic and participatory decision-making procedures are then both an element of, and a condition for, social justice (Young 1990: 23); they simultaneously challenge institutionalized exclusion, a social culture of misrecognition, and current distributional patterns.

So while material distribution and recognition are two absolutely key notions of justice in the contemporary political realm, the focus on the process of justice, including demands for more broad and authentic public participation, is often seen as the tool to achieve both distributional equity and political recognition. Numerous theorists note the direct link between a lack of respect and recognition and a decline in a person's membership and participation in the greater community, including the political and institutional order.

Young, again, was one of the first to make this connection clear. In *Justice and the Politics of Difference*, one of Young's primary emphases is on institutions and the political process. While she argues that distributive justice does not go far enough because it does not include recognition of differences in the social realm—differences which go beyond who has how much; Young goes on to examine the institutional features that lead to injustices *both* in terms of distribution and in terms of recognition. The argument is that a concept of justice needs to focus more generally on the elimination of institutionalized domination and oppression. In order to accomplish this, justice must focus on the political *process* as a way to address a variety of injustices, including both the inequitable distribution of social goods and the conditions undermining social recognition. This leads directly to her insistence on participatory democratic structures to address existing injustices based in both distribution and recognition.

In dealing with issues of justice beyond the distributive, Young (1990: 23) insists on addressing justice in the 'rules and procedures according to which decisions are made'.

> The idea of justice here shifts ... to procedural issues of participation in deliberation and decision making. For a norm to be just, everyone who follows it must in principle have an effective voice in its consideration and be able to agree to it without coercion. For a social condition to be just, it must enable all to meet their needs and exercise their freedom; thus justice requires that all be able to express their needs. (p. 34)

The central focus for Young, in addressing justice both as distribution and the recognition of difference, is on decision-making structures, and she argues for 'democratic decision-making procedures as an element and condition of social justice' (p. 23).[7] Recognition, then, along with inclusion in the political process, become the keys to relieving both social oppression and distributional inequity. As Young argues, such an expansion of the understanding of justice requires more of a state than simply revised distribution patterns.

For Honneth, one form of disrespect or misrecognition—the lack of rights—is directly linked to democratic participation. Citizens are subject to a form of personal disrespect when they are 'structurally excluded from the possession of certain rights within a given society.... [T]he experience of being denied rights is typically coupled with a loss of self-respect, of the ability to relate to oneself as a partner to interaction in possession of equal rights on a par with all other individuals' (1992: 190). There is a direct link, for Honneth, between a lack of respect and recognition and a decline in a person's membership and participation in the greater community, including their right to participate in the institutional order.

Likewise, Carol Gould (1996: 181) insists that taking differences seriously in public life requires 'a radical increase in opportunities for participation in contexts of common activity.... For if individuals have an equal right to determine their own actions and, further, if engaging in common activity is one of the necessary conditions for their self-development, then it follows that there is an equal right to participate in determining the course of such common activity'. Gould, like Young and numerous others who advocate a model of discursive or communicative democracy, insists that this participation needs to happen in a variety of social and cultural institutions, as well as in the more specific context of politics and government.[8] Discourse models and calls for more participatory democracy are thoroughly compatible with the varied notions of justice in both theory and practice; they address the variety of cultural norms, social discourses, and the role of institutions of power in issues of both equity and recognition. In this sense, increased participation can also address issues of distribution and cultural misrecognition.

But perhaps the most thorough discussion of the integration of procedural justice in a broad and inclusive theory of justice is offered by Fraser. When 'patterns of disrespect and disesteem are institutionalized', Fraser argues (1998: 26), 'for example, in law, social welfare, medicine, public education, and/or the social practices and group mores that structure everyday interaction, they impede parity of participation, just as surely as do distributive inequities'.

The point here is absolutely crucial: it is not just that political and cultural institutions create conditions that hamper equity and recognition, but that both distributive inequity and misrecognition hamper real participation in political and cultural institutions. Issues of justice are not just bivalent, but trivalent. In this case, improved participatory mechanisms can help meliorate both other forms of injustice; but those forms of injustice must be addressed in order to improve participation. For a 'parity of participation', Fraser argues, we need both objective and intersubjective conditions to be met. Objective conditions include a distribution of resources to ensure participants' independence and voice. Subjective conditions require 'that institutionalized cultural patterns of interpretation and evaluation express equal respect for all participants and ensure equal opportunity for achieving social esteem' (p. 30). For Fraser, participatory parity comes with the satisfaction of two conditions: the 'respect in institutional patterns of cultural value', and the resources to enable participation (2001: 29). It is absolutely crucial to tie together social subordination and misrecognition with maldistribution. It is not a question of one or the other as the focus of justice, but of both simultaneously. Fraser is adamant on this: to remedy maldistribution we must focus on political–economic restructuring; but such considerations will only come along with recognition, where the remedy is in cultural and symbolic changes in how we regard the presently misrecognized. Only then will participatory parity, and procedural justice, be attained.

As many discursive and communicative democrats argue, moral respect and the recognition of the right of all to participate are key principles for improving and extending democratic action. Justice, then, requires not just an understanding of unjust distribution and a lack of recognition, but, importantly, the way the two are tied together in political and social processes.[9] These notions and experiences of injustice are not competing notions, nor are they contradictory or antithetical. Again, justice is a trivalent package.

Liberal theorists, however, are not quite ready to accept either recognition or participation—and in particular their relationship. Brighouse (2004: 155–7), for example, notes that the focus on using the state to include misrecognized groups, even though some citizens' conceptions of the good would lead them to exclude fellow citizens, crosses the line of liberal impartiality. This is also one of Barry's lines of argument (2001) against cultural recognition and inclusion as elements of justice.

This insistence on impartiality to notions of the good, even when those notions devalue and disenfranchise fellow citizens, is both shortsighted and contradictory even for those who remain wed to a singular emphasis on distribution. Inclusion and respect are supposed to be the assumed starting point for a Rawlsian theory of justice. While recognition and participatory parity may be denied for some by those whose notion of the good is offended by their full inclusion in the polity, one cannot deny that such a right of participation is understood as one of the rights granted under Rawls' imaginary original position. The enfranchisement of women and African Americans, and the autonomy of Native American nations, certainly went against the standing notion of the good of many citizens of the time. So why such a status should not be enforced, even if it does interfere with certain notions of the good held by some citizens? And, more importantly, if this right is denied not simply in theory, but in the everyday political life of our fellow citizens—who then have their own notions of the good denied—how can good liberals deny the importance of attending to participation, and the recognition that must accompany it?

Capabilities

There is, importantly, another school of thought that has attempted to expand a conception of justice beyond its sole focus on distribution. Amartya Sen and Martha Nussbaum (Sen 1985,1999a, 1999b; Nussbaum and Sen 1992; Nussbaum 2000, 2006a) have developed an approach that, while grounded in an understanding of the centrality of distribution as an element of justice, also moves us beyond the limitations of standard distributional theory. The central argument of their 'capability' approach is that we should judge just arrangements not only in simple distributive terms, but also more particularly in how those distributions affect our well-being and how we 'function'. Capabilities are about a person's opportunities to do and to be what they choose in the context of a given society; the focus is on individual agency, functioning, and well-being and, rather than more traditional distributive indicators (Pressman and Summerfield 2002). The point for Sen is to move away from a sole concern with the amount of goods we get, and to examine what those goods do for us; he opens *Development as Freedom* by comparing classic Sanskrit and Greek texts, including Aristotle's point that 'wealth is evidently not the good we are seeking; for it is merely useful and for the sake of something else' (Aristotle 1980: 7). The approach examines our specific capabilities, those things that allow or assist us to translate basic goods into the functioning of human life.

Sen primarily uses the concept of capabilities to compare quality of life in different places, especially in developing nations; he sees this attention as a much better indicator of such quality than a simple growth or a wealth-centered GNP rating. 'The central feature of well-being is the ability to achieve valuable functionings. The need for identification and valuation of the important functionings cannot be avoided by looking at something else, such as happiness, desire fulfillment, opulence, or command over primary good (Sen 1985: 200). *Functionings* refer to various doings and beings: these could be activities (like eating or reading or seeing), or states of existence or being (being well nourished, being free from disease) (p. 197). This approach 'concentrates on the *opportunity* to be able to have combinations of functionings...and the person is free to make use of this opportunity or not. A capability reflects the alternative combinations of functionings from which the person can choose one combination' (Sen 2005: 154). The capabilities approach, Nussbaum (2004: 306) argues, is based in wanting to 'see each thing flourish as the sort of thing it is'. So the central measure of justice is not just how much we have, but whether we have what is necessary to enable a more fully functioning life, as we choose to live it.

While such functioning is central, both Sen and Nussbaum are more directly interested in the *capability* of functioning—on the *qualities* that enable individuals to have a fully functioning life. In other words, the approach includes both the qualities and capabilities held by people *and* their ability to express and exercise those capabilities in a functioning life. Broadly put, the focus of this notion of justice is on what it is that either enables or interrupts a living system in its ability to transform primary goods (if they are available) into functionings. For example, if reading is a functioning, then literacy and being educated are the capabilities necessary for that functioning. Distribution of, and access to, those capabilities may be distributed by a state, but the focus of the theory is also on the functioning of citizens; so this understanding of justice is not about the distribution of material goods alone. Sen remains rather broad and vague on the specific capabilities that individual agents should have to enable their own functioning, noting five basic concepts and freedoms that help advance the general capability of people: political freedoms, economic facilities, social opportunities, transparency guarantees, and protective security (1999b: 10). Here, he notes that since 'political and civil freedoms are constitutive elements of human freedom, their denial is a handicap in itself' (pp. 16–17). Sen's theory of justice, then, focuses as much on those capabilities, and the functionings they allow, as on the basic distributional structure of a government.

Nussbaum, in much more detail, defends a basic 'capability set' necessary for this functioning and flourishing (2000: 78–80; 2006a: 76–8). Specifically, the full list includes:

- Life: being able to live to the end of a human life of normal length.
- Bodily health: including health, nourishment, and shelter.
- Bodily integrity: being able to move freely, having sovereign body boundaries, security against assault, opportunity for sexual satisfaction, and reproductive choice.
- Senses imagination and thought: basically being able to use human intelligence and creativity; this includes adequate education, freedom of expression, and freedom of religious exercise.
- Emotions: 'in general, to love, to grieve, to experience longing, gratitude, and justified anger'.
- Practical reason: the basic liberal right to determine one's own notion of the good life.
- Affiliation: two parts here. It starts with recognition, or 'being able to live with and toward others, to recognize and show concern for other human beings' and 'to be able to imagine the situation of another and to have compassion for that situation....' Also includes 'having the social bases of self-respect and non-humiliation; being able to be treated as a dignified being whose worth is equal to that of others.' Nussbaum explicitly notes that this requires protecting institutions that constitute and nourish such forms of affiliation.

- Other species: being able to 'live with concern for and in relation to animals, plants, and the world of nature'.
- Play: 'being able to laugh, to play, to enjoy recreational activities'.
- Control over one's environment: both political, which includes the right of political participation, and material, which includes the real opportunity to own and control property on an equal basis with others.

Importantly, notes Nussbaum, these are separate components, so that having a lot of one capability does not negate the need to attain all of the others. Many of them are what Rawls calls 'natural goods', which are determined, in a substantial amount, by the luck of the genetic and social draw. Governments, however, are to 'deliver the *social* basis of these capabilities' (Nussbaum 2000: 81).

Returning to the question of participation, both Sen and Nussbaum see citizen participation as integral to an understanding of justice. For Sen, participation is part of an understanding of human beings as agents, and not simply recipients of goods. His conception of justice includes participation as both a freedom and function in itself and as something that supports a range of other functions. Likewise, for Nussbaum, participation— or control over one's political environment, as she calls it—is a key capability that supports the overall functioning of the individual, yet it is also a function in its own right. As a capability, a function, or a combination of both, participation is central to a capabilities approach to a definition of justice.

The capabilities approach, in particular the development of specific lists of capabilities such as Nussbaum's, has been charged with being paternalistic and perfectionist. Deneulin (2002), for example, argues that such a list points out what is objectively good, universally and from the point of view of the theorist. The theory is then accused of focusing not on the functionings that people 'choose', but rather on those that people have a good reason to do or be. Both Sen and Nussbaum are quite aware of such charges, and have responded vigorously to them. Sen, for his part, refuses to develop and publish a list of the type that Nussbaum generated, even though in his own various evaluations of development programs such lists are, temporarily, necessary. Sen (2005: 157) notes that he is reluctant to develop such lists for two reasons. First, there is the difficulty 'in seeing how the exact lists and weights would be chosen without appropriate specification of the context of their use;' and second is the fact that a top-down paternalistic approach would diminish the public reasoning and deliberation necessary for generating an appropriate list.

The problem is not with listing important capabilities, but with insisting on one pre-determined canonical list of capabilities, chosen by theorists without any general social discussion or public reasoning. To have such a fixed list, emanating entirely from pure theory, is to deny the possibility of fruitful public participation on what should be included and why. (Sen 2005: 158)

Nussbaum, given both her explicit list and her insistence that she is developing universal principles in the tradition of Rawls's overlapping consensus (Nussbaum 2002: 76), is much more susceptible to the paternalism charge, but I think Nussbaum's claims are weaker than she insists. Rawls meant for his principles of justice to be universal for all peoples at all times, and developed them in isolation. Nussbaum notes the importance of the influence of 'years of cross-cultural discussion' and dialogue with activists and women's movements; she is accepting of such a list changing over the years. This dedication to movements and to contexts makes her list less paternalistic than some might like to argue. Furthermore, the use of capabilities lists does not necessarily tie one to the universalism that Nussbaum claims; Sen is much more realistic and open to the fact of the impact of contextualism and pluralism on any list of capabilities. The more public discourse is brought in to identify and define capabilities, the more paternalism can be avoided. Inclusively developed lists are not paternalistic, and lists that are understood at temporary are neither universalist nor perfectionist.

The larger point is how capabilities are understood in a larger discourse of justice. Both Nussbaum and Sen base ethical significance in the unfolding and flourishing of basic capabilities, however they are defined, and find harm—injustice, in fact—in the limiting of them. In an important sense, Sen and Nussbaum expand the distributional realm as they focus not just on the distribution of goods we need to flourish, but the processes we depend on for that flourishing to occur. Injustice comes not with a particular good denied, but with the capability that is limited. Their focus is on a threshold level for each of the capabilities on their respective lists, or identified by local populations, under which basic functioning would not be possible.

Importantly, what Sen and Nussbaum's capability approach to justice illustrates is not a singular, distribution-based, understanding of justice, but a linked approach; in the capabilities argument, concepts and practices such as recognition and participation are thoroughly tied to distributional concerns. The focus is not simply on a conception of distribution, or of recognition, for example, but more holistically on the importance of individuals functioning within a base of a minimal distribution of goods, social and political recognition, political participation, and other capabilities. Nussbaum's capability set explicitly includes crucial notions such bodily health and integrity, and having the social bases of respect and non-humiliation: such language ties capabilities clearly into discussions of recognition. Nussbaum declares recognition itself a necessary capability on her explicit list, and so creates a structure in which recognition is considered on par with distribution and others in a larger conception of an environment of human justice. In this, the approach makes a key link between the distributional and the cultural and institutional components of justice theory.

As Olson (2001: 7) claims, the capability approach 'simultaneously addresses interconnected problems of economic inequality *and* cultural disrespect'. Likewise, Robeyns (2003) argues that capability theory can accommodate both issues of redistribution and recognition, and yet is broader than even Fraser's bivalent or trivalent approach. In other words, the capabilities approach can be seen as fully incorporating recognition and distribution in a broad theory of justice, yet goes further then either. In addition to distribution and recognition, Sen and Nussbaum's inclusion of participatory rights and freedoms as additional capabilities necessary to transform goods into a good life illustrates the necessity of linking these various conceptions in a larger framework. In a sense, Sen and Nussbaum's approach expands the distributional realm as it focuses not just on the distribution of goods we need to flourish, but the processes we depend on for that flourishing to occur. So rather than examine recognition, distribution, and process as three different conceptions of justice, they understand all of these as necessary components of a more broad set of factors necessary for our lives to function. Whether we can function fully is the key test of justice. Justice then is not simply about distribution, but also about all that it takes—recognition, participation, and more—to be able to fully live the lives we design.

Justice and Groups

The vast majority of justice theory and all strictly liberal and Rawlsian approaches are focused specifically on doing justice to *individuals*. Do individuals get what is fair and what they rightly deserve? Are political systems designed and set up to provide for such a fair and equitable treatment of the individuals within them? There is very little discussion of *groups* in the literature. Even recognition theorists such as Fraser and capabilities theorists such as Sen and Nussbaum—who understand the reality of group-based injustice and the need for group-based recognition and/or capabilities—remain in an individualist framework, focusing on the impact of such issues on individuals and the justice they receive. Kymlicka (1989, 1995, 2001) is perhaps the theorist most well-known for taking on group rights explicitly as an element of justice, but even his calls and explanations stay within a liberal individualist framework.

As much as we understand justice as an individual experience, the fact is that many injustices are done to groups. The most obvious include slavery and the subjugation of indigenous populations, but numerous theorists and social movements address various forms of racial, cultural, religious, sexual preference, and gender-based forms of discrimination and persecution. In their discussions, both Fraser and Young focus on gender discrimination as central to the issue of recognition. Likewise, Kymlicka's work on group rights centers on social groups in Canada such as First Nations and the Quebecois. Of the three, Kymlicka more directly takes on the issue of group rights in his theory.

For Kymlicka, membership in a cultural group or community should be seen as a primary good in a system of justice. The basis of self-respect comes from membership in a group, and one's ideas regarding the goal of a good life comes, in large part, from one's own cultural background. Kymlicka remains tied primarily to an individualist conception of justice, but one that depends much on what we get from groups. Some critics of Kymlicka note that his focus is still on individual flourishing, even if that flourishing happens in the context of groups; group rights are protected for the sake of individualist liberal notions of justice. Others (e.g. Brighouse 2004: 109) note that even the perceived group injustices are actually individual injustices—prohibiting someone to express opinions and participate in political decisions in their own tongue, for example— actually violate individual freedom of expression and due process, and can be addressed as such. But Kymlicka is quite clear that in cases where minority groups are in danger of being consistently outvoted (or outbid in markets), then special attention should be paid specifically to group rights. Kymlicka (2001: 39ff.) describes this as a 'liberal culturalism', where in addition to standard liberal rights, states 'must also adopt various group-specific rights or policies which are intended to recognize and accommodate the distinctive identities and needs of ethnocultural groups' (p. 42).

This focus on group rights as an element of justice has also been taken up by multicultural pluralists looking for a liberal justification for group difference and self-rule. Both Galston (2002) and Tully (1995) note the relationship between demands for recognition and demands for forms of group autonomy. Tully (p. 6) argues that multicultural demands for recognition 'share a traditional political *motif*: the injustice of an alien form of rule and the aspiration to self rule in accord with one's own customs and ways'. Similarly, for Raz, multiculturalism 'emphasizes the role of cultures as a precondition for, and a factor which give shape and content to, individual freedom' (Raz 1994: 163). Such struggles are struggles for liberty, autonomy, and self-rule—certainly enduring characteristics of liberal justice, yet at the level of the group.

While these approaches remain influenced by traditional liberal notions of justice, and Kymlicka in particular works within a Rawlsian paradigm, the capabilities approach offers another avenue for addressing a group-focused notion of justice. While the capabilities listed by Sen and by Nussbaum are almost exclusively proposed and examined solely at the individual level, it is clear that many capabilities are either assisted by association with groups or are only satisfied within groups. Stewart (2005: 185), unique among capability theorists, takes this tack, arguing that 'one should analyze and categorize group capabilities as well as individual capabilities'. She posits that groups are important to capabilities in three ways: because groups 'affect people's sense of well-being', they are 'important instrumentally in determining efficacy and resource shares', and because 'groups influence values and choices, and hence the extent to which individuals choose to pursue valuable capabilities for themselves and for others' (p. 190). Group membership can bring enhanced self-respect and empowerment to individuals; some bring social goods and needs, others are used for economic purposes. Given those qualities, Stewart maintains that groups can either lead to improvement in some capability categories or, in some cases, undermine individual capabilities.

In addition, though Stewart does not discuss them specifically, Nussbaum's capabilities of affiliation and control over one's (political) environment can only happen within the life of groups—while we may individually affiliate and participate, such activity only occurs in a constructed group context. The point here is quite crucial: that while groups are necessary for the improvement of individual capabilities, they are also to be considered in their own category, as group capabilities are so integral to the development of capabilities in any community. As Stewart concludes,

They are essentially collective entities, involving collective action and interaction among individuals. The capabilities and functionings of these collectives, which are group capabilities and group functionings, like those of individuals, are those things they may be or do. Because of the interactive element, the group capabilities of collective entities are not simply the sum of the individual capabilities of members of the group. (p. 200)

So the ongoing capabilities of groups themselves are essential. They provide the necessary environment within which individual capabilities can thrive—without strong groups, community, empowerment, relationships, affiliation, and participation would be diminished. I do not believe it unimportant that Sen insists on *public* reasoning in the definition of capabilities for any particular time and place, or that Nussbaum feels the need to justify her capabilities list by noting the importance of local movements and communities in its construction. In both, communities are naming their own capabilities—things necessary to guarantee the full functioning of the community itself. It is not simply that groups provide individual capabilities; rather, group capabilities and group functioning are absolutely necessary to this conception of justice. It is fully reasonable to extend a theory of justice, of capabilities and functioning, to groups themselves, in addition to individuals.

The point here is that there is room, once we begin to move beyond strict interpretations of distributive theory, to consider the role of groups in conceptualizing justice. Either within a more traditional liberal paradigm, as Kymlicka and other multiculturalists argue, within the conceptions of recognition and participation, or within the growing capabilities framework, groups can be seen as both the environment within which individual justice is experienced and as a realm of justice in its own right. As Stewart concludes (2005: 201), there are some specific implications for policy with this realization. Policy needs to address group inequalities, to address tolerance for difference to coexist and thrive, to support group recognition and empowerment, and to support numerous collective activities that promote both group and individual capabilities.

Social Movements and the Real World of Justice Theory

The previous discussion brings us to a central reason why theories of justice must expand to encompass groups: because groups and communities are demanding justice *for* groups and communities—not only for individuals. These moves in the theoretical realm toward understanding justice as more than simply distributive, and toward becoming more accepting of recognition, participation, and capabilities more generally at both the individual and group level, are a good thing for justice theory, if it wants to consider itself aligned with the real world. Demands for justice of these types are common in the language and discourse of many recent social and political movements. Movement demands, in fact, have had an important impact on much recent justice theory. Importantly, the development of concerns beyond distribution in justice theory has been heavily influenced by the discourse and practice of social movements in the past few decades.

In his recent overview of justice, Brighouse (2004) begins his discussion of Fraser with a frank admission: 'Fraser's starting point, unlike that of all the theorists we have discussed up till now, is the real world. She identifies injustices in the real world, and tries to elaborate a theory which explains what is wrong with those injustices...' (p. 155). Theories of recognition, including both Fraser and Young, specifically address various injustices. Fraser began her foray into the redistribution/recognition debate with the observation that struggles for recognition have become the paradigmatic form of political struggle. Likewise, Young began her *Justice and the Politics of Difference* by asking what the implications of various movements— feminist, black liberation, American Indian, gay and lesbian—could be for political theories of justice. And both Sen and Nussbaum have explicitly expressed an interest in a theory of justice that is more applicable to real struggles for justice in the developing world.

In the move to describe injustices based on a lack of recognition of identity and difference, exclusion from political participation, and decimation of individual and community capabilities, much of contemporary justice theory shifts the focus away from the more traditional territory of distributive justice, toward a focus on the postmaterial demands of new social movements around identity and community generally, and race, gender, sexuality, and sustainability more specifically. Calls for the recognition of group difference and political participation have, at times, eclipsed claims for social and economic equity, yet the different demands more often exist simultaneously in the same movement. A number of social movements have focused on responding to various forms of misrecognition, exclusion, and decimation of capabilities. From the US civil rights activists in the 1960s who marched with signs declaring 'I Am a Man', to native American activists seeking protection for sacred cultural sites, recognition, participation, and community functioning have all been underlying and central demands of justice. The argument here is that there is a relationship between the everyday experience of disrespect, disempowerment, economic debilitation, and the decimation of individual and community capabilities and the emergence of social movements such as civil rights, indigenous rights, gay and lesbian rights, feminism, postcolonialism, and the more general movements for multicultural acceptance.

Importantly, however, these movements do not limit themselves to understanding injustice as faced only by individuals; justice for communities, as well, is often at the forefront of their interests and protests. How might we explain this postliberal focus on community justice? As Connolly (1993) argues, a form of resentment grows with misrecognition, disrespect, and disempowerment. This resentment is not just individual and existential, but becomes civil resentment as well. Social movements arise as responses to disrespect and misrecognition move from the individual and personal to the collective community. Honneth (1995: 164) sees these movements as a 'collective struggle for recognition'. The civil rights activists noted above marched together for both individual and collective community rights. And certainly, the call there went beyond justice as distribution, into the realm of justice at both the individual and community level. While political theorists, especially those within liberal theories of justice, focus on the individual, movement use of the term 'justice' is much broader. It may seem improper, to some theorists, that the theoretical focus has shifted away from the more traditional territory of individual distributive justice toward the more broad and often postmaterial and community-based demands of these social movements. But this shift is, in many ways, not only due to the limits of the theoretical focus on the distributional paradigm, but also simply in response to the empirical reality of the demands of these movements.

The Upshot

Theorists have defined justice in numerous ways; in my eyes, the most interesting and relevant definitions have come when theorists pay attention to what movements that articulate justice as a goal have to say. Again, I am not claiming that distributive notions of justice are passé or irrelevant—simply that they are incomplete. Inequitable distribution, a lack of recognition, limited participation, and a critical lack of capabilities, at both the individual and group level, all work to produce injustice.

Therefore, claims for justice can, and must, be integrated into a thorough, comprehensive, and pluralist political understanding of the term. My argument in the following chapters is that the environmental justice movement represents and exemplifies just such a project. The point of the chapters is to explore how communities are currently articulating their conception of justice when they use the phrase 'environmental justice' in their discourse and organizing. After that, I turn to how these additional dimensions come into play in calls for not only environmental justice in human communities, but also ecological justice with and for nonhuman nature as well.

Notes

1. The literature on distributive justice theory is simply too numerous to list here. Classics, of course, include Rawls (1971 and revised 1999, 2001), Barry (1995), Miller (1999), and Walzer (1983). Brighouse (2004) offers an excellent introduction and overview.
2. See, e.g. Dumm (1994). Taylor is also critical of attempts to deconstruct identity, which often come together with calls for recognition. This is often the case with subjugated and stereotyped identities, such as gays and lesbians or Native Americans.
3. This tripartite distinction among forms of recognition Honneth reads out of Hegel and Mead. The reference to Hegel is interesting, as it demonstrates a concern with the importance of recognition in a much earlier era. For Hegel (1967), the state is a community of individualized subjectivities, bound together while being recognized as individual subjectivities. The dialectical overcoming of individuality comes with recognition from the state.
4. Honneth understands the plurality of meanings of recognition in its various uses. He notes that in feminist ethics it is characterized by 'the kind of loving attention and caring exemplified in the mother–child relationship', in an ethics of discourse it refers to a reciprocal respect for the equal status of others, and in communitarianism it refers to the way we come to respect other ways of life (2001: 45). Yet even in this understanding of plurality, Honneth remains tied to the psychological dimension.
5. Miller, however, also notes that recognition is an integral part of procedural justice. I return to this issue shortly.
6. Unlike Fraser, however, Honneth sees such an integrated notion of justice in past social movements as well (1995: 166–7). He reads a concern for recognition, along with material concerns, in the histories of class activism in England by both E.P. Thompson and Barrington Moore. These studies, Honneth argues, offer empirical support for the theses that 'social confrontations follow the

pattern of a struggle for recognition' in addition to, or alongside of, struggles for distributional equity (p. 168).

7. None of this, argues Young, crosses the liberal no-fly zone into particular pictures of the 'good'. 'The liberal commitment to individual freedom, and the consequent plurality of definitions of the good, must be preserved in any reenlarged conception of justice' (1990: 36). Social justice for Young refers to institutional conditions and the social norms that lead to exclusion from the community of justice. Theories of justice may strive to take place behind a veil of ignorance or impartiality, but actual injustices do not—hence the need to address the cultural and institutional aspects of justice in dealing with real policy issues.

8. See, e.g. Dryzek (2000).

9. There are, however, some significant differences between Fraser and Young, especially given Young's desire to downplay distribution and Fraser's concern that inequitable distribution is at the heart of much of the oppression Young addresses. See Fraser's discussion of Young in chapter 8 of Fraser (1997).

Part II

Movement Definitions of Environmental Justice

3

Defining Environmental Justice in the USA

Theorists, who have attempted to expand the understanding of justice beyond the distributive realm, have all been influenced by the way social movements later in the twentieth century moved beyond a sole focus on material and distributional concerns. In many ways, the discussions of theorists, such as Fraser, Honneth, Taylor, and Young on recognition and Sen and Nussbaum on capabilities, were spawned as reflections on a variety of social movements—civil rights, women's, multicultural, gay and lesbian, sustainable development, anti-neoliberal, and many more. In other words, it has been, in part, the expansion of the understanding of justice in movements that has had a real impact on the understanding of the term in theory. With this in mind, I turned to movements for environmental justice to examine how movements themselves articulate these concepts and issues.

The literature and demands of environmental justice movements, in both the USA and globally, reveal that these movements are less enthralled with defining justice as solely distributional than are many theorists. A critique of the distribution of environmental goods and bads is certainly central to environmental justice movements, but unlike liberal theorists, movements tend to offer a more expansive, plural, and pragmatic notion of justice. The distributional paradigm is not the only articulation of justice, especially in practice. The issue of distribution is always present and central, but is also almost always tied with some discussion of recognition, political participation, and/or capabilities at both the individual and community level. The argument here is that environmental justice movements illustrate not just a concern with recognition, participation, and capabilities in addition to equity issues, but that this movement also shows us the possibility of employing a variety of notions of justice simultaneously in a comprehensive political project.

In this chapter, I want to focus on environmental justice in the USA. In separating the discussion of the USA and more global movements, I do not want to imply a theoretical distinction between them. My overall point, over the next two chapters, is that environmental justice should incorporate more than questions of distribution of environmental goods and bads, and that I derive this argument from the practice and rhetoric of movements in both the USA and elsewhere. While one key distinction between the USA and more global movements is that the former are more likely to self-identify as 'environmental justice' groups, while the latter incorporate environmental justice claims as one issue and concern among many, I simply want to dedicate a chapter to each in order to deal with them in some depth. So I will begin the discussion of the US scene with an examination of the definitions of environmental justice that exist in both the environmental justice movement and the academic literature written about it. After a brief description of the types of groups and organizations that make up the environmental justice movement in the USA, I will start with an overview of how the justice of environmental justice has been defined. I will then go into some more detail in describing equity-based, recognition-focused, procedural, and capability-oriented frames of justice using both examples from the movement and the literature that attempts to explain it.

Defining the Environmental Justice Movement(s)

One of the fastest growing, and most successful, sectors of the environmental movement in the USA is the environmental justice movement—or, rather, the set of movements, groups, and networks that make up a concern with environmental justice. The term 'environmental justice' is used to cover at least two overlapping parts of the grassroots environmental movement: the antitoxics movement and the movement against environmental racism.[1]

As Melosi has illustrated, things like sewage and municipal waste have been concentrated near the working poor, minorities, and politically disempowered groups since ancient Greece, Rome, and Egypt (Melosi 2004, also discussed by Pellow 2000). More recently, there has been a long history, predating the current environmental movement, of urban environmental problems, occupational health matters, and related issues in the USA (see Gottlieb 2005). The recent antitoxics movement got its start with the community reaction to toxins at Love Canal and the concomitant growth of awareness of the prevalence and dangers of unregulated toxic waste dumps in communities. Dumpsites and situations like Love Canal—contaminated communities with threats to human health—were the initial focus of the movement, and this focus continues. But the movement now covers a wide variety of issues relating to environmental threats to human health—not just old industrial waste sites (or new Superfund sites), but also municipal and hazardous waste dumps and incinerators, nuclear waste, industrial pollution in communities, pesticides, dioxin exposure, community sustainability, and brownfields redevelopment. There are a variety of networks that tie the movement together, the largest being The Center for Health, Environment, and Justice (or CHEJ),[2] which began in 1982 as a response to the immense need for information communities were requesting of the Love Canal Homeowners Association. The Center claims to have assisted over 8,000 groups since its work began, and receives about 1,500 requests for assistance each year.[3] But in addition to the CHEJ, there are a variety of networks focused on environmental justice and toxics issues, organized around issues such as, for example, oil refinery pollution and the effects of semiconductor manufacturing.[4]

The movement against environmental racism, which popularized the term environmental justice, focuses on environmental issues as they pertain to communities of color and the disproportionate risk those communities often face. Most academics and activists trace the beginning of this movement to a 1982 protest against the dumping of PCB-laden dirt in a new hazardous waste landfill in Warren county, North Carolina. Warren county was not only one of the poorest counties in North Carolina, but also had a population that was 65 percent African-American—yet it was chosen to receive this statewide waste. Warren county represented one of the first times civil rights groups and environmental groups worked together on issues important to both. This part of the environmental justice movement was empowered and emboldened by studies in the 1980s and early 1990s that showed not just connections between environmental risk and poverty, but specific connections between race and environmental hazards (USGAO 1983; UCC 1987; Bullard 1990; Bryant and Mohai 1992). While many of these race-based environmental justice groups begin in Native American communities, African-American communities, or among Asian textile workers or Latino/farmworkers, they often join together into broader networks (such as the Southern Organizing Committee, the Southwest Network for Economic and Environmental

Justice, the Indigenous Environmental Network (IEN), and the Asian Pacific Environmental Network, or into multiracial networks and organizations. The 1991 National People of Color Environmental Leadership Summit was a crucial organizing event for the movement, and it was there that participants developed a set of seventeen Principles of Environmental Justice (Lee 1992).

A number of authors approach the broad environmental justice movement using these dual origins—antitoxics in working-class communities and the people of color environmental justice movement (see, e.g. Pellow and Brulle 2005). When the question arises whether environmental justice is really about class or race, it is easy to note the history of both sides of the movement and come to the obvious conclusion that environmental justice has always been about both. Still, this duality does not capture all that exists under the broad umbrella of environmental justice activism in the USA. Faber and McCarthy (2003) argue that the movement has emerged out of no fewer than six popular political movements: the civil rights movement, the occupational safety and health movement, the indigenous land rights movement, the public health and safety movement, the solidarity movement (for human rights and self-determination of peoples in the developing world), and the social/economic justice movement. I would have to add that parts of the larger environmental justice movement also come out of the farmworkers, immigrant rights, and urban environmental movements. Certainly, the roots of the concern and action around environmental justice run both wide and deep. Out of this diversity, as well as a desire to eschew a top-down organizational model, have come a number of environmental justice organizations and networks focused on a wide variety of concerns and battles.

When one discusses environmental justice, the topic could be antitoxics movement issues and groups, race-based environmental justice movement issues and groups, or any combination of the list of movements above. There are certainly differences in these parts of the movement, and many authors treat them separately. As discussed in Chapter 1, Getches and Pellow (2002) fear a dilution of the impact of environmental justice movement as it moves away from a focus solely on race and poverty. Others (see, e.g. Epstein 1997; Faber and McCarthy 2003) argue that while the differences between the parts are crucial, they should still be regarded as one large 'environmental justice/toxics movement.' I share this sentiment in my own previous work on the movement (Schlosberg 1997, 1999a, 1999b, 2003), and continue it here.

One of the arguments of the present work is that even given some of the important differences and foci in the greater grassroots environmental justice movement, there is a unity, of sorts, around the conceptions of 'justice.'

The Justice of Environmental Justice

Given the essentially contested nature of the term 'justice' in its name, it is not surprising that there are quite a few varied definitions of what, exactly, is meant by environmental justice in the literature by and about the movement. Much of the literature on environmental justice examines particular cases to tell stories of injustice; explores the argument about whether such injustices are intentional, or racist, in nature; analyses the myriad ways of operationalizing and measuring such injustices; and studies the political structures and movement strategies involved. Throughout this literature, there are bits of definitions of just what 'environmental justice' means in various writings, but relatively few attempts to examine or sum up such a definition in a systematic way. The attempts at defining the term thoroughly, from an academic point of view, seem to have accelerated after Taylor's important study (2000) on the environmental justice frame, coupled with Pellow's attempt (2000) to define environmental injustice in the same issue of *American Behavioral Scientist*. Since then, there have been some important attempts to offer a particular definition of the term.[5]

The movement, of course, defined itself quite early on, with a statement of seventeen principles of environmental justice developed at the 1991 First National People of Color Environmental Leadership Summit.[6] Taylor (2000: 539–40) identifies no less than twenty-five different issues in this document, and it is truly a broad statement, covering not just protection from contamination and the cessation of the production of toxic materials, but also environmental policies based on mutual respect (as opposed to discrimination), the right to participate, and self-determination. Interestingly, nowhere in those seventeen principles is there any reference to an equitable distribution of environmental risks, which is what most observers of the movement take as the central meaning of environmental justice. And against those that see the environmental justice movement as solely anthropocentric, the principles link cultural integrity with environmental sustainability, and sustainability for humans along with other living beings.

Leaders of the movement, in their own writings, also offered numerous definitions of the central terms of environmental justice. Benjamin Chavis, then head of the United Church of Christ's Commission on Racial Justice (1987), defined the term 'environmental racism' as racial discrimination in the enforcement of environmental laws, the siting of toxic waste disposal and polluting industries, and the exclusion of people of color from environmental decision-making (Chavis 1993: 3). Key founding academic scholar-activists in the movement, such as Robert Bullard and Bunyan Bryant, added their own definitions of movement terms. Bullard's focus has always been on the relationship between race and environmental inequities, though his own works also include reference to the related issues of oppression and political disenfranchisement that are the core of recognition-based and procedural notions of justice.

In Bullard's two early edited collections (1993, 1994*a*) on the movement, as well as other early collections on the topic (Bryant and Mohai 1992; Hofrichter 1993; Bryant 1995), there is rarely a systematic attempt to define the broad term environmental justice. Still, mentions of equity (in the distribution of environmental ills), recognition (with a focus on cultural and racial recognition), and participation (particularly authentic, as opposed to inauthentic or token, inclusion) are numerous and ever-present; in addition, the capabilities and overall functioning of both affected individuals and, importantly, communities, is consistently addressed, if not in those exact terms. Throughout this literature, there is very little agreement on exactly what environmental justice means. Or, more accurately, there are a variety of notions put forward, with very little *dis*agreement; environmental justice becomes what its documenters and examiners have put forward, en masse.

Bryant's eloquent differentiation (1995) between environmental racism and environmental justice is the exception here, and it set the tone for a movement that focuses on both a broad range of injustices and a complex notion of justice itself. Bryant makes the claim that environmental justice is broader in scope than either environmental racism or environmental equity.

It refers to those cultural norms and values, rules, regulations, behaviors, policies, and decisions to support sustainable communities, where people can interact with confidence that their environment is safe, nurturing, and productive. Environmental justice is served when people can realize their highest potential, without experiencing the 'isms.' Environmental justice is supported by decent paying and safe jobs; quality schools and recreation; decent housing and adequate health care;

democratic decision-making and personal empowerment; and communities free of violence, drugs, and poverty. These are communities where both cultural and biological diversity are respected and highly revered and where distributed justice prevails. (p. 6)

I will return to this definition, but its beauty is in the breadth and integration of numerous issues that embody the movement's own understanding of justice.

Obviously, the environmental justice movement in the USA focuses on justice as an issue of distributional inequity. Studies that demonstrated such inequity, such as a 1983 United States General Accounting Office report and the 1987 study by the United Church of Christ, *Toxic Wastes and Race*, spurred the movement in its early years. But Bryant and others illustrate that also central to environmental justice struggles is an engagement of issues of individual and cultural meaning and identity. Individuals and communities insist on recognition as an integral part of their political demands. Struggles for environmental justice 'are embedded in the larger struggle against oppression and dehumanization that exists in the larger society' (Pulido 1996: 25). The bottom line here is that environmental justice activists often see their identities devalued and make a direct connection between the defense of their communities and the demand for respect. And the response to this is not solely a focus on redistribution, or even on the demands for recognition. It is also about participation, empowerment, and voice, which brings us directly to the procedures used in making decisions on environmental policies; and it is about the essence of the public, collective realm, which relates directly to capabilities and the functioning of communities and their residents.

Academics, however, have not always been so expansive and pluralistic in their attempts at defining environmental justice. Lake (1996) was one of the earliest academics to directly examine the conception of justice in the environmental justice movement; he does this in a quite critical manner. Lake complains that the movement 'generally overemphasizes issues of distributive justice' and 'adopts an unnecessarily truncated notion of procedural justice' (p. 162). He argues, following Young's discussion of the limits of the distributive paradigm, that one simply cannot have a thorough distributive justice without having justice in the *procedures* for producing that distribution. Lake suggests that the movement's focus on distributional equity not only takes away from procedural equity, but also misses the centrality of procedure in producing inequitable distribution. But Lake seems not to have recognized the amount of attention actually given to the issue of procedural equity in the movement, even in its early years. While Lake argues that the concern with procedural equity in the environmental justice movement is both limited and truncated, the principles, activists, and scholars within the movement show otherwise. There is much within both the movement's literature and its political action that demonstrates the very key focus on participatory process.

Young herself, with Hunold (Hunold and Young 1998), illustrates the importance of the combination of distributive and procedural justice in an examination of case studies of hazardous waste siting. Distributive equity is absolutely central, they argue, but it cannot answer who has a right to make a decision and by what procedures. Too often discussions of distributional equity simply assume just and workable institutions, but this is often not the case. Importantly, Hunold and Young note that public participation and discussion transforms the understanding of a problem, and often helps the public to come to a distributively fair solution. Likewise, Hampton (1999) discusses the necessity of linking equity with stakeholder involvement in decision-making. He argues that 'the promotion of environmental equity requires the provision of conditions and resources which enable communities to freely express their opinions' (p. 165). Various involved publics, he notes, should have the procedural opportunity to make their values explicit, and such participation should have an impact on policy, in order to promote a full sense of justice in the community. In both of these works, in contrast to Lake, the focus is not a critique of the movement's understanding of justice, but a description of the way that different notions of justice can be combined in practice.

Shrader-Frechette (2002) continues this dual focus on equity and participation in her important book on the topic. Specifically, she sees environmental injustice when an individual or group suffers 'disproportionate environmental risks . . . or has less opportunity to participate in environmental decision-making' (p. 3). Central to Shrader-Frechette is what she calls the 'principle of prima facie political equality;' this 'includes components of both distributive justice and participative justice' (p. 24).[7] Figueroa (2003) combines economic distribution with cultural recognition in his dualistic definition of environmental justice; he brings Fraser's theoretical discussions of a bivalent notion of justice to bear on the concept.

A number of academic examiners of environmental justice, however, articulate one or another notion of justice in their works. Still, even with these specific foci, the terms are understood in quite broad and integrated ways. Cable, Mix, and Hastings (2005) offer an example. While they still refer to environmental justice as focused on disproportionate exposure by class and race, and state that the goal of the movement is equitable distribution (p. 60), they also discuss, in depth, the importance of respect, recognition of local expertise, and participation. Pellow's work (2000) offers another example. While he begins with a stated focus on environmental inequality, Pellow, in many ways, reflects Young and others' insistence on seeing ties between inequity and institutional barriers. Pellow demands we understand environmental inequality as a sociohistorical process, one that involves multiple stakeholder groups with contradictory and conflicting interests and allegiances. In this, he wants to examine environmental justice through a life-cycle analysis of production and consumption (and disposal). So an initial focus in inequality becomes quite broad. Yet later, Getches and Pellow (2002) return to earlier themes expressed by Bullard and Chavis specifically on environmental racism. Here, the definition of environmental justice is limited to its beginnings 'at the intersection of racial discrimination and environmental insult'. As noted in Chapter 1, Getches and Pellow argue for limiting the operational definition of environmental justice for pragmatic, political reasons. They want the definition linked to policy agendas that can be reasonably accomplished, rather than to a broad and integrated notion that, they believe, would dilute the movement and its potential accomplishments.

While some purposefully narrow their definition, others, however, seem to let one particular facet of justice dominate their conception of environmental justice. Peña (2005), for example, makes the essential argument that environmental justice is, centrally, about autonomy, in addition to equity. While discussing the importance of other notions of justice, he elevates autonomy, and specifically community autonomy, overall else. Autonomy is 'about the ability of local cultures to assert control over their own space (and places) by exercising freedoms to organize production and consumption in sustainable and equitable patters that derive from self-generated ecologically and culturally appropriate norms' (p. 144). This, for Peña, is the essence of environmental justice. Ultimately, however, Peña leaves autonomy, well, autonomous, tying it with localism and the privileging of local views; this seems to leave us incapable of tying autonomy with other elements in a larger view of justice. For Peña, in other words, autonomy is necessary and sufficient as a master frame for justice; my argument is that it is necessary, but insufficient. For both a more full claim and experience of justice, and for the connection to environmental ends, autonomy needs to be tied to a number of other capabilities.

Bryner (2002) offers one of the most comprehensive definitions of environmental justice, and is in many ways closest to my own view, though closer in terms of a pluralistic approach if not in all of the included notions of justice. Bryner lays out five different ways of framing environmental justice, noting that they are not mutually exclusive, and can certainly overlap. The civil rights framework, noting a general lack of power in minority communities, is first. Second and third are the familiar questions of distributive and participatory justice. But these simply do not capture what communities are articulating, and so Bryner notes the importance of a more broad social justice framework. Here, Bryner understands that for many activists, 'environmental justice is mostly about the fundamental distribution of political power' and the need for structural change. Finally, given that Bryner lays out this definition in a book on the relationship between justice and natural resources policy, his fifth model of understanding environmental justice is within a sustainability framework. Again, it is crucial that Bryner brings this up, not only because it is a way to link environmental and ecological justice, but because numerous activists themselves address sustainability in their discussions of environmental justice (e.g. Agyeman, Bullard, and Evans 2003). This also illustrates that the line that Dobson (2003) draws between environmental justice and environmental sustainability is not one at which EJ activists stop. Many understand, as Bryner points out, that pollution prevention is one step better than distributional equity; it means less pollution for all involved, including the natural environment, which means more of a chance for true environmental sustainability.

My central point in this work is that this breadth of concepts used in defining environmental justice illustrates that the term is quite broad, integrated, expansive, and inclusive, embodying a variety of understandings of justice itself. Early on, activists in the movement took on the definition of 'environment', broadening it beyond the more mainstream organizations' notion of parks, wilderness, and the lands of the 'big outside', to an understanding of where people live, work, and play everyday (Novotny 1995). A refusal of narrow definitions is at the heart of the movement; this is explicitly stated in the case of the term 'environment,' but is no less evident in the notion of justice as well. In both theoretical and case-study approaches, we see a wide variety of meanings being used to describe the experience of environmental injustice and the calls for more just arrangements. What one sees in the literature is a variety of framings of the issue, by a rich assortment of both academics and activists. Let me examine some of those as they relate to specific, though interrelated, notions of justice.

Environmental Justice and Distribution

Even with this broad definition of environmental justice coming through in both the movement and the literature about it, the most often cited, and most obvious, evidence of environmental injustice is in the realm of distribution—specifically the inequitable share of environmental ills that poor communities and communities of color live with. Here, the focus is on how the distribution of environmental risks mirrors the inequity in socioeconomic and cultural status. As Dowie (1995: 141) has noted, '[w]hile created equal, all Americans were not, as things turned out, being poisoned equally'.

Benjamin Chavis's early argument (1993: 3) outlining 'environmental racism' makes the point bluntly: 'People of color bear the brunt of the nation's pollution problem'. Bullard's classic *Dumping in Dixie* (1990) was also thoroughly focused on distributional inequity. As noted earlier, the 1983 GAO report and the 1987 UCC study motivated and empowered the movement. The UCC study found race 'to be the most significant among variables tested in association with the location of commercial hazardous waste facilities. This represented a consistent national pattern' (UCC 1987: 9). Similar conclusions have been found in studies done with regard to hazardous waste disposal sites, various types of incinerators, polluted water, toxic releases from industry, lead poisoning, and other types of environmental dangers.[8] This line of research continues; recently, an Associated Press analysis illustrated that African-Americans are '79% more likely than whites to live in neighborhoods where industrial pollution is suspected of posing the greatest health danger' (Pace 2005).

The antitoxics side of the environmental justice movement makes the same argument along class lines: that it is not just race, but poverty that is a central indicator of the presence of environmental bads in a community. In addition, studies have shown that agencies such as the EPA enforce environmental laws in poor communities and communities of color less stringently than they do in wealthy white communities (Lavelle and Coyle 1992). Boyce et al. (1999) argue that states with greater inequalities in power (illustrated by differences in voter participation, tax fairness, Medicaid access, and education) had less stringent environmental policies and greater levels of environmental stress.

Overall, the inequity argument covers a large range of issues. From the first major collections on the issue (Bryant and Mohai 1992; Bullard 1993) to more recent discussions (e.g. Agyeman, Bullard, and Evans 2003) the discussion of inequity in the distribution of environmental goods and bads has included the disproportionate siting of hazardous waste sites, incinerators, landfills, polluting industries and facilities, nuclear facilities; the disproportionate numbers of minority workers in hazardous occupations, such as farm work, dry cleaning, and electronics; the disproportionate consumption of toxic-contaminated fish by minorities and immigrants, as well as the concomitant disproportionate exposure to pollutants and occupational illnesses as a result.[9] Critics also continue to note the inequity in the application of environmental laws and standards in poor and minority communities, including lower rates of environmental cleanup and enforcement. Finally, many authors discuss inequities in the exposure to environmental *goods* (such as parks, playgrounds, green space, clean water and air, and healthy foods). The bottom line here is that the 'unifying insight of environmental justice recognizes that neither the costs of pollution nor the benefits of environmental protection are evenly distributed throughout our society' (Edwards 1995: 36).[10]

The distributional approach, which makes up the vast majority of environmental justice research, illustrates that communities of color and poor communities are simply inequitably burdened by environmental hazards and risks, and argues against this injustice. Very basically, from this perspective, environmental inequality occurs when the costs of environmental risk, and the benefits of good environmental policy, are not shared across the demographic and geographic spectrums. As Shrader-Frechette notes (2002: 24–5), distributive justice 'requires a fair or equitable distribution of society's technological and environmental risks and impacts. It refers to the morally proper apportionment of benefits and burdens . . .'. Presumably, she continues, distributive equity requires that 'all things being equal, rich and poor, colored and white, educated and non-educated, be treated equally in the distributions of society's environmental benefits and burdens'.

The specific cases here are simply too many to mention, and they are thoroughly covered in numerous collections and descriptions of the movement. Illustration, however, is the key to understanding, so let me briefly describe just one of these cases from my own backyard in Northern Arizona. Native American nations, for example, are disproportionately and inequitably impacted by every point in the nuclear cycle, from uranium mining, to nuclear testing, to waste disposal. The Navajo Nation, the largest Native American reservation in the USA, was home to uranium mining for much of the cold war. Yet the mining companies paid Navajo miners less than the national norm, did not enforce basic safety standards in Navajo mines as they did elsewhere (such as repairing mine-shaft ventilators), left large contaminated tailings piles throughout the reservation, and discharged radioactive water into surface and well water supplies. Other uranium mining operations in the region certainly had problems, but the Navajos were disproportionately impacted; wells on the reservation are still contaminated, studies have shown lung cancer risk is doubled for people living near tailings piles, and organ cancer rates for Navajo teens are seventeen times the national average (see Pasternak 2006). The plan for the disposal of the inevitable waste produced by the nuclear plants using this mined uranium is burial at Yucca Mountain in Nevada, on the traditional home of the Shoshone nation. The Shoshone are one of the most bombed out nations on the planet, as their land became the Nevada Test Site (LaDuke 2002: 27), and, like the Navajo, tribal members suffer disproportionately from nuclear-related diseases. Environmental inequity in the nuclear cycle is a real and potent problem.

But this discussion, and this case, illustrates two very important additional points. First, environmental justice is not simply an individual experience; it is embedded in one's community. It is crucial to note that much of the environmental justice research focuses at the community level—the whole argument between focusing on zip codes versus census tracks for more accurate data masks a more important agreement: both define environmental justice in collective, geographic terms, and not individual ones. Communities are as much the victim of inequity as individuals; many authors state this without examining the implications. In addition, it is not just individuals that have mobilized for environmental justice, it is communities. Getches and Pellow (2002: 24) offer one of the few analyses to make this clear, as they argue that if 'the wrongs to be addressed are essentially community wrongs, then communities, not individuals, can stake a claim to environmental justice'. In the Navajo case, it is not just the individual experience of inequity that comes to the surface with a case of a contaminated well, or even an illness; it has become part of the community experience, the community identity and definition, the community burden, and the community response. In this, the traditional center of attention on distributive justice, or equity, becomes obviously limited in terms of the usual liberal rights that focus on individuals alone.

57

The second important point here is that there is much more to environmental justice in these cases than the framework of equity, alone, can cover. Even within the movement, there is an understanding of the limitation of the equity approach. Between the early movement activities in the 1980s and the beginning of reflection on the movement in the 1990s, both activists within, and scholars writing about, the environmental justice movement replaced the term equity with that of justice. Both practitioners and researchers began to understand that justice was broader than the singular question of equity. 'The former concept was too limiting for the job that needed to be done. By making connections between environmental and social issues, environmental justice provides an opportunity for building broad-based coalitions in order to make profound changes to enhance the quality of life of people . . . ' (Bryant 1995: 7). The term justice replaced equity in the literature of the movement because those involved in, and reflecting on, the movement understood *justice* as a more inclusive term that incorporated equity and much more (Taylor 2000: 537). Even theorists understood this shift; Shrader-Frechette's work is based on the realization that '[d]istributive justice in the allocation of environmental impacts, however, is necessary but not sufficient in order to promote environmental justice' (2002: 27).

Environmental Justice and Recognition: People, Culture, and Communities

Still, given that seeming realization that a fuller definition of environmental justice must move beyond equity, it is disappointing that most of the otherwise insightful theoretical attempts to examine environmental justice do not go into the issue of recognition. Shrader-Frechette (2002), for example, while otherwise quite thorough in her own description of why equity is incomplete, and inclusive of Young's critique of distributive justice (1990), does not address the issue of recognition. Dobson's insistence (1998) that all injustice is about inequity, likewise, misses the opportunity to fully understand and encompass how environmental justice is articulated by the movement itself. Others (Bryner 2002; Pellow and Brulle 2005) begin to touch on the issue, but without a thorough examination of the importance of recognition. Those whose work focuses on, and is informed by, the experience of affected communities, and of the importance of individual and community identity in understanding the motivations of environmental justice activists, have begun to grasp the relevance of recognition—broadly defined. Figueroa (2003, 2004) is the only academic I have encountered who explicitly examines recognition as an integral element of justice in his (Fraser-influenced) discussions of the bivalent nature of environmental justice.

While distributional equity is often the first and central definition of justice noted by activists and groups within the environmental justice movement, it certainly does not encompass all of the critiques or desires of the movement. Initially, descriptions and critiques of misrecognition focused most explicitly around issues of race and racism. As Bullard (1993: 7–8) argues, the 'focus of activists of color and their constituents reflects their life experiences of social, economic, and political disenfranchisement'. Struggles for environmental justice are motivated by various forms of oppression in the community. Krauss's study of women (1994) in the environmental justice movement demonstrates that for both white activists and activists of color, 'the starting places for and subsequent development of their analyses of toxic waste protests are mediated by issues of class, race, and ethnicity'.

It should be noted that this focus on racism has been countered by both industry and government with the argument that discrimination is not intended. For example, arguments have been offered that low-income citizens and people of color move to already polluted areas because of low-property costs, or those immigrants are simply more likely to work in agriculture or fish for subsistence. In these cases, the argument goes, there is no racist intent on the part of industry or government; and without intent, one does not have deliberate racism or misrecognition.[11] Yet this view is easily countered with a basic structural analysis. Even if racism is not explicitly intended, it remains structurally embedded. Merely because the distribution is caused by, for example, market forces rather than targeting minorities does not mean that the overall process is just. Whether an industry purposefully locates in an overwhelmingly minority area, the very existence of so many polluting sites in poor and minority areas illustrates institutionalized racism, classism, and misrecognition. As Cole and Foster (2001: 65–6) assert, if 'existing racially discriminatory processes in the housing market, for example, contribute to the distribution of environmental hazards, or of people of color, then it is entirely appropriate to call such outcomes unjust, and even racist'.

One can look to a lack of recognition and validation of identity as a central factor in the distribution of environmental risks. Hamilton, for example, notes that land use decisions reflect class and racial bias.

'Because they reflect the distribution of power in society, they cannot be expected to produce an equitable distribution of goods' (Hamilton 1993: 69). The simple point here is that there is a crucial link between a lack of recognition and the inequitable distribution of environmental bads; it is a general lack of value of the poor and people of color that leads to this distributional inequity. We can use Honneth, on the theoretical level, to examine this link. One of the central notions of respect and recognition for Honneth is physical integrity. 'The forms of practical maltreatment in which a person is forcibly deprived of any opportunity freely to dispose over his or her own body represent the most fundamental sort of personal degradation' (Honneth 1995: 132). While Honneth refers to how acts such as physical injury, torture, and rape deny recognition, we can certainly add unwanted exposure to environmental risks as an example of seizing control of a person's body against their will. Exposure to risk is a type of physical abuse, especially given the direct health effects shown to be produced by, for example, exposure to lead in urban housing or uranium mine tailings on Native American reservations. Again, there is a direct relationship between a lack of recognition and environmental degradation. These events are not independent, nor should they be considered as such. Activists in the movement understand this linkage; hence their interest, and insistence, for both environmental equity and cultural recognition.

Winona LaDuke (2002: 60), a prominent Native American activist-scholar gives another clear example of the relationship between structural inequity and the lack of recognition. EPA standards limit the level of dioxin releases from paper mills into rivers and streams. These releases are known to contaminate fish, and so the EPA based its release levels on the average consumption of such fish. Yet Native American consumption is well known to be higher than the average American, making the dioxin release a much greater health risk to native Americans.[12] Whether the EPA is deliberately racist is beside the point here; the fact is that there is structural discrimination in the setting of pollution limits by the EPA, based on a lack of recognition and acknowledgement of Native American practices of subsistence fishing.

This issue of cultural misrecognition is illustrative of the fact that much in the environmental justice literature goes beyond a focus on race alone in examining the central concern with recognition. This broad interest in the recognition of culture and identity is notable throughout the environmental justice movement's literature and political action. Laura Pulido (1996: 13) argues that central to environmental justice struggles is an engagement of issues of cultural meaning, including, but not limited to, identity. Tesh and Williams (1996) argue that identity is crucial for the movement as well, especially in its insistence on the validity of the experiential, subjective knowledge of grassroots activists and communities. Peña (2003) stresses the importance of the role of place-based community identity in environmental justice discourses. Likewise, Figueroa's recent work (2004) attempts to link issues of equity and recognition through a notion of community environmental identity. The impetus for this concern is that environmental justice activists often see themselves as outside the cultural mainstream. As such, their identities are misrecognized, malrecognized, devalued, and/or ignored. Movement groups have turned to demands for recognition as a key component of the justice of environmental justice.

This question of recognition is discussed in the movement both at the personal level and at the level of community; misrecognition is experienced in both realms. The more personal side comes up in numerous activist testimonials. Cora Tucker, an African-American activist, discussed her reaction at a town board meeting, when white women were addressed as 'Mrs. So and So', while she was addressed simply as 'Cora' by the all-white, all-male board: 'I said, "What did you call me?" He said, "Cora", and I said, "The name is Mrs. Tucker' and I had the floor until he said "Mrs. Tucker".... It's not that—I mean it's not like you've got to call me Mrs. Tucker, but it was the respect' (quoted in Krauss 1994: 267). Lois Gibbs (1982), of the CHEJ, tells a similar story of a public hearing in which representatives appeared not to be listening to her testimony. She stopped speaking, and when the hearing official finally noticed the silence and asked if she was through, simply said that she was just waiting until someone was listening. Gibbs then continued her testimony. During the campaign to halt a proposed incinerator in south central Los Angeles, women's concerns were often dismissed as irrational, uniformed, and disruptive. As Hamilton (1994: 215) argues, male city and corporate officials 'used gender as the basis for discrediting women's concerns.' In hearings regarding a proposal to build a hazardous waste incinerator in Kettleman City, California, observers noted the different body language county commissioners expressed when Mexican-American residents and representatives of ChemWaste were at the microphone—patronizing on the one hand, and respectful on the other. Vernon Masayesva, a Hopi and executive director of the Black Mesa Trust, an organization dedicated to preserving reservation water from mining use, tells of his own motivation to act as based in witnessing such misrecognition. In 1973, when

Masayesva was young, the Hopi sued mine owners and the Department of Interior to stop the world's only water-propelled coal slurry pipeline. What Masayesva remembers most clearly, and what inspired his own future activism, was 'the way the elders were being treated, ignored, and ridiculed throughout that process' (quoted in Reily 2004). This practice of misrecognition and disrespect on the individual level is an everyday experience for these activists; yet it is also motivating, and authentic recognition is a key element of their demand for justice.

But the issue of recognition obviously goes beyond individual experiences and needs; questions about, and demands for, community and cultural recognition permeate the movement as well. Certainly, activists make a direct connection between the defense of their communities and the demand for respect. An understanding of collective identity is central to social movements (Melluci 1989); this is why they are *social* movements, and not simply individual actions or collections of individual actions. One of the main reasons for the attraction and success of the environmental justice movement is its link with the civil rights framework (Camacho 1998; Taylor 2000; Faber and McCarthy 2003); key to this link is the common focus on the dignity of recognition of both individuals and communities (Agyeman, Bullard, and Evans 2003: 7).

The central concern of many environmental justice groups is community and cultural survival in a system where recognition is denied and communities and cultures are thoroughly devalued. Pulido (1996: 25) argues that one main difference between the members of mainstream environmental organizations and members of environmental justice organizations is that the latter 'draw people who already exist as a social or spatial entity in some way', as workers, a class, or community—and these communities insist on recognition.[13] A demand for community recognition was obvious in the battle of the Mothers of East Los Angeles (MELA) against the construction of a toxic waste incinerator. As Pardo (1990: 4–6) notes, the 'Mexican American women living east of downtown Los Angeles exemplify the tendency of women to enter into environmental struggles in defense of their community'. She offers a quote from MELA activist Juana Gutierrez: 'As a mother and resident of East L.A., I shall continue fighting tirelessly, so we will be respected.'

Peña's work (1999, 2002, 2003) focuses on the acequia (literally, irrigation ditch) farming communities of northern New Mexico and southern Colorado. These identities are communal, with long, embedded, and grounded histories, often stretching back to the Spanish land grants of the seventeenth century. As the places are disturbed and disrupted by environmental impacts, so are the identities of the individuals and communities that make up that place. 'To the extent that we construct our identities *in place*, whenever the biophysical conditions of a place are threatened, undermined, or radically transformed, we also see these changes as attacks on our identity and personal integrity' (Peña 1999: 6). These communities often feel like endangered species, and environmental justice battles are battles for the preservation of the 'homeland environment' and the local knowledges and senses of place that exist in those communities (Peña 1998).

For these communities, and many others in the environmental justice movement, this defense of community is nothing less than a matter of cultural survival. This is certainly central to Native American and other indigenous communities and activists. Lance Hughes, the director of Native Americans for a Clean Environment, made clear the reason for his organization's focus on environmental issues: 'We are not an environmental organization, and this is not an environmental issue. This is about our survival' (quoted in Johnson 1993: 12). LaDuke cites sovereignty issues and cultural survival as key reasons for her participation in the environmental justice movement (Di Chiro 1992: 117). LaDuke founded the White Earth Recovery Project, which seeks in part to purchase traditional tribal lands back from nontribal owners and to reestablish a traditional tribal economy; her top-stated reason for this project is the reestablishment of the dignity of the community (LaDuke 2002: 48). In one study, interviews of a variety of Native American activists show that they have 'a genocidal analysis rooted in the Native American cultural identification, the experience of colonialism, and the imminent endangerment of their culture' (Krauss 1994: 267). For activists interviewed in another study of indigenous and Chicana women in the southwest, threats 'to the environment are interpreted as threats to their families and communities'. They see 'toxic contamination of their communities as systematic genocide' (Bretting and Prindeville 1998: 149). The top motive cited by these women activists is cultural preservation, making it equal to their concern with public health (Prindeville 2004).

The case of uranium mining on the Navajo reservation can be reexamined from this perspective. One can focus on the maldistribution of environmental risk, but it is the basic racism and lack of recognition of the equality of Navajo miners that is central. This is the key to explaining the differences in attention to safety in uranium mines off versus on the reservation. This injury is not just individual, but community-impacting as well; as mining has contaminated many wells that were used for religious ceremonies, those practices at the center of communal identity and functioning are impacted. Interestingly, however, early in the battle, the main environmental justice organization on the Navajo nation, DineCare,[14] focused on the health impacts on individual miners, their families, and native communities, rather than on the cultural impacts. They did this to win individual legal rights for miners and their descendants.

More recently, however, threats to Navajo, and the nearby Hopi, religious identities are being directly confronted. While native cultures see the home landscape of these nations as sacred ground, the majority culture sees the land as a national sacrifice zone (Kuletz 1998: 7). The main argument against the continued use of pure and increasingly rare aquifer water to slurry coal from mines on Black Mesa through a pipeline to an electricity generating station 273 miles away in Nevada is that the drawdown of the aquifer is impacting springs used for religious ceremonies and agriculture. In this arid area, the tribes consider water a centerpiece of their physical and spiritual existence. Simply put, the disappearance of the water is threatening the traditional practices and lifestyle of the Navajo and Hopi. The mining and power companies' lack of recognition of these impacts on the native communities literally adds insult to injury.[15] In another example, increased oil and natural gas drilling near the reservation, on a mountain site that is sacred to the Navajo, is also causing distress. The president of the Navajo nation, Joe Shirley Jr., complained that 'because of their significance to Dine life, any desecration through oil and gas drilling on or near the two mountains will have a devastating effect on Navajo beliefs.' Another Navajo official noted that 'it's like putting a gas well on top of the Lincoln Memorial...The insensitivity of the gas companies when it comes to our culture is hard to fathom' (both quoted in Romero 2003).

So, in addition to equity, the environmental justice movement focuses on individual and community recognition; the point is to gain recognition for oneself, for one's own community, and for the movement as a whole. The self-respect and autonomy demanded by individuals and communities fighting for environmental justice includes gaining recognition from others, and mutual respect for various communities, identities, and cultures. Importantly, however, such recognition is also clearly tied to participation and self-determination.

Environmental Justice and the Centrality of Participation

The African-American feminist scholar Patricia Hill Collins (1998: 46) notes that the phrase 'coming to voice' is being increasingly used in both feminist and black feminist writing; this notion includes breaking silence, developing self-reflexive speech, and confronting or talking back to oppressors. As with much in contemporary theory, this move is simultaneously occurring in many social movements as well; demands for individual and community voice and self-empowerment have become a central part of the environmental justice movement. Benjamin Chavis's definition of environmental racism (1993: 3) includes 'the history of excluding people of color from the mainstream environmental groups, decision-making boards, commissions, and regulatory bodies'. In addition, one can certainly see a link between a lack of individual or cultural recognition and a lack of valid participation in the political process. Simply put, misrecognition due to racism and/or classism creates real structural obstacles to political participation. In response, one of the earliest slogans of the movement, and a mainstay since, is the notion that 'we speak for ourselves' (Alston 1991). As Di Chiro (1992: 98) argued at the time, the question of agency inherent in 'speaking for ourselves' is a principal issue for activists in the movement. For Lee (1993: 39) self-determination and participation in decision-making about one's own environment is central to environmental justice; it brings with it an appreciation of diverse cultural perspectives and an honoring of cultural integrity. For Bullard (1993: 13), the reason for insistence on speaking for ourselves is the empowerment of disenfranchised people and their inclusion in a more fully democratized process. Again, activists in the movement understand the linkage between recognition and participation in the political process. Bullard (1993: 202) argues that 'African-Americans and other people of color must be empowered through their own organizations and institutions if they are to effectively address the problem' of environmental injustice. Coming to voice, and to participation, is central to environmental and social justice as it breaches a range of structural and cultural obstacles—including cultural degradation, oppression, and lack of political access. This holds not just for communities of color, but all individuals and communities fighting the injustice of misrecognition.

Without a doubt, the demand for political participation in decisions governing communities has been essential to the environmental justice movement from its inception. The construction of inclusive, participatory decision-making institutions—speaking for ourselves, a 'place at the table,'[16] equal, informed, respectful participation—has consistently been at the center of environmental justice demands. Environmental justice activists call for policymaking procedures that encourage active community participation, institutionalize public participation, recognize community knowledge, and utilize cross-cultural formats and exchanges to enable the participation of as much diversity as exists in a community. Through the development of various principles and policy suggestions, a shared and respected role in the decision-making process has been well documented and expressed as a key demand of the movement.

The Principles of Environmental Justice, developed at the First National People of Color Environmental Leadership Conference in 1991, include calls for procedural equity that were on par with calls for other forms of justice. The Principles include demands that 'public policy be based on mutual respect and justice for all peoples', 'the right to participate as equal partners at every level of decision-making including needs assessment, planning, implementation, enforcement and evaluation', and 'the fundamental right to political, economic, cultural and environmental self-determination for all peoples'. These calls for procedural justice permeate the demands, and the practices, of a variety of environmental justice organizations. For example, the Southwest Organizing Project (SWOP 1995) developed a 'Community Environmental Bill of Rights'. It includes 'the right to participate as equals in all negotiations and decisions affecting our lives, children, homes and jobs', and the 'right of access without cost to information and assistance that will make our participation meaningful, and to have our needs and concerns be the major factor in all policy decisions'.

Movement groups, such as SWOP, have been calling for thorough and authentic public participation in environmental decision-making throughout the history of environmental justice in the USA. From the classic early battles, such as against incinerators in south central Los Angeles (Hamilton 1994) and community contamination in Carver Terrace, Texas (Oliver 1994), the right to participate in decisions has been central. In Carver Terrace, there was anger over the fact that information regarding health risks had been available to the EPA in the form of a report for over a year, but was not released to the local community most impacted by these risks. While a government buyout of the community was the primary goal of the neighborhood group, participatory claims were central to the process. The residents insisted on accurate information; a prompt, respectful, and unbiased hearing on contamination claims; and democratic participation in deciding the future of the community (which was eventually bought out by the federal government) (Capek 1993: 8). These demands for participation continue to be central throughout the environmental justice movement.

One of the earliest political victories for environmental justice advocates in the USA was the establishment in 1992 of the Office of Environmental Justice in the Environmental Protection Agency; this office serves as the home of the National Environmental Justice Advisory Council (NEJAC), which is chartered to provide advice to the EPA and the federal government on a range of issues. The NEJAC established a subcommittee on Public Participation, which developed a 'Model Plan for Public Participation' to be used by federal agencies in designing a process for participation for communities affected by environmental policies under consideration (USEPA 1996, updated 2000a). The Model Plan suggests that policymaking procedures must encourage active community participation, institutionalize public participation, recognize community knowledge, and utilize cross-cultural formats and exchanges to enable the participation of as much diversity as exists in a community. A variety of other publications by the NEJAC include recommendations on public participation in federal permitting processes (USEPA 2000b), and two guides for consultation, collaboration, and meaningful involvement for indigenous groups and tribal members in environmental decision-making and regulatory processes (NEJAC 2000, 2004).

Academic studies of the movement over the years have steadily highlighted this particular type of demand for justice. In Freudenberg and Steinsapir's early study of the movement, the first and major shared perspective across the grassroots is the 'right of citizens to participate in making environmental decisions—emphasis on process as well as content of decision making' (1992: 31). Capek's environmental justice 'frame' (1993: 8) includes a demand for accurate information, respectful and unbiased hearing of claim, and democratic participation in deciding the future of contaminated communities. Hamilton (1993: 67) notes the movement's expansion of the conception and practice of democracy to be more inclusive of community input. She argues that the focus of the movement is on a broad notion of ecological democracy, including new forms of citizen participation in governance. Bullard (1994b: xvii) also lays it out clearly: 'What do grass-roots leaders want? These leaders are demanding a shared role in the decision-making processes that affect their communities. They want participatory democracy to work for them.' The focus is on fully realizing democratic participation in environmental and community decision-making. Gould, Schnaiberg, and Weinberg (1996: 4) state that '[f]rom our perspective, these groups are attempting to exercise their rights as citizens. They seek to have some say in the local development of their communities, in order to ensure that the quality of their lives will be protected.' Hunold and Young (1998) look to hazardous waste protests and see questions of both material distribution and the injustice of decision-making procedures. Bretting and Prindeville (1998: 153) found a strong belief in the rights of citizens to participate in making environmental decisions common among all activists interviewed. Part of my own previous work (Schlosberg 1999*b*) focused on the participatory demands and practices of movement groups and networks. And Bryner (2002) analyzes the public participation framework as one of the key frameworks of environmental justice. Participation of those previously left out of environmental decision-making is an absolutely essential part of the movement. 'Justice may require the right to participate in a decision making process, the right to have one's interest included in the analysis, or the right to be represented by others' (Bryner 2002: 46). Obviously, through these principles, group demands, and policy suggestions, a shared and respected role in the decision-making process is central to the movement. This demand for procedural equity is not just in the principles of the movement, but in actions on the range of diverse issues the environmental justice movement addresses.[17]

The demand for this type of authentic, community-based participation comes out of the experience of disenfranchisement—the combination of misrecognition and political exclusion. The lack of participation in environmental decision-making comes, in very large part, from the limitations of race, class, and gender. These present a range of structural obstacles—including less access to political, legal, scientific, economic, and other resources—to full participation in environmental decisions. Environmental justice groups often argue that the injustices they suffer come from a lack of oversight; the demand to counter this is not just a call for a recognition of the problem, but also a call for more thorough and participatory local input into, and control over, environmental decisions. Groups do not want others—either mainstream environmental groups or governmental agencies—simply saying that they will take care of the community's interests; they wish to be consulted from the start, speak for themselves, work with a variety of other groups and agencies, and be offered a full partnership in the making of decisions.

There are a number of specific types of participatory practices that movement groups see as part of their demand for environmental justice.

First, and most basically, communities demand information about the issues and risks that affect them. Information is an essential part of informed consent, which is included in the list of principles of environmental justice from 1991. As Shrader-Frechette argues (2002: 77), central to a right of informed consent is both the protection of individual autonomy and protection from harm. In medical ethics, she explains, there are four conditions which must be met in order to satisfy informed consent: those creating a risk must disclose full information, the potential victims must be competent to evaluate that information, they must understand the danger involved, and they must voluntarily accept the risk. Environmental justice groups focus on getting information from governments and industry, and sharing this information with the community, in order to be more competent decision makers. The lack of information is seen as not only a violation of informed consent and procedural justice, but also as an act of individual and community deception. While political and economic actors often claim that community members are not qualified to make judgments on technical issues, those community members insist that they should have all of the information available to other decision makers.

Second, and most obviously, environmental justice groups insist on inclusion in the traditional policymaking and environmental decision-making processes. Again, the original principles of environmental justice include statements about political and environmental self-determination, and the right to participate as equal partners at every level of decision-making. These two aspects of participation—information and inclusion in decision-making—are easily found within the demands of the vast majority of environmental justice organizations; in fact, it would be difficult to find an issue where public participation is not a movement demand. Why? Hunold and Young (1998: 87) argue that public deliberation is not only the most likely way to a distributively fair solution, but that the process itself respects the interests and autonomy of people. That is, if it meets certain procedural criteria. In addition to access to information, Hunold and Young (pp. 88–9) insist that participants have equal resources to examine information, that all affected perspectives are included, that consultation occur over time (rather than in a single public hearing), that decision-making authority be shared, and that public decision-making be authoritative (rather than symbolic). This type of informed, ongoing inclusion and authority are at the center of environmental justice demands. Even those critical of the movement and its underlying claims of environmental risk (e.g. Bowen and Wells 2002) see the movement's prevailing concerns focused on procedural inclusion and community empowerment.[18]

Third, and increasingly, a notion of community-based participatory research as a part of procedural justice is taking hold in the movement. In this process, 'scientists work in close collaboration with community partners involved in all phases of the research, from the inception of the research questions and the study design, to the collection of the data, monitoring of ethical concerns, and the interpretation of the study results' (Shepard et al. 2002). The related practice of popular epidemiology (Brown and Mikkelsen 1990; Brown 1992) was at the heart of a couple of key environmental justice battles—community health surveys done with community involvement were crucial to understanding cases of contamination in Love Canal and Woburn. A number of academics and EJ activists see participatory research as a way for the movement to build relationships with researchers. While the idea of a 'communiversity' (Wright 1995) was idealistic, it was the impetus for environmental justice research centers at universities such as Clark and Xavier. More often, partnerships develop between researchers and communities on particular issues, where communities participate as partners and research subjects simultaneously. This model of more full, authentic participation goes beyond just informed consent in environmental justice research, into full partnership in the creation of community knowledge.

Interestingly, while we do not see in many definitions of environmental justice the emphasis on liberal individualism that is at the heart of many theories of liberal justice, the focus on procedure illustrates the importance and resonance of those theories and their focus on impartiality and just procedures to adjudicate among different substantive goals and conceptions of life. Yet, again, as with both equity and recognition, the issues involved in participatory justice need to be understood and addressed at both the individual and community level. The relationship between individual experience and community achievement is crucial to the practice of participation as an element of environmental justice, and empowerment is the key here. Gottlieb (1993: 210–11) argues that the individual transformative experiences and the focus on one's own community create a very powerful image of that community. As Austin and Schill (1991: 74) observed very early in the movement, grassroots people have proven that they are capable of leading, speaking, and doing for themselves and for their communities. This practice has been central in the history of a wide variety of environmental justice groups in the USA. And those individual and group achievements have an impact on both individual and community. Camacho (1998: 27) notes that the various actions of individuals and community groups have brought a sense of efficacy in the political process.

The Role of Capabilities and Functioning

The capabilities argument, where justice includes these elements in a larger picture of the basic functioning of individuals and communities, is also articulated, if not in Sen and Nussbaum's own words.[19] Bryant's early definition of environmental justice serves as an example here. Environmental justice refers to places 'where people can interact with confidence that the environment is safe, nurturing, and productive. Environmental justice is served when people can realize their highest potential' (Bryant 1995: 6). Bryant includes decent paying and safe jobs, quality schools, recreation, housing, and health care, democratic decision-making and personal empowerment—all in addition to distributive justice. Here is one of the founders and intellectual pillars of the movement, articulating a notion of environmental justice based, essentially, in a notion of community capabilities and functioning. As Taylor argues (2000: 535), one of the reasons why environmental justice originally had resonance in black communities is because those communities had long supported struggles for better housing conditions, more worker rights, and less segregation of public places. In other words, there was a long-standing understanding of justice having to do, more generally, with the general functioning of community, in addition to specific forms of discrimination and inequity.

More recently, Faber and McCarthy (2003: 58) note that the most important part of environmental justice activism is building community and community capacity, and facilitating community empowerment. Di Chiro (2008) discusses the focus on 'social reproduction' in the movement.[20] Prindeville's interviews with activists illustrate that they are mobilized to political action by a desire to empower their communities and preserve their cultures, in addition to achieving distributional equality (2004: 93). The overall emphasis of environmental justice groups is on community functioning—including the basics of health, safety, and well-being, along with equality, recognition, and participation. Environmental justice activists work to achieve economic equity, social justice, and environmental quality for their communities.

Let me briefly lay out two specific examples of capabilities and functioning as central to environmental justice organizing. The growth of asthma in many communities has become a motivator for environmental justice organizing. Asthma in children, in particular in cities, increased by 52 percent between 1982 and 1996 (Sze 2004), and has become a major issue for environmental justice organizations such as West Harlem Environmental Action (WEACT) in New York and Alternatives for Community and Environment (ACE) in Boston. As Brown et al. (2005) argue, asthma has become a politicized illness experience. Many environmental justice groups attempt to help sufferers of asthma understand the social, structural, and environmental determinants of their health issues. Importantly, and as Brown et al. argue, environmental justice groups focus not on the individual experience of asthma, but instead on the collective identity and the community cost of the spreading illness. ACE, for example, focuses on housing, transportation, access to health care, pollution sources, and industrial policy in addition to health education. Here, the issue of the asthma epidemic is understood and addressed in terms of its impact on, and threat to, the functioning of both individuals and the greater community. In response, movement groups emphasize the community capabilities—pollution control, transportation policy, health policy, and access—that are necessary to improve both individual and community functioning. While equity is discussed, recognition is demanded, and participation in policymaking is sought, asthma campaigns in the environmental justice community are more generally about reestablishing the capabilities necessary for a healthy, functioning community.

Cultural preservation for Native American environmental justice activists is also not just an issue of recognition, but of community functioning. As noted earlier in discussing recognition, many activists see threats to native lands as direct assaults on native peoples and long-standing cultural practices. Land destruction is seen as an erosion of traditional lifestyle, health, and culture—in a word, genocidal.[21] Many Native American activists discuss the loss of sacred sites and cultural practices, and the impact on community functioning. The mining examples earlier exemplify this focus, but threats to community capabilities and continuity come up throughout Native American environmental justice activism. For example, Ojibwe culture believes that the creator provided fish to feed both belly and soul. But given the contamination of much fish in the region with PCBs and mercury, the state advises people to eat only one fish per week. So the Ojibwe are torn between sustaining their cultural beliefs and practices on the one hand, and preserving the health of their children on the other—if you cut back fish intake, you decimate culture, and if you eat them, you poison the next generation. Either practice threatens the viability of one's community, and decimates the capabilities necessary for the culture and people to continue to function and thrive. In another example, a recent decision by the US Forest Service to allow reclaimed water (i.e. treated sewage) to be used for snowmaking on local mountains seen as sacred by thirteen tribes was described simply as 'cultural genocide' by the president of the Navajo Nation—in other words a direct attack on the cultural capabilities and functioning of the tribe.[22] These types of threats to the functioning of community are repeated throughout Native American environmental justice battles— for traditional fishing, for the protection of sacred sites and practices, and for the preservation of traditional economic and cultural activities. Important in all of these cases is a focus on community, in addition to individuals.

The Interplay of Equity, Recognition, Participation, and Capabilities in Environmental Justice

While it is convenient to offer discussions of equity, recognition, participation, and capabilities in distinct sections, above, one very rarely sees movement groups discuss one of these dimensions of justice in isolation. Groups integrate these notions of justice, and while a group may call for equal distribution of environmental risks, it will also complain about the lack of recognition of community members, the lack of participatory opportunities, and/or the decimation of community functioning. As in the discussion of justice on the theoretical level, these notions of justice in the environmental justice movement are thoroughly integrated in practice. Conceptions of justice, and, more importantly, the experiences of injustice, are experienced in numerous ways at once.

Within the environmental justice movement, one simply cannot talk of one aspect of justice without it leading to another. This dedication to a broad understanding of justice was apparent—in both the process and the results—very early in the movement at the First National People of Color Leadership Summit and in the principles that were developed there. As Dana Alston argued at the summit: 'Our vision of the environment is woven into an overall framework of social, racial, and economic justice' (Alston 1992: 50). Taylor (1993: 57) notes that the environmental justice movement 'integrates both social and ecological concerns much more readily [than the traditional environmental movement] and pays particular attention to questions of distributive justice, community empowerment, and democratic accountability.' And, as noted earlier, Bryant

(1995: 6), one of the academic founders of the movement, insists that a thorough definition of 'environmental justice' (as distinguished from environmental racism and environmental equity) is broad, referring to cultural norms, people realizing their highest potential, personal empowerment, and democratic decision-making.[23] Unfortunately, these statements are often lost in the wealth of literature available on environmental justice, and many still misread the conception of justice in the movement as purely equity-based. The argument here, however, is that not only are there different conceptions of justice apparent in the movement, but the movement also recognizes that these notions of justice must be interrelated: one must have recognition in order to have real participation; one must have participation in order to get equity; further equity would make more participation possible, which would strengthen community functioning, and so on.

One possible critique of the inclusive approach to justice is that everything flows from the maldistribution of risks and resources, or that redistribution will satisfy all such broader demands. Indeed, some argue that environmental justice activists would be satisfied if the government simply improved the distribution of environmental bads. The common objection raised to this expansion of the environmental justice discourse here is usually articulated like this: 'Members of environmental justice organizations desire recognition and demand participation to be sure, but they would trade them in a heartbeat for distributional equity.' But there are two problems with this response. First, it simply assumes that (re)distributional equity can occur within existing social, economic, and institutional conditions. The point of including issues of recognition, participation, and capabilities in a larger theory of justice is that distributional equity simply *cannot* come about otherwise. Environmental justice groups *will never have the opportunity* to trade recognition for a better distribution of environmental bads; such a distribution will not come about without satisfaction of the broader elements of justice: recognition, participation in environmental decision-making, and the capabilities necessary for communities to flourish. Second, given the broad focus of environmental justice, I do not see activists being satisfied without all aspects of justice being achieved; more importantly, activists recognize that such government capitulation *will not simply happen* without a broader cultural recognition of the victims of environmental injustice, their inclusion in problem-solving and policymaking, and functioning communities. There are definite relationships between inequity, misrecognition, lack of participation, and capabilities; the integration of these concerns in the achievement of environmental justice is at the heart of the movement, in both its critiques and its intended solutions.

And this relationship is understood within the movement. Pulido (1996) argues that environmental justice movements are 'simultaneously about both material concerns and systems of meaning' (p. 13) and how the various forms of injustice suffered are mutually constitutive. 'The task is to identify the ways in which racism, cultural oppression and identity interact with economic forces to create unique forms of domination and exploitation;' such a concern with this linkage leads to a need to challenge 'the various lines of domination that produce the environmental conflict or problem experienced by the oppressed group in the first place' (pp. 32, 192–3). This means confronting material inequality, cultural misrecognition, capabilities, and other power relations that deny meaningful participation. For the environmental justice movement, the demand for more public participation and procedural equity in the development, implementation, and oversight of environmental policy is the key to address issues of distributional equity, recognition, and capabilities. It is a focus on the political process, specifically demands for public participation and community empowerment, which is seen as the tool to achieve the broad aims of justice.

Again, the point here is that the movement embodies a comprehensive integration of numerous conceptions of justice. The integration of notions of justice is evident throughout these cases. The environmental justice discourse, or frame, in these cases encompasses inequity, the lack of recognition, and exclusion from decision-making; but the discourse also includes important reference to both individual and community capabilities, overall functioning, and the potential of individuals and communities to thrive.

Conclusion

The movement for environmental justice may not add anything to the theoretical literature of the study of justice, but its analyses, practices, and demands undoubtedly offer a real-world illustration of these theoretical concepts in political action. Certainly, and at the very least, it should be clear that environmental justice means much more than a lack of equity in the distribution of environmental ills. More broadly, what the environmental justice movement demonstrates is the possibility of addressing different conceptions of justice simultaneously, and bringing numerous notions of justice into a singular political project. In this, I would argue that the movement demonstrates that it is, indeed, possible to incorporate both material and postmaterial demands in a single and comprehensive political movement. As Pulido has noted, environmental justice offers 'a positive example of how postmodern identity politics can be linked to concrete material struggle' (1996: xvii). The project of environmental justice goes much further, however, combining elements of economic and quality of life issues, along with identity politics, within a context of a struggle for political participation and the functioning of communities. 'Environmental Justice' in the USA illustrates that the theoretical arguments about the nature of justice are more than academic exercises; the issues surrounding a struggle for justice on all fronts has been brought to life clearly, comprehensively, and forcefully by a very active and passionate political movement.

Notes

1. For overviews see: Adamson, Evans, and Stein (2002), Agyeman, Bullard, and Evans (2003), Bryant and Mohai (1992), Bryant (1995), Bullard (1993), Bullard (2005), Cole and Foster (2001), Faber (1998), Hofrichter (1993), Pellow and Brulle (2005), Roberts and Weiss (2001), Stein (2004), and Szasz (1994).
2. Previously the Citizen's Clearinghouse for Hazardous Waste (CCHW).
3. See http://www.chej.org
4. The Refinery Reform Campaign, at http://www.refineryreform.org, and the Campaign for Responsible Technology (CRT), at http://www.svtc.org
5. See, e.g. Agyeman (2005), Bryner (2002), Cole and Foster (2001: ch. 3); Figueroa (2003, 2004), Getches and Pellow (2002), Peña (2002), Schlosberg (2003, 2004), and Shrader-Frechette (2002).
6. The principles have been published in numerous places. See Lee (1992) for a description of the summit and the development of the principles. See Agyeman (2005), Dryzek and Schlosberg (2005), or the Web site of the Environmental Justice Resource Center [www.ejrc.cau.edu/princej.html] for the full list of principles.
7. Shrader-Frechette approaches the definition of environmental justice a bit differently than my tack in this work. Her method is to define the term through an exploration of philosophical principles illustrated with environmental justice cases. Through thought experiments, she explores principles that could support the attainment of environmental justice. But this philosophical focus moves away from the original concerns with distribution and informed consent, and into questions of paternalism, compensating wage differential, and moral heroism, e.g. In this, Shrader-Frechette offers keen insights into how

notions of environmental justice are often philosophically difficult, yet she distances herself from the stated concerns and language of groups organized to articulate their woes and fight environmental injustice.

8. See also, e.g. Bryant and Mohai (1992) and Bullard (1993).
9. This includes the experience of environmental blackmail, or having to accept hazardous jobs and industries in the face of the threat of no jobs at all.
10. There are numerous arguments about the accuracy of these equity claims, as some studies have attempted to show no racial or class bias. Differences in findings occur depending on the level of analysis (from state-level data down to census tract) and the nature of the environmental problem (toxic releases, incinerators, waste dumps, etc.). For a discussion of the earliest criticisms of the inequity approach, and a response from one of the researchers on the United Church of Christ study, see Goldman (1996). For constructive overviews of the equity literature, see Szasz and Meuser (1997), Lester and Allen (1999), and Bowen (2001). While I, personally, am convinced by the data, the empirical disagreements are immaterial to the argument here regarding the overall conception of justice constructed by the movement.
11. There are numerous examples of this argument. See Starkey (1994) and Boerner and Lambert (2000). Also see the excellent discussions of this issue in Shrader-Frechette (2002: 15–16), and in Cole and Foster (2001: ch. 3).
12. A 1 in 8,600 risks of cancer, rather than the EPA standard one in a million risks, claims LaDuke.
13. I discussed these preexisting social relations as part of a larger discussion of movement networks in previous work (Schlosberg 1999*a*, 1999*b*).
14. On the Web at dinecare.indigenousnative.org/history.html
15. Interestingly, one of the other points is the lack of recognition of traditional ecological knowledge; tribal critics note that the companies only pay attention to Western science. See Reily (2004) and blackmesatrust.org
16. See, in particular, the early discussion among Anthony et al. (1993).
17. It is also crucial to note that the emphasis on procedural justice and participation is evident not just in the external demands made by the movement, but also in the *internal* processes many groups and networks set out for themselves. See the discussion in Schlosberg (1999*b*: ch. 6). Brulle and Essoka (2005) counter with the claim that EJ organizations are not, in fact, very democratic or participatory, but their narrow study relies on an analysis of the printed bylaws of a limited number of organizations, which do not always reflect the real internal structures and practices of groups.
18. But, problematically, Bowen and Wells (2002) classify the motivation as merely 'power politics' and go on to dismiss the demand on the basis that decisions should be made by trained professionals in the public sector, based solely on 'sound' science, rather than the seeming irrationality of the uneducated community. Such a position violates not only environmental justice, but most models of democracy as well.

19. No activist writings that I am familiar with mention the capability approach by name, and Bryner (2002) is the only academic who has mentioned Sen in his attempt to define environmental justice as practices in the USA However, Bryner focuses very broadly on Sen's conception of development as freedom, and not specifically on how such a focus translates into attention to the capabilities and functioning of individuals and communities.

20. Di Chiro (2008) uses a feminist framework very close to the capabilities approach, on 'social reproduction', to understand environmental justice movements (see also Bakker and Gill 2003, Katz 2001). Her argument is that these movements work to preserve processes required to maintain everyday life and sustain cultures and communities—in other words, community functioning.

21. See, e.g. stories in Weaver (1996) and LaDuke (2002).

22. For more information on this case, see www.savethepeaks.org

23. Still, it is odd that a number of academics who study various conceptions of justice in the movement continue a focus on presenting or defining environmental justice as purely equity-based. Pulido (1996), for example, focuses thoroughly on cultural recognition and the forms of institutional power that deny that recognition to groups, but the title of the work—*Environmentalism and Economic Justice*—does not reflect this complexity. Certainly, Pulido understands the movement in more thorough terms than that. Others, however, seem not to recognize their own limited definition. Bretting and Prindeville (1998) specifically study the threat of cultural destruction faced by Chicana and indigenous women activists, yet define environmental justice as purely distributional in the introduction to their work.

4

Environmental Justice and Global Movements

The environmental justice movement within the USA certainly developed and popularized the concept(s) of environmental justice. But the phrase has been readily adopted by a number of movements outside the USA, both those global in nature and those based in, or incorporating, the Global South. As with the American movement, the literature and discourse of movement groups that articulate demands for environmental justice reveal a concept that includes distributional concerns—and much more. As with environmental justice groups in the USA, the most obvious and oft-cited evidence of environmental injustice in the global realm is distributive—specifically the inequitable share of environmental ills with which poor communities, indigenous communities, communities of color, and communities with economies outside the neoliberal model must live. Here, the call for environmental justice focuses on how the distribution of environmental risks mirrors the inequity in socioeconomic and cultural status. But while distributional inequity is crucial to the definition of environmental justice, it is a necessary yet insufficient factor in that definition at the global scale. Again, a critique of the distribution of environmental goods and bads is central to groups that invoke environmental justice, but they offer a much more broad definition of justice which includes conceptions of, and demands for, recognition, participation, and capabilities for both individuals and communities.

The question of recognition is discussed by groups at both the personal level and at the level of community—recognition for cultures, traditions, and ways of economic, social, and religious life. Misrecognition is seen as both the cause and the effect; on the one hand it is the lack of recognition that leads to distributional inequity, exclusion, and devastated communities, and on the other hand it is the continued inequity and exclusion that creates the conditions for continued mis- or malrecognition. Additionally, the construction of inclusive, participatory decision-making institutions is at the center of environmental justice demands globally, as it is in the USA. Activists use the claim of environmental injustice to call for policymaking procedures that encourage active community participation, institutionalize public participation, recognize community knowledge, and utilize cross-cultural formats and exchanges to enable the participation of diverse, and traditionally excluded, communities. To challenge a range of cultural, political, and structural obstacles constructed by cultural degradation, political oppression, and lack of political access, communities and movement groups are coming to demand a voice and authentic participation. The demand for this type of authentic, community-based participation comes out of the process of disenfranchisement, the experience of mis- or malrecognition and/or a frustration with the debilitation of capabilities.

At the global level, discussions of capabilities and explicit references to the functioning of both individuals and communities are central to arguments for environmental justice. The literature and demands of movement groups are full of descriptions of the loss of health, the decimation of economies, and the destruction of traditional cultures and practices. In addition, and as with both recognition and participation, the discussion of capabilities and the related loss of functioning is articulated at both the individual and community level. Environmental injustice is seen as a process that takes away the ability of individuals and their communities to fully function, through poor health, destruction of economic livelihoods, and general and widespread environmental threats.

Overall, and once again, the justice of environmental justice is made up of a broad array of claims and demands, including equity, recognition, participation, and capabilities. And as with environmental justice in the USA, these global groups demonstrate that one can hold together a broad and integrated notion of justice, and use a variety of theoretical approaches and frames, in the discourse of a pragmatic and engaging political project.

While the claims are similar, it is important to note that environmental justice outside the USA, however, is quite different from the movement within the USA. The US movement was made possible by the confluence of a number of factors that simply do not exist, in tandem, elsewhere (Carruthers, forthcoming). First, the strong, preexisting, race-based civil rights movement in the USA is rarely matched, though indigenous movements in various places certainly use the language and tactics. More problematically, the US movement had access to clear demographic evidence illustrating the inequitable distribution of environmental hazards and risk; movements in the Global South rarely have the kind of data used in environmental justice studies in the USA. In addition, one must always pay attention to localized discourses of social movements; while some groups may be dealing with issues of environmental contamination, they may articulate their concerns with localized discourses unrelated to those used by the US movement. Yet environmental justice as a phrase and a call does have resonance at the global level, and in the Global South; environmental concerns are often brought within the larger (or local) discourse of social justice—and the movements associated with such general calls for justice. Environmental justice is much more a component discourse in these social justice movements, or one of many organizing concerns, than it is a stand-alone movement of its own. Still, in the developing world, from India to Africa to Latin America, environmental justice has become a theme, and a demand, of numerous movements.[1]

Given this difference in environmental justice organizing outside the USA, I address the justice of environmental justice differently in this chapter. Rather than attempt an analysis of the thousands of NGOs and grassroots organizations in the global realm doing some sort of work identified with a theme of environmental justice, I want to briefly focus on a few of the most potent issues of the moment, and illustrate how the term is defined and addressed within each by movement groups that articulate demands for environmental justice. Certainly, recent actions against the most visible institutions of the new global economy—the World Trade Organization (WTO), the International Monetary Fund (IMF), and the World Bank—encompass and articulate themes of environmental justice. Related, movements for food autonomy and security are also expressed with the language of justice for both people and nature. Additionally, and again related, numerous movements for indigenous rights in both the North and South are imbued with the variety of issues of environmental justice I am discussing. Finally, the cause of climate justice has been taken up by many groups over the past decade; their conception of justice is illustrative of all of the themes and concepts noted above. These movements encompass notions of *environmental* justice because in each of the individual foci, part of what is to be distributed are environmental goods and bads, part of what is to be recognized are cultural and/or traditional ways of living with nature, one aspect of participatory demands relate to environmental decision-making, and capabilities and individual and community functioning are seen as threatened by environmental ills.

Equity and Distribution

Certainly, at the center of the recent protests against global financial and trade institutions, against the globalization of the food system, and for climate justice and indigenous rights, is the issue of equity; economic or distributive injustice is a key and constant rallying cry. The most basic critique of the currently favored neoliberal model of globalization and development is that it increases and exacerbates inequity, both between the North and the South and between elites and the impoverished in southern nations. Critics point out that countries praised for adopting this model often saw a growth in the fortunes of a rich minority, at the expense of the majority of the population, for whom conditions of life often deteriorated.[2] Public Citizen's Global Trade Watch (1999), one of the major organizers of events related to the WTO meeting in Seattle in 1999 and after, makes the point quite directly: 'the WTO has contributed to the concentration of wealth in the hands of the rich few, increasing poverty for the majority of the world's population'. Questions regarding who benefits and at whose expense, as well as a demand for the accounting of the full costs of trade to communities, workers, and nature, are key. This is also illustrated in Global Exchange's 'Top Ten Reasons to Oppose the IMF' (Global Exchange 2000*a*). Here, another of the key leading NGOs of the recent protests argues that the IMF 'caters to wealthy countries and Wall Street' while increasing poverty and hurting workers, women, and the environment.

Importantly, this critique regarding inequity addresses not just the distribution of economic goods but environmental goods and bads as well. Many groups criticize the strain on natural resources as nations move to an export-led economy, and note the inequity in the distribution of natural resources, including potable water, as they are privatized. The '50 Years Is Enough' campaign of the US Network for Global Economic Justice (USNGEJ) insists on the suspension of policies and practices of the IMF and World Bank that have 'caused widespread poverty, inequality, and suffering among the world's peoples and damage to the world's environment;' they also demand reparations for both social and ecological devastation (USNGEJ, n.d.). The Porto Alegre Manifesto, put out by a group of nineteen organizations attending the World Social Forum in that city in 2004, includes a statement calling for an alternative development model that stresses energy conservation and democratic control of natural resources (Group of Nineteen 2005). Some groups have urged specific policies to 'green' trade and development, including those that address pollution, waste treatment, chemical and pesticide runoff, forest protection, GMOs, agriculture and intellectual property, and biodiversity (FOE, n.d.).

On all of these issues, goes the argument, there is not only inequity in the distribution of the profits that such environmentally destructive practices bring, but also inequity in terms of who receives the bads—the pollution, waste, lack of resources, and theft of intellectual property related to local environmental knowledge. The central critique of the institutions of this new world economy is that they promote an inherently inequitable distribution of economic goods and related social and environmental bads. Social justice, environmental justice, and ecological justice are tied together in these critiques, as the poor suffer both social and environmental inequity and nature is drained of resources for economic gain. This distributional element of the injustice of economic globalization is clear enough, and much has been written on the issue from the point of view of the antiglobalization movement.[3]

Likewise, in the movements for democratic food security, criticism is leveled at systems and processes that deprive people of their land-based livelihood while enriching others, particularly large corporations based in the north. Again, there is a link between economic, social, and environmental inequity; groups claim that people are driven from traditional farming techniques that sustained individuals, communities, and the land and into wage-based work and a cash economy, where the poor cannot afford to buy food or water. Numerous movement groups—global groups such as the World Social Forum, northern NGOs such as Greenpeace and Oxfam, and southern groups such as the Third World Network—argue that neoliberal globalization is a threat to food security and sustainable livelihoods, and impacts the least well-off populations to a much greater extent.

Related, food security groups articulate their criticism of genetically modified food with the language of inequity. While GM foods are supposedly to bring more food and food security to more peoples, especially in the south, the critique is that 'GM crops are ineffective in tackling the underlying political and economic causes of food insecurity: poverty and inequality' (Orton 2003). A food development strategy based on GM foods does not address the lack of access to land, water, energy, training, credit, markets, and other goods and services that would allow poor individuals and communities to develop their own food security; rather, a technology-based strategy directs resources away from these existing inequities and needs.

These same criticisms regarding inequity as an element of environmental justice come from the indigenous rights movement. Groups complain that indigenous communities face disproportionate impacts due to the environmental degradation of development and resource extraction, practices such as bioprospecting (or biopiracy) and the patenting of indigenous knowledge for corporate profit, and the militarization and violence that come with such development. In addition, peoples are often forced off of their lands by development or contamination. The IEN claims that '[t]rade liberalization and export-oriented development . . . are creating the most adverse impacts on the lives of Indigenous peoples . . .' (IEN, n.d.). The Penan people of Sarawak, Malaysia, for example, insist that increased logging for export—a practice expanded as a part of neoliberal development—has silted rivers, killing fish, and spreading disease (Global Response 2005). Numerous indigenous communities across the globe have fought the disproportionate impacts of energy development, from coal to uranium to oil, on their lands (see Obiora 1999; IEN 2001).

Finally, climate justice has often been articulated in the language of equity. The International Climate Justice Network's (ICJN) widely circulated Bali Principles of Climate Justice declare that 'the impacts of climate change are disproportionately felt by small island states, women, youth, coastal peoples, local communities, indigenous peoples, fisherfolk, poor people and the elderly' and that 'the impacts will be most devastating to the vast majority of the people in the South, as well as the "South" within the North' (ICJN 2002). Robert Bullard, a major figure in academic environmental justice in the USA, wrote on his experience at the Sixth Conference of the Parties to the United Nations Framework Convention on Climate Change (UNFCCC) (COP6); there, his focus was a description of how the most adverse effects of changing climate 'fall heaviest on the poor'. Likewise, a Climate Justice Declaration developed from the second People of Color Environmental Justice Leadership Summit in 2002 (Environmental Justice and Climate Change Initiative 2002) and updated at a 2004 conference on environmental justice and climate change at the University of Michigan starts with the claim that the effects of climate change will be felt unequally.

Poor nations, people of color, Indigenous peoples, and low-income communities in all nations are the first to experience negative climate change impacts such as sea level rise, flooding, drought, heat-death and illness, respiratory illness, infectious disease, and economic and cultural displacement. (Climate Justice Declaration 2004)

Greenpeace's discussion of the impacts of climate change insists that the 'greatest impacts will be on the poorer countries least able to protect themselves from rising sea levels, spread of disease and declines in agricultural production in the developing countries of Africa, Asia and the Pacific. At all scales of climate change, developing countries will suffer the most' (Greenpeace, n.d.).

Inequity is also cited not just as a result of climate change but as a cause as well. Rising Tide, a coalition of numerous NGOs in Europe, South America, Africa, and Asia, writes, using the language of equity, that climate change 'is a direct result of the economic domination of Northern interests and transnational corporations. We call for climate justice through solutions that address structural inequalities and recognize the historical responsibility of the rich nations for the problem' (Rising Tide, n.d.). In another political statement, the network states that 'social and economic equity between and within countries lies at the heart of all solutions to climate change' (Rising Tide 2002). Their suggestions for addressing climate change focus on alleviating inequity, including a transition to renewable energy which does not fall hardest on low-income communities or communities of color, and a repayment of 'ecological debt' (the destruction and exploitation of resources) from the North to the South.

In addition, and related to the indigenous rights issues above, many indigenous communities and nations, especially those in the Arctic, note that they are disproportionately impacted by climate change; the Inuit feel so strongly that they have filed a human rights lawsuit against the USA as the biggest contributor to climate change (Gertz 2005). Again, key here is the language of concern with differential impacts of climate change, as well as proactive suggestions to address inequity in responding to the problem.

Importantly, it is crucial to understand that, just as with the US case, while the concept of equity is central to the definition of justice in the academic literature, movements demonstrate that environmental justice at a global scale has a much broader meaning in practice than academics usually acknowledge. In all of these issues of global environmental justice, for example, movements apply the concept of equity to their own groups and communities, not simply to individuals. The concern is with the poor, communities of color, indigenous communities, and/or communities that have suffered a disproportionate burden of globalization, food insecurity, a lack of rights, and the impact of climate change. Justice in practice, or justice as articulated in movements using the discourse of social and environmental justice, is as much about communities as it is about individuals. But it is also about much more than equity.

Recognition

Simply put, equity is not the only issue of justice addressed by various groups and movements identifying with, and articulating, a call for environmental justice. Other fundamental critiques apparent in the literature of global movements invoking environmental justice include the relationship between social, cultural, and ecological misrecognition and community devastation, the lack of democratic participation in the construction and ongoing processes of governing institutions, and the debilitation of many individual and community capacities necessary for healthy functioning.

As for the first, there are many references, in the literature critical of the global economy, to the danger of a growing global monoculture. This is not just a critique of the singular vision of neoliberal globalization, but a lament for the present and coming loss of diverse cultures. The call for justice, in this instance, is a call for recognition and preservation of diverse cultures, identities, economies, and ways of knowing. The argument is that a process of homogenization both contributes to the breakdown of the cultural and social networks in local communities and also destroys the essence and meaning of local cultures. An anti-WTO declaration by the global network Peoples Global Action (1999) makes this position quite clear:

This unaccountable and notoriously undemocratic body called the WTO has the potential not only to suck the sweat and blood of the masses of the two-thirds of the world, but also has started destroying our natural habitats, and traditional agricultural and other knowledge systems developed over centuries and our cultural diversity by converting us into objects....

More recently, in organizing against the WTO ministerial conference in Hong Kong at the end of 2005, Peoples Global Action (PGA) claimed that the WTO's 'single global market agenda poses a great threat to the diversities of the world' (PGA 2005). A lack of recognition of the validity of local cultural identities, and forms of economic organization, is a key problem of the WTO specifically and the globalizing economy more generally, from the perspective of the grassroots groups associated with PGA.

This is particularly the critique that comes from those concerned with food security. The argument is that traditional and culturally specific forms of food production and distribution are seen as backwards or inefficient by western policymakers, food producers, and distributors. Shiva (1997, 2000) has spent much of the past decade criticizing the links between economic globalization and cultural threats, specifically by examining the development of the global food supply system and its effects on local communities.[4] Shiva notes the crucial link between food diversity and cultural diversity; many cultures are defined by their particular local diet—for example, some are rice-based, others cereal-based or millet-based. But globalizing the food supply in a way that does not recognize such traditional practices destroys local production and market practices, and local cultural identity suffers. Shiva cites the example of different Indian regions being defined in part by the base cooking oil used (which differs according to the local flora); the ban on the local production of oil and the move to imported soybean oil was, for Shiva, an outright attack on diverse local cultures, identities, and practices. Another important cultural injustice of the globalization of the food system is the destruction of the current localized culture of farming, to be replaced by a singular, corporate, and highly engineered process. Local seed banks, for example, are seen as saving not just biodiversity, but cultural diversity as well; but these banks are replaced with a practice of monocropping with seeds owned and controlled by multinational seed corporations. At the base of such injustices is a straightforward lack of recognition of the validity and value of traditional systems of providing food to populations. The lack of recognition leads to an upheaval of existing food production systems and, argue critics like Shiva, less food security.

And again, cultural recognition is certainly central to the definition, and attainment, of social and environmental justice by indigenous movements. For many Native American environmental justice activists in the USA and other indigenous activists around the world, the defense of community is bound to recognition from majority culture and governments. The concerns of Native Americans on this point were addressed in Chapter 3, but the same argument holds for other indigenous movements worldwide. There are two key related demands here. The first is a simple call for the recognition that indigenous populations exist in places where the majority culture does not necessarily see them; the second is that indigenous traditions, cultures, and ways of life need to be recognized and respected as alive, valid, and on par with other cultures.

A key statement by the Coordinating Body for the Indigenous People's Organizations of the Amazon Basin (COICA) insists that both governments and NGOs 'must recognize the existence of the population' indigenous to the region (quoted in Conca and Dabelko 1998: 338). Indigenous groups such as COICA work to get both governments and NGOs to understand that nature is not empty and devoid of peoples and culture—that indigenous peoples exist and occupy their own territory, and this should be recognized and respected. A vision of the natural world devoid of the indigenous peoples that populate it simply makes those cultures invisible. COICA's statement is full of demands for cultural recognition, autonomy, and respect for indigenous laws and practices, and the organization insists that a recognition of the peoples of the region lead to an acceptance of indigenous organizations as legitimate and equal partners (p. 342). The point is not just recognition of peoples, but respect for them; a representative of indigenous groups in Guatemala, for example, points out that indigenous peoples do not have legal rights, and are most often 'just used as cheap labor, almost slaves or indentured servants. . . . We are seen as resources and folklore. Our fundamental rights are not recognized. . . . We will keep struggling so that our cultural rights as indigenous peoples are recognized' (Oxfam 2005).

The IEN understands environmental injustices, specifically, as a 'new form of racial discrimination against Indigenous Peoples' (Indigenous Environmental Network, n.d.). Related, the lack of recognition of, and religious intolerance toward, traditional indigenous beliefs and practices has led to the 'denigration, prohibition, and persecution of Indigenous spiritual beliefs and ceremony' (Indigenous Environmental Network, n.d.). In another example, the Zapatista movement in Mexico, made up primarily of indigenous peoples of Mayan descent, has from the start combined a critique of the globalizing economy (and Mexico's adoption of the neoliberal model) with a demand for recognition of indigenous peoples and environmentally sustainable ways of life. The movement's most popular spokesperson, Marcos, demands a world 'where we can be respected for the work that we do, the value that we have as human beings' (quoted in McKinley 2006). It is absolutely crucial to understand that the concept of inequity simply does not capture the understanding of environmental injustice articulated by indigenous movements; recognition of culture, of value, of rights, and of alternative ways of life is central to their discourse of justice.

As for climate justice, a number of the Bali Principles of Climate Justice (ICJN 2002) directly address recognition. There, climate justice 'demands that public policy be based on mutual respect and justice for all peoples, free from any form of discrimination or bias' as well as 'an appreciation of diverse cultural perspectives'. The principles also explicitly call for solutions that address women's rights, affirm the right of youth as equal partners in the movement, and prevent the extinction of cultures and biodiversity due to climate change. In the eyes of the actors in the movement, recognition is integral to environmental and climate justice.

Again, climate justice is integrally linked to indigenous peoples, and recognition and respect for indigenous practices and land rights is central to the demand for social and environmental justice on the issue. A statement from the Sixth International Indigenous Peoples' Forum on Climate Change calls upon the (UNFCCC) to 'to recognize that through the protection and promotion of Indigenous Peoples' rights and through recognizing and integrating our dynamic and holistic visions, we are securing not only our future, but the future of humanity and social and environmental justice for all' (International Indigenous Peoples' Forum on Climate Change 2003).

In these cases, as articulated by these environmental justice movements, one major step toward justice is through recognition. The basic argument is that ways of life are being threatened simply because they are not recognized and are devalued as ways of life. That is an issue of recognition, not simply equity. In addition, and as with the discussion of equity, it is crucial to understand that this discourse of recognition, as I have laid out above, is applied not solely to individuals, but to communities as well.

Participation and Procedural Justice

In all of these cases, in addition, justice includes a dimension of participation on environmental and other issues—participation by those at the short end of distributional inequity and participation by those suffering the injustice of the lack of cultural recognition. For example, by far the most oft-discussed critique of the WTO, IMF, and World Bank beyond the issue of inequity is that of the lack of meaningful participation offered to the public, various opponents, or even the nations of the South, in both the everyday practices of the organizations and their various attempts at meetings and negotiations. A statement signed by over 1,120 organizations from 87 countries, and published by Public Citizen's Global Trade Watch (1999) includes not only issues of equity (see above), but also crucial issues of participation. WTO 'rules and procedures are undemocratic, untransparent and non-accountable and have operated to marginalize the majority of the world's people'. The statement calls for a review of WTO policies and impacts, with the full participation of civil society; this has been an ongoing demand of movement groups since before the 1999 Seattle protests.

In fact, one of the underreported events at the 1999 WTO meeting in Seattle was the rebellion of many smaller and southern nations. 'We came here with high expectations from our countries in the Caribbean,' said Clement Rohee, Guyana's minister of foreign affairs. 'We are very much disappointed over the fact that coming from small economies we ended up with a situation where we are totally marginalized in a process that has been virtually hijacked by the more wealthy developed countries.'[5] Global Exchange (2000b: 2) has argued that 'developing countries have relatively little power within the institution, which through the programs and policies they decide to finance, have tremendous impact throughout local economies and societies'. These nations are suffering not only growing impoverishment through the inequitable policies of these institutions, but also decreasing control over global decisions regarding their own economies, including their environments and natural resources. These criticisms, while marginalized in 1999, were central to the breakdown of WTO negotiations in Cancun 2003.

The lack of democratic participation is also a major part of the critique of the current transition of food production from the local to the global. The injustice is not just that cultures and ways of life are ignored, dismissed, disrespected, and ultimately destroyed; it is also the key that local communities have no say in this process. The concern is that with the entry of multinational corporations into food production, in places where food has always been locally produced and managed, those corporations will become the sole decision-makers with regard to food, excluding local input. The example most often cited is that poor farmers and communities have been sidelined in the decision-making regarding the introduction of genetically modified food; the technology has been introduced in many areas without the consultation or involvement of the public. The international peasant group Via Campesina insists that '[p]easants and small farmers must have direct input into formulating agricultural policies at all levels. . . . Everyone has the right to honest, accurate information and open and democratic decision-making' (Via Campesina 2002: 4). Shiva's conclusion in *Stolen Harvest*, after chapters of critique of the globalization of farming and the food supply, is a demand—expressed, she argues, by citizens' movements North and South—for democratic control over the food system (2000: 117). Food democracy is 'the new agenda for ecological sustainability and social justice' (p. 18).

Finally, demands for expanded and more authentic public participation in the development of responses to climate change are present in climate justice principles put forth by numerous NGOs.[6] The Environmental Justice and Climate Change Initiative (EJCC) include community participation as one of its ten key principles: 'At all levels and in all realms, people must have a say in the decisions that affect their lives. Decision makers must include communities in the policy process' (EJCC 2002). In the Bali Principles, climate justice 'affirms the rights of indigenous peoples and affected communities to represent and speak for themselves', and 'demands that communities, particularly affected communities, play a leading role in national and international processes to address climate change'. Centrally, 'Climate Justice affirms the right of indigenous peoples and local communities to participate effectively at every level of decision-making, including needs assessment, planning, implementation, enforcement and evaluation, the strict enforcement of principles of prior informed consent, and the right to say "No"' (International Climate Justice Network 2002). The document also criticizes the role of transnational corporations 'in unduly influencing national and international decision-making'. The principles are clear that public and community participation should be accountable, authentic, and effective at every level of decision-making. The Milan Declaration of Indigenous Peoples (International Indigenous Peoples' Forum on Climate Change 2003) combines a concern with participation with that of indigenous recognition, as well as existing inequity. The declaration demands the provision of 'necessary support to indigenous peoples for their full and effective participation in all levels of discussion, decision making, and implementation as well as ensuring that the necessary funding will be provided to guarantee such participation and to strengthen their capacities'. Here, it is understood that full and authentic participation simply cannot happen without a concomitant effort to address the inequity that either excludes indigenous communities from, or disadvantages them at, the negotiating table.

Capabilities and Functioning

The above cases, however, also illustrate how inequity, a lack of recognition, and exclusion from participation do not completely cover the sense of injustice expressed by movement groups and NGOs. In addition to these concerns, groups articulate a more broad focus on the destruction of the capabilities and functioning of both individuals and communities. For example, one of the principle points regarding the injustice wrought by the WTO is a destruction of various cultural capabilities, which debilitate those cultures' functioning and ties to the land. People's Global Action argues that the WTO-led model of globalization expands monopolies and corporate control through privatization, and 'means that access to water, land, seeds, forests, natural resources and energy is a constant struggle for the poor of the world. This is devastating lives in many ways...' (People's Global Action 2005). The PGA notes that inhabitants of rural areas are uprooted from their traditional rural cultures and livelihoods, and move into urban slums for work in the international economy. In the transition to a neoliberal economic model, individuals lose their traditional community support, and are deprived of the capabilities they had in their rural homes and economies. The point here is that neoliberal globalization uproots not just individuals, but communities as well, and makes those communities much less likely to provide the capabilities necessary for a fully functioning life.

One item in Nussbaum's capability set (2000, 2006a) includes health and nourishment; this is an obvious and key necessity for a fully functioning life. NGOs involved in food security campaigns often bring this capability forth as a right. Oxfam's official declaration to the World Food Summit in 2002 demands not just a right to *access* to food, but a right to food, period. Yet the criticism is that the often imposed move to a more industrialized, globalized, and neoliberal agricultural system leads to less food security, and so less health and nourishment. Via Campesina argues that with such industrialization, 'local production systems are destroyed, often resulting in greater food insecurity in the community' (Via Campesina 2002). The complaint is that it is not just a livelihood that is to be destroyed (and a sustainable one at that), but various regional peoples' and cultures' ways of life. The argument for food security as a basis of community capability, and the defense of actions to protect it, was made clear by Korean peasant activists at the 2005 WTO meeting in Hong Kong:

Agriculture is...a central part of our culture. Agriculture is the foundation of our lives, it is like our mother. We fight against the WTO with a level of urgency and desperation because we are trying to protect our mother, the giver of our life. We are not here as rebels, but as sons and daughters defending our mother whose life is threatened. (Via Campesina 2005)

Along the same lines, Shiva (1997, 2000) has argued that globalization creates 'development' and 'growth' by the destruction of the local environment, culture, and sustainable ways of living. While Shiva does not explicitly refer to the capabilities framework, her focus certainly is on those capabilities surrounding food production that are crucial to individual, community, and cultural functioning. The argument from critics such as these is for systems of 'food sovereignty', or the right and ability 'of each nation to maintain and develop its own capacity to produce its basic foods respecting cultural and productive diversity' (Via Campesina 2002).

Similarly, for many indigenous movements calling for environmental justice, the issue is nothing less than a matter of cultural survival. As noted in Chapter 3, Native American activists see environmental justice as a response to the experience of cultural genocide—threats to individuals, families, communities, and cultures. Environmental discrimination is an

assault on Indigenous People's human rights and public health, including their right to their unique and special social, cultural, spiritual and historical life ways and worldviews. Environmental racism results in the devastation, contamination, dispossession, loss, or denial of access, to Indigenous Peoples' biodiversity, their waters and traditional lands and territories. Environmental racism is now the primary cause of impaired human health . . . and the forced separation and removal of Indigenous Peoples from their lands and territories, their major means of subsistence, their language, culture, and spirituality . . . (IEN, n.d.).

The mining, biopiracy, deforestation, oil and gas drilling, and dumping of waste on indigenous lands impacts ceremonies, traditional medicines and ways of life, indigenous economies and means of subsistence, and individual and community health (IEN, n.d.).

Indigenous movements in the south articulate the same demands around individual and, just as importantly, community capability and functioning. Generally, environmental contamination and devastation caused by, for example, oil or gas drilling, impacts game, fish, and the quality of drinking water; all of this has had a severe impact on the health of local indigenous peoples (see, e.g. Amazon Watch, n.d.). Too much logging and the culture's ability to provide fish for itself, plants for medicines, and trees for its shelter or art forms are destroyed (see, e.g. Council of the Haida Nation, n.d.). Rodolfo Pocop, the National Coordinator of the National Indigenous and Peasant Council (CONIC) in Guatemala, notes this type of critique with regard to mining, as he argues that a 'whole system of life and culture is being destroyed. Scientific data and analysis show one impact on nature, but to us it is deeper. We feel like this kind of mining represents a destruction of life and culture' (Oxfam America 2005). In another example, the U'wa campaign to stop oil drilling on traditional indigenous lands in Columbia linked the expected environmental damage to the cultural destruction of the U'wa. Communiqués publicized through the Rainforest Action Network focused on this very issue.[7] The U'wa rejected the Columbian government's support of Occidental Petroleum, 'whose plan seeks to subdue the U'wa culture by spearheading an oil exploration project on our ancestral territory'. The capabilities and functioning of a culture were the primary things to be defended.

The response to such examples of environmental injustice is similar to that offered in response to neoliberalization generally, or to the destruction of food security. Often, indigenous peoples will propose an alternative to the model of economic development they see as harmful to their communities and traditions; forms of sustainable development in line with traditional economies are suggested that will not impact the ongoing functioning of cultures.

On the issue of climate change, capabilities and functioning are also central to the definition of the justice of climate justice. The argument is that global warming reduces 'peoples' ability to sustain themselves' and that '[i]n the face of rapid change the integrity of community ties are of paramount importance' (Miller and Sisco 2002: 1). In other words, both individual and community ability to function is threatened. The Bali Principles of Climate Justice also directly link the question of climate change to the capabilities of local communities to sustain their ways of life. '[Th]e impacts of climate change threaten food sovereignty and the security of livelihoods of natural resource-based local economies', and 'threaten the health of communities around the world...' (International Climate Justice Network 2002). Communities 'have the right to be free from climate change, its related impacts, and other forms of ecological destruction'. Climate justice means being 'committed to preventing the extinction of cultures and biodiversity' and the Bali Principles demand 'fundamental rights to clean air, water, food, and healthy ecosystems' (International Climate Justice Network 2002)—the essential capabilities necessary for individual and community functioning.

Bringing together the indigenous and climate change issues, numerous indigenous groups have noted the threat, and the injustice, to native peoples and cultures posed by climate change. As Goldtooth (2005) bluntly states, '[c]limate change is a genuine threat to our health, our physical and cultural survival and our future generations.' The IEN (2001) notes that indigenous peoples 'crucially depend upon healthy, diverse, and intact habitats for subsistence. We suffer most immediately and directly from the adverse effects of climate change.' In the example noted above, the Inuit have recently initiated a suit against the USA for its direct impact on the undermining, due to climate change, of Inuit culture. They argue that global warming, led by the practices of the USA, is threatening their way of life and destroying Inuit sea ice culture.

Overall, in all of these movement examples of environmental justice, capabilities and functioning are incorporated as part of the argument for environmental and social justice. And again, as with the environmental justice movement in the USA, these capabilities are discussed and claimed as much—if not more so—at the community level as they are at the individual level. In addition to the general claim here that the understanding of justice, as articulated by environmental justice movements in practice, is broad and inclusive of distribution, recognition, procedure, and capabilities, the other major point is that justice is understood and articulated both in terms of individuals and their communities. This examination of the way that both justice and capabilities are articulated in movement practice is a pragmatic critique of the way that the capabilities approach is individualized as it is presented and embodied in the work of Sen and Nussbaum—though it is also an inherent critique of individualized liberal notions of justice generally. Given the articulations of various movements around issues of environmental justice, it seems quite obvious that a major concern, across a number of issues, is not just individual, but community capability and functioning—or more particularly, the threats to those capabilities and continued functioning of communities.

Finally, there has been some discussion in the theoretical literature about the paternalism present in the capabilities approach, in particular that a list of capabilities can be seen as universalist or ethnocentric, and developed outside the communities in which they are to be applied.[8] Paternalism, in this sense, refers to outside parties defining an individual's conception of the good, something good liberals would not stand for. As discussed in Chapter 2, both Sen and Nussbaum are very cautious about appearing paternalistic—Sen by refusing to develop a specific and universal list for pluralistic reasons, and Nussbaum insisting that her capabilities list was developed with movements and problems in developing countries in mind. One way of responding to such charges is to more fully involve communities and movements in the definitions of their own capability set and policy desires, related to their own understanding of, or desires for, individual and community functioning. The previous illustrations of those that refer to capabilities and functioning within a discourse of environmental justice do just this; the capabilities laid out above, and the alternative policies suggested, are defined by the communities and movement groups articulating their opposition to environmental injustices.

Conclusion: Linking Notions of Justice

Beyond simply indicating that demands for social and environmental justice include elements of equity, recognition, participation, and capabilities, this exploration of articulations of global environmental justice on the part of global and southern NGOs illustrates that these conceptions are thoroughly linked. It is not simply that the justice of environmental justice in political practice includes these varied issues and conceptions; the broader argument here is that the movement represents an *integration* of these various claims into a broad call for justice. In the various organizations that articulate environmental justice at a global scale, such as those I have discussed here, one simply cannot talk of one aspect of justice without it leading to another. Not only are the different conceptions of justice apparent in the environmental justice discourse, but the literature and actions of the groups imply that these notions of justice must be interrelated. In fact, I did not discuss calls for participation by indigenous groups in the appropriate section above because I simply could not find such calls that were distinct from the demands for recognition; they are, in the literature of indigenous groups fighting for environmental justice, integrally related.

For the indigenous movements calling for environmental and social justice, equity, recognition, political participation, and individual and community capabilities are intricately woven together. In both the U'wa and COICA cases noted above, the indigenous organizations insist on not only cultural recognition but also the democratic and participatory rights that come with that recognition; the two are inseparable elements of justice. Kiefer and Benjamin (1993) note that in a meeting of NGOs dedicated to indigenous issues in 1992, a list of critical needs was developed; those included attention to existing indigenous knowledge and skills in relation to nature, representation at various levels of government, and respect for indigenous self-government. Again, the issue is not just that of equity, but of many other aspects of justice as well. Indigenous nations in North America argue that there are numerous barriers to participation by indigenous peoples in the governance of environments. 'These obstacles preclude the articulation and acceptance of Indigenous knowledge' (Borrows 1997: 426). Borrows argues that bringing in indigenous ways of knowing nature would not only expand participation, but also demonstrate the 'socially constructed notions of space' and the cultural contingency of these ways of knowing the land. In other words, broadening participation would bring a recognition of, and validity to, diverse ways of understanding and valuing (in numerous senses) the land. Likewise, in the case of the transition of food production, the affront to culture, the violation of basic democratic processes, and the debilitation of community functioning are linked; there is a direct relationship between the destruction of local cultural practices, the domination of food production systems, and the lack of local participation.

In the WTO, IMF, and World Bank case, the critique of these institutions follows the complex nature of justice I have been discussing. Obviously, the issue of equity is central, but other key critiques include the social and ecological devastation the development model engenders—the destruction of nature, culture, and existing modes of relation between the two—and, obviously, the lack of democratic participation in the planning of development. Protesters from Seattle to Cancun were quite clear that there would not be satisfaction with minimal participation—a seat at the table or participation in an unempowered working group on one issue or another. The current development model cannot be 'fixed' simply by letting some folks speak at WTO meetings, as that would not guarantee full participation, let alone the recognition and validation of other cultures or ways of living or economic equity. Ultimately, there is a direct link between justice as equity, cultural recognition, capabilities, and democratic participation; focusing on one notion at the expense of others, or while ignoring others, simply cannot satisfy the multiple and complex nature of justice sought by the movement. Justice, as defined by the movements present at the protests, will not be fully reached without addressing justice in each realm.

In the climate justice discourse, the links between distributive inequity and other notions of injustice are constant. An ongoing complaint is that the cultural disruptions predicted for climate change will only happen to some; some communities will be denied the capabilities necessary for ongoing survival. 'The economic, cultural, and health costs associated with global warming also fall hardest on those with the least resources' (Miller and Sisco 2002: 1). This combination of equity, recognition, and capabilities themes continues in the discussion of remedies. There, an

97

attempt at equity through redistribution is not seen as enough to remedy injustice; compensation is dismissed if it does not contribute to lowering the vulnerabilities of communities—that is protecting their capability to function—as the globe warms.

I am not trying to argue that all of those groups that use environmental justice as an organizing discourse address all of these notions of justice, and have ultimately developed a broad and harmonious definition. Rather, the argument here is that the public discourse of environmental justice is broad and varied, with groups tapping into different understandings and approaches to the concept of environmental depending on issue, situation, and tactics. The metaphor might be overused, but we can see these groups reaching into the same justice toolbox, using, and articulating, the same tools from place to place, and case to case. Rather than a broad, universal, and unitary notion of environmental justice, what there is in practice is a set of important discourses which are repeatedly raised—equity, recognition, participation, capabilities, and functioning; these concepts are consistently discussed at both the individual and community level, and they are most often discussed in relation to one another. At most, from an examination of the definition of environmental justice through global movements, we get an understanding of a broad and unified notion of the term, though not a singular, universal, and unitary definition.

Yet we also see that these various forms of injustice are intricately linked, and must be addressed simultaneously. It may be the case that improved participatory mechanisms can help meliorate other forms of injustice; but those forms of injustice must be addressed in order to improve participation. Justice, then, requires not just an understanding of unjust distribution, limited capabilities, and a lack of recognition, but, importantly, the way they are tied together in political and social processes. These notions and experiences of injustice are not competing notions, nor are they contradictory or antithetical. Inequitable distribution, a lack of recognition, destruction of capabilities, and limited participation all work to produce injustice, and claims for justice are integrated into a comprehensive political project in the calls for environmental justice at a global level.

Notes

1. Sources on environmental justice in the developing world include Adeola (2000), Agyeman, Bullard, and Evans (2003), Byrne, Glover, and Martinez

(2002), Carruthers (forthcoming), Guha and Alier (1997), Roberts and Thanos (2003), and Westra and Lawson (2001).

2. For evidence supporting this claim, see the United Nations Development Programme (UNDP) *Human Development Report 2005.*

3. See, e.g. Greider (1996), or essays in Mander and Goldsmith (1996), as well as the websites of the leading NGOs involved in the protests: www. globalexchange.org, www.citizen.org/trade, and www.ourworldisnotforsale.org.

4. In addition to the work cited above, see the various publications at www.vshiva.net

5. Quoted in *World Trade Observer*, 3 December 1999, p. 1. This daily was published in print and online during the Seattle WTO meetings; it is now archived at http://depts.washington.edu/wtohist/Research/academic.htm.

6. See, e.g. the 10 Principles for Just Climate Change Policies in the USA (Environmental Justice and Climate Change Initiative 2002), the Bali Principles of Climate Justice (International Climate Justice Network 2002), and the Milan Declaration (International Indigenous Peoples' Forum on Climate Change 2003).

7. Information on the U'wa/Occidental Petroleum battle is available at <www.ran.org/ran_campaigns/beyond_oil/oxy/>. Occidental announced in May 2002 that it would pull out of its claim on U'wa lands.

8. See, e.g. the discussion—and defense of Sen and Nussbaum—in Deneulin (2002).

Part III

Doing Justice to Nature

5

Justice to Nature 1:
Distributive Approaches

Doing Justice to Nature

As I discussed at the outset, one of the tasks of this book is to explore how the broad discourse of justice generated and used by environmental justice movements can also be applied to doing justice to nature itself. The point of such an effort is, on the one hand, a pragmatic and strategic one; the goal is to offer a discourse of justice that is attractive to movements interested in both environmental and ecological justice. But there is also a straightforward academic task here as well. Both academics and activists are developing and using varied conceptions of justice, while focusing on two very different sets of issues. The question is whether it makes sense to use those same conceptions in both the human realm and as applied to nonhuman nature. I believe that it is, and argue that such a set of conceptions, then, can be brought together in a wide-ranging discourse of environmental and ecological justice, applicable to human and nonhuman alike.

As with many of the discussions in the environmental justice literature, the vast majority of academic forays into defining ecological justice remains tied to a distributional approach, paradigm, and discourse. I want to spend this chapter examining the variety of ways that distributional conceptions of justice can be used to outline a theory and practice of ecological justice.

Many have tried to use the language of liberal distributional justice in looking at justice to nature. Without doubt, and to the credit of environmental political theorists, the discussions of environmental and ecological justice within the equity framework are vast, rich, and complex. I am very appreciative of the work of people like Baxter (2000*a*, 2005),

Bell (2002), Dobson (1998), Low and Gleeson (1998), de-Shalit (1995), and Wissenburg (1998), for example. Still, as thorough as these works are, I find them incomplete, especially as the distributive conception of justice itself has come under intense critical inquiry by political theorists. My overall task is to expand the current discourse about environmental and ecological justice using a theory of justice that includes recognition, participation, and capabilities as integral, and explicit, components; I get to those conceptions in Chapter 6. Such an expanded discourse, I argue, can be used in defining both justice between humans on environmental issues and justice between the human and nonhuman worlds; it can also help build discursive links between the two demands. But before getting to either of these discussions, I address a range of theoretical obstacles that need to be breeched before we can begin to apply *any* conception of justice to the nonhuman world.

Obstacles

When discussing environmental justice movements in the USA or else-where, were there is a demand for recognition and political participa-tion as a way of attaining distributional equity, the main objection one encounters is the argument that all justice is distributional, and move-ments are mistaken to address recognition, participation, or capabilities as a primary focus of justice. I hope I have addressed this objection in the previous chapters. But in extending the discourse of justice into the realm of nature, one first runs into the question of whether justice as a concept can apply to nature at all, as either the subject of justice or simply its recip-ient. The second, inevitable, objection is that to address justice to nature is to cross the forbidden line in liberalism between an overlapping con-sensus on political procedures and a value-based notion of the good life.

There are numerous, constant objections to nature as *subject* of justice within liberal theory. For many theorists, nonhuman nature is simply beyond the bounds of relationships that can be based on justice. For Rawls (1971: 512), our relations with animals, plants, and the environment are outside a relation of justice, as we cannot 'extend the contract doctrine so as to include them in a natural way.' In his expansive theory, our inter-action with nature is simply not acknowledged as a question of justice. Likewise, Brian Barry's extension of Rawls's theory of justice excludes a place for nature. Rather than focus on the ability to enter a contract, however, Barry has articulated the problem a little differently, arguing that 'justice and injustice can be predicated only of relations among creatures who are regarded as moral equals in the sense that they weigh equally in the moral scales' (1999: 95). Given this, he argues, the concept of justice cannot be 'deployed intelligibly' outside human relations (Barry 1999: 95).

It is not that these theorists are disinterested in the way humans treat nature. Both Rawls and Barry argue that it is wrong to be cruel to nature, and the capacity of animals for feelings of pain and pleasure means we should have some compassion for them—but not justice. Rawls (1971: 512) believes that we have 'duties of compassion and humanity' in the case of animals. Barry (1999: 114) argues that it is 'inappropriate—cosmically unfitting, in some sense—to regard nature as nothing more than something to be exploited for the benefit of human beings'. But because it is *wrong* does not mean it is *unjust*, he argues. So in the view of two major figures in liberal distributional theories of justice, while we can certainly do wrong to nature, there is simply no victim of injustice in relations between human beings and the natural world.[1]

In other words, liberal justice theorists have come up with a number of objections to extending the range of justice to the nonhuman realm. Baxter (2005: 77) has examined various 'objections of principle' for not extending distributive justice to the nonhuman world, and argues that the three key reasons rely on the basic claim, made by Rawls, Barry, and others, that there are simply no moral agents outside the human realm. As Baxter classifies them, the first category of objection is that justice is a relationship among a group of beings that cooperate voluntarily, the second is that justice involves an assignment of property rights, and the third is that justice requires reciprocity. In all of these, nature is on the outside, lacking ability for voluntary cooperation, unfit as an owner of property rights, and incapable of offering justice in return for receiving it. While these objections seem rather straightforward, Dobson (1998) has also examined the variety of reasons for the traditional liberal exclusion of nature from theories of justice in some depth, and poses some interesting questions regarding the rather flimsy justifications of this exclusion on the part of some theorists. Dobson argues (p. 168), for example, that in Walzer's theory of justice (1983), the exclusion seems to come down solely to the human capacity to 'hope'.

But it is not just the traditional liberals who exclude nature from the sphere of justice; many of my colleagues—theorists of environmental and ecological justice—do the same. These theorists often draw a line between nature as a *subject* of a theory and practice of justice and nature as a *recipient* of various schemes of justice. As with more traditional liberal theorists, it is the former that many environmental theorists are uncomfortable with. Wissenburg, for example, argues that in order to adapt distributive justice to the environmental agenda, we would need to include parts of nature and future generations as subjects of justice; he simply does not believe such an inclusion would work. He critiques but eventually gives up to Rawls's contract argument: '[A]s long as humans can argue for the existence of relevant differences between themselves and animals, the status of animals as subjects [of justice] cannot a priori be taken as part of our considered judgments' (Wissenburg 2001: 196). Likewise, Talshir (2001: 38–9) argues that nature is by definition a 'nonsocial' agent, and so 'injustice' can only be used in a metaphorical sense in environmental cases.

Bringing nonhuman nature into the realm of subjects of justice, then, is one major challenge—but this is not the only objection. By this time, good classic liberals are probably steaming about one of the major standard criticisms of bringing environment into the discussion of justice: that anything having to do with environmental issues crosses into the liberal no-fly zone of impartiality and neutrality. In this view, the basic idea of the 'preservation' of nature is a good, and as a litmus test of an impartial definition of justice is illiberal. 'Ecological Justice', then, is a taboo oxymoron within the context of universal and impartial notions and procedures for justice. The central problem between liberalism and environmental advocacy of any type is quite clear: neutrality on notions of the good life supposedly precludes a state focus on sustainability. For example, the biocentric argument that we should consider non-human nature, or at least animals and species, as moral equals in political decision-making is often used as an example of a notion of the good. Biocentrism is an approach that is based on recognition and respect for an intrinsically valuable nature, but such an idea, argue liberal critics, is a *preference* not shared by others. The inclusion of nonhuman nature in considerations of justice may simply not be acceptable to many members of the liberal state; if so, then, it remains a question of the conflict between different notions of the good. Justice theorists focused on impartiality, such as Rawls or Barry, would keep the conceptualization of *justice* out of such conflicts about the *good*.

Any version of environmental or ecological justice, in this classic liberal view, must be a generally agreed on good. In other words, liberal ecocentrics might try to persuade their fellow citizens to adopt their principles, and may express or vote their ecocentric beliefs in the various battles on preferences and notions of the good that occur through the democratic process. Ecological justice, then, would simply be a good agreed on by the majority. As I discuss below, Rawls understood environmental issues in this way, and Miller (1999*b*) agrees. Yet, as de-Shalit notes, for this approach to work, believers would also have to get everyone (or at least a majority) to believe that notion, and that is often simply too difficult a task (de-Shalit 1995: 7).[2] Dobson (1998) thought this conflict between a desire for environmental ends and the insistence of liberal impartiality was a serious enough problem to argue that this may be where liberalism and environmentalism part company. If a minority believes in justice, and that justice is denied by the majority, a crisis in the liberal polity may ensue—as it has over a number of objections from various human populations about their exclusion from liberal justice.

Dryzek (1987), however, argues that the paradox in this insistence of calling environmental ends 'goods' in liberalism is that unless the members of the state accept a common ecological purpose, then all other human purposes and notions of the good are endangered. In this case, then, we should not sacrifice the flourishing of many for the sake of the perception of the good life of some whose conceptions would undermine the ecological order. There is a key difference between reducing available notions of the good life in order to protect the possibility of justice for all, and insisting on particular notions of the good that would deny that. Justice extended to nature may do the former, but certainly not the latter.[3] In this view, sustainability, at least, is a prerequisite for liberal democracy. The underlying conditions under which a number of different conceptions of the good life can flourish is a state of ecological justice. The impartiality of liberalism can only really thrive within the *context* of that protection and flourishing of the greater community of justice. I return to this point below.

But I think the best response to the objection that environmental foci, as goods, are not impartial is the argument that liberalism itself, in both theory and practice, is not neutral. Young, for example, argues that impartiality is an idealist fiction; it is impossible to adopt an unsituated point of view, and if a point of view is situated, then it cannot be universal (1990: 104). The purist impartiality argument is also attacked by numerous folks in the environmental community. Attfield (2001) notes that liberal democracy in practice is not neutral on a host of issues, not just environmental. Eckersley (1996: 214) says liberalism is 'systematically biased against the interests of "non-citizens",' that is future generations and nonhuman nature. And obviously, the economic system tied to political liberalism, market liberalism, is not neutral, especially on environmental issues (Bell 2002). Liberal states are rarely impartial; instead, they advocate particular notions of the good all the time. Spreading 'democracy' abroad, insisting on denying the institution of marriage to gay couples, favoring the market over social welfare, denying equal pay for women, etc. are policies, based on particular notions of the good, pushed by supposedly impartial liberal states. Given this consistent hypocrisy, a focus on ecological justice is no more illiberal than other state policies.[4]

But it is not just states that violate impartiality; partiality is evident even in supposedly impartial liberal theories of justice. As noted above, classic liberal justice theorists such as Rawls or Barry would not include nature as a subject of, or partner in, justice. But note the lack of impartiality here: some cultures and cosmologies assume sentience, a soul, and consciousness to nature—both individual critters and the larger landscapes. Any theory of justice that excludes parts of the world from consideration that some cultures would include begins under a very partial cultural bias; and assuming one cultural bias over the other is not how one should ground an impartial theory of justice. In essence, much liberal justice, including the specific question of how nature fits in such a conception of justice, is inherently partial. So neutrality in both the applied and the theoretical sense is a fiction. This problem, however, may be resolved through the application of an element of recognition, which I return to in Chapter 6. For now, we will assume we must address the impartiality question as we examine the application of distributive models to nature and ecological justice.

Expanding the Traditional Approach

These obstacles to the consideration of nature in a scheme of liberal justice are challenged by a number of recent authors. As Rawls is the major figure in justice theory over the past three decades, it is not surprising that many environmental theorists have taken his ideas on directly, looking for ways to insert a conception of ecological justice in his liberal distributional theory. Various theorists have used different parts of Rawls's theory—primarily the potential of overlapping consensus, but also extensions of the restraint principle and the veil of ignorance—to attempt to justify a notion of ecological justice that remains within Rawls's larger framework.

Again, for Rawls justice is only possible between moral equals who can enter into contracts. Rawls is pretty clear that humans' relation to nature 'is not a constitutional essential or a basic question of justice'

(Rawls 1993: 246). So any conception of justice to nature is beyond the proper range of justice. Yet ecological concerns can come into the relationship of justice between humans, as Rawls himself acknowledged. In a political sense, liberal citizens may try to use various values to persuade others of their ecological notions of the good, or they may vote their ecological beliefs. Then again, Rawls leaves a door open to a broader conception of ecological justice with a footnoted caveat: 'Of course, these questions may become ones of constitutional essentials and basic justice once our duties and obligations to future generations and other societies are involved' (Rawls 1993: *n* 35). And they could remain in Rawls' greater framework, as citizens may be able to develop *political* reasons for a broad ecological concern, as opposed to moral or religious ones; such a political conception could be acceptable to all citizens as part of a greater overlapping consensus.

Bell (2002, 2003) reads much into this opportunity, and defends it thoroughly. Ultimately, Bell simply lays out how environmental concerns should not violate objections of neutrality in the eyes of more purists, if mistaken, Rawlsians. He argues that there is nothing in Rawls's political liberalism that rules out ecological justice in a democratic liberal state. A concern for, and inclusion of, nature in a framework of justice would not necessarily be an endorsement of a particular conception of the good. Rather, supporters of such policies could persuade citizens to include theses concerns in an overlapping political consensus. This would result in what Bell calls a 'green neutralist liberalism' (Bell 2002: 721) or a 'liberal ecologism' (Bell 2003: 2). This is not substantively different than what Brian Barry (1999) has suggested. Barry's basic conclusion regarding the place of nature and sustainability in liberal justice is noted above—that environmental ends are conceptions of the good, and the best proponents of environmental justice can do is to try to convince enough people that we should consider nature as having some moral weight in our own decision-making. Here, in other words, even if the question of nature is one of the good, not justice, and so is subject to citizen debate, ecological justice can still prevail. For both Bell and Barry, the point is that while liberalism might not embrace justice to nature, it certainly does not *preclude* it. Yet even if environmental justice advocates were able to convince enough of their fellow citizens to establish a green liberalism, Bell notes that it would be 'substantively and procedurally biased toward humans' (Barry 1999; Bell 2003: 2). Still, this is nonetheless a better situation than a liberalism that is incapable of considering ecological justice at all.[5]

Wissenburg offers another approach to greening Rawlsian justice—focusing on the duty we have to restraint. 'Whenever there is a choice between destroying a good, thus depriving others of present or future options to realize legitimate plans, or merely using it without limiting other peoples' options, we have a duty to do the latter' (1998: 124). This restraint principle can be used in various environmental matters, both domestic and international, as a way to bring a notion of sustainability into liberal decision-making. In Fraser's very limited discussion of environmental matters (2001: 36–7), she comes to a similar conclusion. Fraser argues that if one group wants sustainability and the other does not, we cannot write the conflict off as simply two different notions of the good. As she argues, if the anti-environmental parties get their way, they will deny parity to both contemporary others and future generations.

This may, indeed, rule out some pictures of the good by acknowledging the unjust or unsustainable implications. Admittedly, the range of available and acceptable pictures of the good life would certainly be narrowed. Liberals may simply look to a classic theorist such as J.S. Mill for a supportive liberal principle regarding limiting the freedom of some to live a particular notion of the good if it brings harm to others. There are plenty of historical examples of limiting some notions of the good to support the ongoing and overall good of the nation, as when the franchise was expanded to African-Americans, women, and indigenous peoples. A restraint principle could be used to justify an environmental focus on the part of a liberal state, without a violation of the principle of impartiality. Of course, and as Wissenburg notes, this idea is still 'consistent with the psychological transformation of nature into resources' (p. 172), and so, remains solely within a Rawlsian framework of the distribution of goods among humans, without any recognition of nature itself as a subject of justice. In other words, it is more in the realm of environmental rather than ecological justice.

Others (such as van deVeer 1979; Wenz 1988) offer another, more radical, proposal for expanding a Rawlsian approach; one could 'thicken' the veil of ignorance Rawls asks us to imagine as we develop the original set of justice principles. Behind this veil, we should not only be blind to our future position in society, our abilities and talents, and our possible lot in life, but we should also consider that we might not even be human on the other side of the veil. Wissenburg (1993: 17) argues that this idea really does not work in theory, as he argues that we cannot imagine what it means to be irrational; even if we could, we could not use that irrationality to plan the rational set of rules Rawls asks us to. Still, the idea that we could thicken the veil in this way makes as much sense as the imaginary original position itself does; we could attempt to represent nature in this imaginary space, just as we are to represent the idea of a disembodied and unencumbered person. Such an imaginary practice might be useful in establishing an overlapping consensus or basis for justice; still, the first task would be to come up with a justification for the inclusion of nature as an agent or subject of justice, which Rawls explicitly denied.

David Miller, another of the major figures writing in the liberal tradition, has also explored the environmental implications of justice theory, and offers a different approach (Miller 1999b). Rather than examine ways of justifying ecological ends, or of including nature in an overlapping consensus, Miller examines the possibility of including environmental goods along with other primary goods in calculations of distributive justice. Miller concludes by dividing environmental goods into three categories. There are some environmental goods that can be easily and directly attached to other primary goods. Ill health, caused by pollution, for example, would reduce the value of (not to mention access to) other primary goods. There are other environmental goods about which we can generate, through democratic procedure, enough public agreement that they would not generate issues of distributive justice. And finally, there are a number of environmental goods that are valued differently by different people, and would have to be counted as primary goods only by those who value them as such. In this case, in order to apply some principles of distributive justice, Miller argues that a form of cost–benefit analysis would be a crucial, if difficult, way to measure the desire, the losses, and the willingness of the public to pay for environmental goods.[6] So Miller offers a way to include various environmental goods (necessarily defined as *goods*, amenable to distribution) in a distributional calculus. Again, and as with attempts to stretch Rawls, this approach simply brings environmental goods into a distributional framework; nature, more broadly construed, is something simply not considered in this framework.

These discussions regarding how environment and/or nature fit in traditional conceptions of liberal justice are, however, thoroughly constraining. We have a premade set of theories of justice, developed with certain considerations of liberal societies in mind; yet environment and nature are quite difficult to simply add on, as the justifications are difficult to find *within* such theories of justice. Certainly, it is an interesting and crucial debate within the liberal distributional justice community—how can we bring these new considerations of environmental and ecological justice to bear in theories that did not consider such issues at the outset. And it is heartening there are ways that recent theorists have seen to use and/or expand the framework of traditional liberal justice theory to include environmental concerns in a number of ways. Still, this approach is quite confining, and there may be much more potential in addressing distributional justice in broader ways.

Broader Approaches to Distribution and Ecological Justice

Beyond simply looking for ways to find openings for environmental and ecological justice in existing theorists' works and frameworks, a number of environmental political theorists have offered additional and innovative approaches. Many authors who focus on the concept of ecological justice—doing justice to nature—move beyond the confining questions addressed above, and examine ways of extending distributive justice so that it can encompass environmental and ecological questions. Three key approaches focus on preserving the context of human justice for future generations, paying attention to specifically ecological indicators in a distributional conception of justice, and expanding the notion of the human community to include its ecological support system. What this literature shows is that there are at least a few routes to a conception and practice of ecological justice within the liberal limitations of justice— one that addresses environmental concerns while continuing to exclude nature as a subject.

Future Generations

Attention to future generations is probably the most discussed approach to expanding distributive in a way that brings attention to the natural world.[7] While this tactic does not extend justice to the natural world directly, it does acknowledge our justice responsibilities for future generations of human beings. The discussion of future generations allows an inclusion of the environment of the future without a particular dedication to that environment or to nature itself—just to the humans who will occupy it. Justice, in this sense, requires an intergenerational principle of equal opportunity; various authors argue that we cannot leave less to future generations than we ourselves enjoy, we cannot leave them without enough to construct their own conceptions of the good, and we cannot leave them with their lives endangered. The approach is specifically distributional, focusing on the distribution of natural and environmental goods to future generations of humans—addressing what we in the present generation consume, and what we leave to our progeny. For many justice theorists, this human and distributional focus enables us to thoroughly broaden the application of justice while remaining firmly grounded in the familiar ground of contemporary liberal justice theory.

Brian Barry has discussed the possible impact of environmental damage on our provision of justice to future generations. We should, he argues, 'provide future generations with the opportunity to live good lives according to their conception of what constitutes a good life' (Barry 1999: 104). Here, in order to do justice to future generations of human beings, we must leave them an environment that does not diminish their choices of the good life. Barry is really not all that concerned about the *specific* types of choices available in the future—even a preference for plastic trees may be a valid choice. A focus on the types of choices takes us away from the key issue, which, to Barry, is simply that for future generations the 'conditions must be such as to sustain a range of possible conceptions of the good life' (p. 105). Barry notes a particular concern with the consumption of nonrenewable resources in this case, as the depletion of nonrenewables could lead to our limiting possible choices in the future. Likewise, Norton (1999: 149) makes an argument that we have an obligation not to diminish the opportunities of future generations; the best way to achieve this is to specify certain aspects or features of the natural world and insist they be protected. Sustainability, then, is a necessary condition of justice to future generations.

An extrapolation of how Rawls might be used to extend environmental justice to future generations is offered by de-Shalit (1995). While Rawls does not allow us to discuss animals or nonhuman nature within a theory of justice, he does acknowledge that we can actually do environmental harm to future generations. In response, Rawls (1973: 293) suggests a savings principle: 'Saving is achieved by accepting as a political judgment those policies designed to improve the standard of life of later generations of the least advantaged.' Here, Rawls extends his difference principle to the least well-off of the future.[8] If we accept that the least advantaged of the future may be least advantaged in environmental goods—access to food, clean water and air, an environment free of toxins and full of resources—this savings principle can bring a form of environmental justice to future generations.

113

de-Shalit himself offers perhaps the most thorough discussion of *Why Posterity Matters* (1995) in an exploration of justice and environmental affairs, though he takes a different tack. The focus of de-Shalit's environmental dedication to posterity comes with an extension of our conception of community to generations in the future—a communitarian theory of intergenerational justice. Here, 'our obligations to future generations derive from a sense of a community that stretches and extends over generations and into the future' (p. 13). Simply put, we should consider this extended community when making environmental decisions. We should not overburden the future with environmental problems; rather, we should leave them with an ample supply of environmental goods. For those very far in the future, we are still obligated to 'relieve any potential and foreseeable distress' (de-Shalit 1995).

de-Shalit makes an argument, beyond the contractarian one of Rawls and others, that suggests our obligations to generations both now and far in the future, not just our immediate progeny. The 'constitutive community extends over several generations and into the future, and that just as many people think of the past as part of what constitutes their "selves", they do and should regard the *future* as part of their selves' (de-Shalit 1995: 15–16). Our community spreads out over time, not just place; this is the essence of our obligation to the future, and the environment of the future.

One of the strengths of de-Shalit's approach here is that, unlike the various discussions of notions of the good, or of savings or difference principles, this is how many in the real, and pragmatic, political world view our obligations to the future. It is a theory of intergenerational justice that goes beyond the individualistic and atomistic focus of so much justice theory, into an understanding of groups and communities and their condition both now and into the future. Even conservatives, going back to Burke, often discuss our obligations to past and future generations on more or less communitarian grounds; Burke notes the 'partnership between those who are living, those who are dead, and those who are to be born' (Burke [1970] 1999: 96). But this concept of a transgenerational obligation should also appeal to a variety of other ideologies as well.

This concern with future generations, however, also must be used to illuminate the need to provide justice in the present. In this, de-Shalit follows others who argue that we simply cannot think of intergenerational environmental justice without also incorporating environmental justice among contemporaries. As Attfield (1999: 156) notes, 'to sell future generations short is both wrong and inequitable. So too is a preoccupation with justice between generations at the cost of a neglect of justice between contemporaries.' In essence, he argues, we need to rectify existing injustices as a prerequisite for doing environmental justice to future generations (p. 163). This concern is also expressed by de-Shalit (1995: 11), who refers to the need to balance our obligation to future generations with our obligations to less well-off contemporaries.

Yet as helpful as this model of justice to future generations is, it is still not an extension of the community of justice to nature—it is not ecological justice. The approach does not recognize nature *for itself*, or as a full member of our community, but solely as it supports the *human* systems that are nested within it. Recognizing and valuing that support system is central to the future generations approach; any decline in the quality or standard of the natural world that supports future generations will limit the choices, and notions of the good, of those generations. But while the extension of justice to future generations includes a concern for the future environment of those future generations, the extension of the scope of justice remains centered on human needs and definitions of the good. Others, however, are not as hesitant in actually extending the community of justice beyond humans to nonhuman nature in some way; I will return to these shortly. First, though, I need to address another, recently popularized, way distributive justice can be used to protect the human environment.

Distributive Justice and Ecological Space

Some theorists remain focused on applying innovative models of distributive justice to provide for more environmental justice to those in the present. Pogge (2002), for example, has developed an idea of a 'global resources dividend'. Here, the idea is that the 'global poor' own an inalienable stake in all limited resources; if a state or government sells their own natural resources, a small part of that value is to be shared with the poor. In a sense, Pogge insists on redistribution as a duty of justice rather than as a matter of charity; he expands the conception of justice to the environment on the assertion that all human beings share in the development, sale, and use of natural resources. In many ways, this is simply an implementation of the Rawlsian difference principle, that any benefit to the well off must also benefit the least well off. And this is not really about ecological justice, or doing justice to nature; rather it is about the costs and benefits of the use of nature being shared in the human community. It may, however, be the case that such a tax or dividend would be a disincentive to take resources out of the natural world, or to be efficient in any such use of resources.

Hayward (2005a), however, offers a critique, and a quite creative expansion, of Pogge's proposal, and his response illustrates another opening for a consideration of nature in a theory and practice of global distributive justice. Basically, Hayward argues for a tax based on 'a nation's per capita utilization of ecological space' (2005a: 318). The idea here is to determine just how many resources are consumed in production, and how much space is necessary to absorb the waste of such production. Here, Hayward refers to the increasingly popular notions of 'ecological space' and an 'ecological footprint', or the occupation of ecological space; yet he expands the use of the concept in important ways.[9]

Focusing exclusively on the extraction of primary resources, as does Pogge, could hurt the poor more than it helps, suggests Hayward. The burden should not be on simple extraction, but on the overall economic benefit, and ecological cost, of the use of resources. Such a focus has the benefit of including both the extraction of resources and the 'disbenefits' in the form of pollution and other ecological externalities. For Hayward (p. 325), the point is that the concept of ecological space should be conceived of as addressing the 'ongoing initial appropriation of nature by humans'. The normative justification for levying such a tax is based on the degree of *excess* use of ecological space (p. 330) rather than simply the use of resources. In this way, distributive justice is served by requiring those who occupy more, and disproportionate, ecological space to compensate others who do not.

The discussion of the use of a concept of ecological space in a distributional theory of social justice is one key way we can extend the conception of distributional justice to include the natural world. Here, the use of nature is brought into the everyday calculus of redistributive justice, into a consideration of what is distributed, and what the costs to both humans and the natural world that distribution brings. Staying within the bounds of liberalism, it focuses on what everyone needs to live the type of life they value and desire. Yet beyond fair distribution, the concept also introduces sustainability, or at least the full ecological costs of such life choices; it has an eye toward both social and ecological justice. Incorporating the concept of ecological space into global distributive justice illustrates a commitment to ecological and environmental justice, in addition to social justice.

Expanding the Community of Justice to Nature

Still, such efforts, though they expand our conceptualization of justice to include ecological *impacts*, do not explicitly address how to include aspects of nature itself as participants in a larger community of justice. As difficult as such an expansion sounds initially, theoretical efforts to do so are not new. For decades, those who have argued for animal rights have broken much ground in this direction, extending the scope of moral applications, including justice, to some nonhuman animals with interests or preferences. This is most often done by expanding either a utilitarian notion of pain and pleasure (Singer 1975), or by applying a Kantian notion of inherent value, so that we expand the list of those that are to be considered ends in themselves (Regan 1983). The most popular author of expanding scope in the environmental literature, at least in the US context, is Leopold (1949) and his conception of a 'land ethic'. Interestingly, the land ethic aims to expand both the moral community and to extend our own conception of ourselves within that community. Simply put, Leopold's ethic is about enlarging the boundary of our own moral community to include the natural world. Leopold's efforts are aimed to get us to understand the role of the natural community in supporting human moral practices, but he insists that we accept this larger system and ecological community as both part of our own being, and also as an end in itself.

More recent authors have moved beyond a concern with including parts of nature in a moral community to a more specific concern with its inclusion in the community of justice. For Low and Gleeson (1998), as with Leopold, in order to conceive of extending distributive justice to nature, we either need to expand the scope of the moral community to include some nonhuman animals or the broader environment, or we need to expand the scope of the 'self' of liberalism. At the very least, this extension simply brings nonhuman nature into consideration as the place where human justice occurs. Habermas brings such a concern for the 'lifeworld' into his understanding of social movements such as environmentalism (1981); he sees these movements arguing for protection of the context of the lifeworld, which is necessary for solidarity, and, so, justice. With such a concern comes the need to include the nonhuman world in theories of justice, both as an object and a precondition of justice (Dobson 1998: 187–8).

Given the long genealogy of the 'expand the community of justice to nature' approach, it is not surprising that there is also a long history of objections. The standard criticism is that such a notion puts nature on an equal moral footing with humans. In reality, however, there is only very rarely an appearance of this language of equality. At most, the conception championed by Leopold, for example, asks for moral *consideration* of nonhuman nature; but such a consideration does not require a previous conclusion of equality. As Sagoff (1993: 86–7) notes, Leopold's bold proclamation of a land ethic was articulated without the need to advocate an egalitarian moral system with nature, or even a demand for equal rights for animals. Taylor's *Respect for Nature* (1986), coming in the early years of environmental ethics, revived the idea that we can invoke a thorough consideration of nature without proclaiming human–nonhuman equality. We can make the claim for the moral consideration of nature as part of our extended community, and the inclusion of that nature in a theory of justice, without insisting that every part of nature has moral worth identical and equal to our own.

Baxter (2005) is perhaps the most thorough and articulate recent exploration of the extension of the community of justice to parts of nonhuman nature. Influenced by Barry's conception of impartiality, Baxter argues that we can extend the idea of the community of justice to at least some of nonhuman nature, while detaching this extended community from any conception of the good (Baxter 2000b: 50). To stay within Barry's conception of justice as impartiality, Baxter argues that an extension of the community of justice is simply a procedural move. Admission to the community of justice is not based on any particular notion of the good, but rather on the characteristics of candidates—in particular whether they have interests (p. 57). If we can detach the notion of the community of justice from the notion of the good, we can remain impartial and within the rest of Barry's conception of justice as impartial proceduralism.

Baxter is not making a claim that members of nonhuman nature are moral agents; and certainly not insisting that animals reach the threshold Barry holds for entry to the community of justice—equality of moral standing. Instead, Baxter argues that nonhuman nature should be considered recipients, rather than agents, of justice; as such, they 'may intelligibly be said to have claims upon the actions of moral agents' (2005: 7). Baxter includes a moral status for 'the "merely living" which rests on the property of being a living organism with, therefore, welfare interests' (p. 65). For some, this extension of the community of justice is an important and paradigm-shifting notion—that some members of the community of justice are recipients only rather than both recipients and agents of justice. Wissenburg (1998), for example, has argued for this extension of community to recipients as well as agents. But Baxter argues that this shift is not as radical a paradigm shift as it may seem. He examines how Barry incorporates human beings who cannot articulate their own conceptions of the good, such as infants and those with cognitive handicaps. Rawls, and nearly every other liberal justice theorist, makes the same exception for humans who have interests but cannot fully articulate them or be full agents of reciprocal justice. Here, we expand the community of justice to include these examples of individuals with interests, even if they cannot formulate a conception of the good or fully participate as agents in the community of justice. The fact that nonhuman nature cannot defend its own interests or reciprocate moral concern or practice 'will no more justify excluding them from the community of justice than it will justify excluding "inarticulate" humans who are similarly situated' (Baxter 2005: 119).

Baxter makes two central claims in this argument to extend justice to some nonhuman nature, both based on the premise that nonhuman nature has interests. First, 'all non humans, sentient and non-sentient, are members of the community of justice,' and second, 'all members of the community of justice are proper recipients of distributive justice with respect to environmental goods and bads—that is, to ecological justice' (Baxter 2005: 9). He goes on to argue that once we accept that 'the interests and needs of nonhuman nature should be represented in the formulation of the basic structure of impartial justice . . . then their extermination, including that produced indirectly by habitat destruction, will prima facie have to be regarded as unjust' (p. 114).

It is important to note a crucial addition Baxter makes to the ecological justice discourse. Baxter extends the community of justice to what he calls 'merely living' *species*, or those nonsentient and 'too lacking in individuality for it to make much sense to attribute the rights to individuals of the species' (Baxter 2005: 127). In these species, as no individual member possesses ambitions or interests that differentiate it from other members, there can be no moral differentiation between those individuals. This does not mean that the individuals in this species are totally devoid of moral standing. Baxter suggests we admit not just individuals and species to the community of justice, but 'viable populations' (p. 128) of species as well. Ecological justice, he insists, defends the claim that viable populations of merely living organisms have a right to environmental resources necessary for those populations to exist and survive (p. 131). Again, this is an expansion of the community of justice, not only to sentient animals, but to groups and populations.

Finally, Baxter insists that even if we expand the community of justice, we still do not have any kind of agreement on what is good for members, or how to balance interests. This issue remains in the category of competing notions of the good. We simply expand the community of consideration, and open the procedural outlines of a just, yet still impartial, society to their inclusion. As Baxter (2005: 124) puts it:

> What the amended version of justice as impartiality, which admits nonhuman nature to the community of justice, can plausibly aim for is to push moral thinking in a certain direction—one which requires the interests of nonhuman nature to be considered in human policy-making, which underpins constitutional provision for this, and which allows human interests to trump those of nonhuman nature only under certain fairly stringent conditions.

In other words, there is still no guarantee of a beneficial outcome for nature over humans, which would be a violation of impartiality. All we have is a guarantee of *consideration* of nonhuman living nature in human deliberation of distributive justice. Ultimately, what Baxter seeks is a theory that all members of the extended community of justice are justified in making claims against other members; the task is to determine the level of resources various organisms or populations are entitled to claim against one another. The larger point here is that distributive justice can no longer take place under the assumption that impacts to nature do not exist, or do not affect the larger community of justice. Within the distributive paradigm, nature is incorporated as both a recipient of, and, importantly, context for, justice.

In some ways, though, this approach is not as broad in including nonliving nature as, for example, is the ecological space approach. Unlike that approach, Baxter offers no moral accountability for the *nonliving* aspects of the natural world. Baxter limits his extension of the community of justice to living organisms with interests. Even though various nonliving entities—mountains, rivers, and clouds—make contributions to the sum total of environmental benefits, they have no interests, argues Baxter. While such a distinction makes sense in terms of how we understand a recipient of the moral consideration of justice—Baxter is referring to individual nonhuman animals with welfare interests—it unnecessarily limits the extension of justice to nature. Nonhuman, nonliving nature remains the environment in which all other beings exist, sustain themselves, develop interests, and, for humans, develop preferences for the good life. We are still left with the task of finding a way to include a larger consideration of nature in a conception of justice.

Limitations of Distributive Theories of Ecological Justice

The closest these distributional theorists of justice get to the arguments of environmental justice movements is in the discussion of future generations of humans. But those arguments do not address the issue raised by movements of the recognition of particular ways of life and ways of relating to nature. Rather, the point of the focus on future generations is to find a way of using liberal theories of distributional justice to justify the protection of the natural world. While this is an admirable way of opening a theory in a direction many thought it could not go, it remains squarely in the distributive paradigm—and distant from many of the demands and articulations of movement groups. Furthermore, and unfortunately, most of these attempts at expanding environmental justice, or of establishing ecological justice, ignore the realms of justice theory that have been moving away from a strict distributional focus. In other words, there are other potential conceptions and discourses of justice that may be more useful in establishing justice to nature.

Most advocates and practitioners of green theory and philosophy have not really picked up on either the calls of other theorists or environmental justice movements to extend analyses of justice beyond the distributive realm. Green political theorists have engaged traditional liberal justice theorists on these questions of distributional justice, and many have gone much further than simply applying questions of nature to existing frameworks. Still, given theoretical and movement calls to extend an analysis of justice beyond the distributive realm, theories of environmental and ecological justice have been disappointing to date. For much of the past two decades, most authors in the field have avoided an examination of the interface between justice and the environment, focusing instead on environmental values or ethics. More recently, however, authors such as those discussed above have begun to use the language of distribution to frame sustainability and environmental justice. Yet even these authors, dedicated to expanding the existing discourse of justice to future generations and nature, rarely stray from a distributive approach. Most remain tied to a limited distributive paradigm, and a one-dimensional conception of justice. While we would expect such dedication to distribution from the more traditional liberal theorists who developed their theories around the concept, it is disappointing to see more recent and creative theorists captured by this limited conceptions. As examples, I focus here on Dobson (1998) and Low and Gleeson (1998), in addition to Baxter (2005).

121

Dobson (1998) offers a groundbreaking attempt to find common ground between social justice and environmental sustainability. This is a thorough and comprehensive study, and it begins with Dobson's clear and explicit agreement with Barry's more 'narrow' conception of justice (1999), that 'all justice is distributive' (Dobson 1998: 17). This bias toward the distributive is made quite continuously clear by Dobson's interchangeable use of 'social justice' and 'distributive justice' throughout his work. Dobson (1998: 235–6) also explicitly argues that issues of respect and affinity, as they have been raised by numerous theorists of justice critical of the distributional focus, are *not* issues of justice, as they go beyond distribution. He remains within the distributional paradigm of justice, and does not address key issues of how identity, recognition, and political process play into environmental justice. All environmental injustice, then, is a matter of the maldistribution of environmental goods and bads. As important a contribution Dobson's work is to the literature on environmental and ecological justice, it is hampered by his insistence on remaining within the realm of distributive justice.

Dobson begins with his agreement with the Brundtland Report in its claim that 'inequality is the planet's main "environmental" problem' (WCED 1987: 6; Dobson 1998: 14). He goes on to offer a comprehensive examination of possible relationships between the varied discourses of distributive justice and environmental sustainability. He takes apart various elements of the distributive model proposed by a wealth of authors in political and social theory, examining the 'community' of justice (dispensers and recipients), what is distributed, the principles of distribution (utility, need, desert, entitlement, etc.), and whether the theory is partial or impartial, proceduralist or consequentialist, and particular or universal. The central task of Dobson's book is a comparison of possible relationships between different pictures of distributive justice and various ideas regarding environmental sustainability, with an eye toward discovering some compatibility. Ultimately, Dobson finds very little common ground. He concludes that distributive justice and environmental sustainability are only compatible within particular (and limited) definitions and frameworks of both justice and sustainability.

Dobson's work is much more of an examination than a prescription, as it explores the possible relationships between the varied discourses of distributive justice and environmental sustainability. The comparisons and matchups are thorough and exhaustive, and the myriad relations make for a complex, though illuminating, matrix. These conclusions, though, regarding the limited possible relationships between theories of social justice and models of environmental sustainability, are limited by the sole focus on justice as distributional. By remaining in the distributive paradigm, Dobson misses important notions of justice, including those examined by theorists of recognition, participation, and capabilities, as well as notions articulated under the broad banner of the environmental justice movement—including academics and activists he cites in his text. This needlessly limits the possible convergences between social justice and environmental sustainability.

One of the key concerns that motivated Dobson to take on this project was that environmentalists and social justice activists lack a common discursive ground, and so often talk past one another. His own response is to more thoroughly lay out the theoretical and discursive realms where the movements can meet. Yet it seems counterproductive to ignore additional theoretical and discursive realms—additional conceptions of justice—where the two might find room to talk. My own suggestion is to expand the discourse of environmental and ecological justice to enable talk that has previously gone 'past' to make sense to all the parties involved.

Like Dobson, Low and Gleeson (1998) take on an environmental analysis of various notions of distributive justice. Again, the result is thorough and admirable, demonstrating once again that the issues that come out of the intersection of discussions of environment and justice are quite challenging, interesting, and full of potential. Low and Gleeson's goals differ a bit from Dobson, as they aim both to develop general principles of ecological justice, and to suggest cosmopolitan and global institutions charged with carrying them out. But I also find their efforts incomplete. Like Dobson, they resist a move beyond the distributive paradigm, and proudly so. 'The distribution of environmental quality is the core of "environmental justice"—with the emphasis on *distribution*' (Low and Gleeson 1998: 133). Low and Gleeson develop two key principles of environmental justice (p. 156), three 'rules of thumb' (pp. 156–7), and two international environmental institutions along the lines of Held's cosmopolitan democracy (p. 191).[10] Again, the focus, and so the conclusions, are limited.

But like Dobson, Low and Gleeson also miss the opportunity to use their own concerns to move beyond a narrow conception of distributive justice. This is especially frustrating given the fact that their two key principles of environmental justice only indirectly affect distribution. Those principles are, first, '[e]very natural entity is entitled to enjoy the fullness of its own form of life,' and second, that 'all life forms are mutually dependent and dependent on non-life forms' (Low and Gleeson 1998: 156). Rather than address distribution, these principles are really about recognizing and respecting (*a*) the potential of nature and (*b*) the dependence of humans on the realization of this potential in nature. While Low and Gleeson proudly declare their adherence to a tradition of distributive justice, their own discussions and these central principles demonstrate the centrality of underlying social and cultural practices and beliefs that lead to the distribution of environmental ills—and the centrality of recognition in addressing those ills.

Low and Gleeson are also quite attentive to, and supportive of the arguments regarding political participation as a means to environmental justice. They certainly see the link between participation, inclusive procedures, empowerment, and good environmental ends. They quote approvingly from some who have addressed the issue of participation and public discourse, speak positively of participatory and discursive procedures to attain environmental justice, and so seemingly understand the claim for a larger venue of justice. Yet these realizations regarding participation are not incorporated into their ideal principles or practices of ecological justice; rather, their proposed global cosmopolitan institutions leave little room for expanded participation, and would seem to diminish, rather than extend, political inclusion on environmental issues at the local level.

Finally, Low and Gleeson acknowledge the contextual and cultural bases of the meanings of both of the terms 'environment' and 'justice' (pp. 46, 48, 67), but cannot bring this notion of cultural difference into their definition of either environmental or ecological justice. Justice is understood as a 'universal moral relationship we share with other humans' but one that 'has to be interpreted through culturally specific institutions which will vary' (p. 67). So they seem to see the importance of acknowledging the variety of cultural contexts from which meaning is derived, and insist that autonomy is a key principle of justice (p. 199). Yet Low and Gleeson are blinded by their fear of 'postmodernism', which they simply equate with relativism. Acceptance of different notions of justice, to them, means accepting that 'your conceptions of justice are true for you, in your cultural context, but mine are true in my context;' this makes justice 'meaningless' (p. 197). There is no middle ground for Low and Gleeson; there is only universalism or relativism. No matter that this supposed dichotomy has been denied from William James (1909) to Richard Bernstein (1988) and, most recently, David Miller (1999*a*, 2003) specifically on justice. Low and Gleeson, in their focus on justice in the distributive paradigm, fail to see the possibility of *engagement* across notions of justice—something crucial to notions of justice as recognition and political process. As I argue in Chapter 7, there is still the possibility of *unity* on notions of environmental justice, even if there is not *uniformity* of cultural definitions of the term.

Reading much of this distributive literature on the question of environmental and/or ecological justice is frustrating, however, as authors such as Dobson, Low and Gleeson, and Baxter acknowledge and discuss valid issues of justice that the distributive paradigm simply cannot encompass. As noted above, Low and Gleeson's key principles of ecological justice are all about recognition rather than distribution—though they themselves do not recognize that. Dobson also alludes to many of the issues raised by movements regarding recognition; for example, he approvingly cites the work of Laura Pulido (1996). Pulido has focused on environmental justice struggles in the US southwest, and has argued that environmental movements of the poor focus not only on economic justice, but also on cultural identity and survival as an element of environmental justice. It may be true that the victims of environmental injustice encounter environmental problems through their economic inequality, but that economic inequality is also tied to cultural inequality. Pulido (1996: 29–30) suggests that resolutions to environmental justice will be found not only through economic restructuring or redistribution, but also through the alteration of power relations, cultural practices, and systems of meaning. While attempting to encompass the articulations and discourse of what Pulido calls 'subaltern environmentalism', Dobson's adherence to the distributive paradigm simply cannot cover challenges made by Pulido—and the environmental justice movement—in the realms of power, culture, and social meaning.

Likewise, Baxter's text is focused squarely and insistently in the realm of distributional justice; nowhere are the justice theories of Fraser, Young, Sen, or Nussbaum raised. As with the Dobson and Low and Gleeson works, there are important references to other approaches, but they are not explicitly addressed or incorporated. For example, Baxter argues that we can justify extending justice to nature by 'recognizing their claim to a fair share of the environmental resources which all life-forms need to survive and flourish' (Baxter 2005: 4). I examine these types of claim in depth in Chapter 6; the point here is that while notions of recognition and capabilities are raised in Baxter's text, he does not attempt to bring such concerns and themes into a conception of ecological justice beyond the obviously distributive.

Beyond the Distributive Approach to Nature

The underlying concerns of many of the theorists I address here simply cannot be contained with a focus on distributional theories of justice. For example, Dobson (1998: 64) notes that the key question of how the community of justice gets determined is not thoroughly discussed in distributive theories of justice. Baxter wants to extend this community, but insists that such a discussion remains within the context of distribution. Rather, my argument is that once we begin to extend the community of justice beyond humans, even when we are exploring loopholes in existing distributional theories, we are stepping beyond distribution into the realms of recognition, procedural justice, and capability theory. Further, if it is necessary, as Young, Fraser, Nussbaum, Sen, and many others argue, to take into consideration institutional, cultural, and symbolic limits to attaining distributive justice, then even if we focus on weaker forms of environmental sustainability we still must examine why we treat both exposed human communities and nature as we do to cause the environmental inequities we have. None of the above approaches does this. The misrecognition of communities, noted by the movement for environmental justice, and the misrecognition of nature, noted in a number of ecological discourses (social ecology, ecocentrism, and even ecological economics) are integral not only to the condition of human communities and of nature generally, but also to this distributive approach to conceptions of sustainability as well. Any attempt to find common ground between sustainability and justice necessitates an examination and understanding of the misrecognition—not just maldistribution—of both those communities striving for environmental justice and the natural world. Likewise, any attempt to theorize doing justice to nature itself must focus on the capabilities necessary for that natural world to both flourish and be sustained. And all must address how we incorporate all of these concerns into just procedures for environmental decision-making, especially as we expand the concerns, and community of, justice. It is to those issues that I now turn.

Notes

1. That said Barry (2005: 261ff.) is concerned with a theory of justice addressing environmental issues; his approach, however, is a distributive one that applies only to human relations, and not to nature—environmental, rather than ecological, justice.

126

2. The problem is not simply getting people to agree to such a notion, but also overcoming the distortions brought by those with power and economic interests—witness, e.g. the discussion of climate change in the USA over the past decade.

3. This idea is not uncommon in the literature. See, e.g. Dobson's discussion (1998: 202) and B. Barry's similar argument (1999). Interestingly, Benton made this same argument about ecocentrism (1993: 104). Ecocentrics, he argues, do not insist on a particular notion of the good, but they do rule out some pictures of the good by pointing out the implications of them; there is the possibility of an ordered, but still plural, social life beyond unsustainability.

4. In more pragmatic moments, theorists recognize this fact. de-Shalit (1997: 88), e.g. notes that this imagined impartial liberalism is more of an American model, while the 'social liberalism' of many other nations is not hostile to the idea of advancing certain ideas of the good, including conservation, and is generally more open to state intervention in such matters.

5. Actually, Bell and Barry revisit a similar call by Achterberg (1993) early on in the development of ecological political thought; he argued that the neutral ground all liberal citizens can agree to is the fertile ground for the relationship between liberal justice and ecological sustainability.

6. Humphrey (2003) takes Miller to task for this last issue; he argues that *irreplaceable* loses should be an important part of any such calculus, thus tipping the scale in favor of preservation.

7. There are many examples here, including Barry (1999), de-Shalit (1995), and Page (2006).

8. Well, at least the immediate progeny of those developing justice in the original position behind the veil of ignorance. Rawls notes the existence of a family relationship to immediate descendants that would be part of the consideration of participants (Rawls 1973: 292; discussed in de-Shalit 1995: 100).

9. In addition to Hayward (2005a), see Wackernagel and Rees (1996) and Redefining Progress (n.d.) for more on the ecological footprint.

10. Interestingly, Low and Gleeson's pragmatic and incremental solutions for both environmental and ecological justice focus on global political institutions rather than organization in civil society (where, presumably, the demand for environmental and ecological justice originate).

6

Justice to Nature 2: Incorporating Recognition, Capabilities, and Participation

Introduction

The aim of this chapter is to offer a theory of ecological justice—justice to nature—that moves beyond a sole focus on the distributive paradigm of justice and encompasses innovative ideas in both recent theories of justice and the political demands of relevant social movements. The central focus will be on bringing notions of recognition and capabilities into a broad and comprehensive theory of ecological justice. My task here is not to lay out one single and universal theory of ecological justice; rather, the point is to examine the potential of a few additional discourses of justice, and a variety of approaches within each, that we can use to understand and extend practices of justice to include the nonhuman natural world—individual animals, communities, and the whole of nature.

The project here is informed by a number of influences, issues, and questions. First, as laid out in Chapter 2, there is much recent justice theory outside distributive and Rawlsian frameworks, in particular the arguments of theorists who focus on recognition as a key element of any notion of justice, and those that have expanded the distributional paradigm with a capabilities approach. The works of Young (1990, 2000), Fraser (1997, 1998, 2000, 2001), and Honneth (1992, 1995) among others, have engendered debates about the place of recognition in a theory and practice of justice. Young's focus on oppression caused by misrecognition, and Fraser's development of a 'trivalent' understanding of justice having distributive, recognitional, and participatory elements, are of particular value. Recognition, I argue, has a particularly useful part to play in expanding conceptions of justice to nature. In addition, Sen (1985, 1999*a*, 1999*b*), Nussbaum (2000, 2004, 2006*a*), and Nussbaum and Sen's conceptions of capacity and functioning (1992) are innovative ways of rethinking theories of justice, as they focus not simply on distribution, but on how we translate that distribution into functioning lives. As Nussbaum has begun to apply these ideas to a discussion of justice to animals, it is especially enticing to think about ecological justice from a capabilities perspective.

The second major influence here is how *movements* for environmental justice define what they mean by justice. As discussed in Chapters 3 and 4, environmental justice movements generally look at environmental justice—their concern is most often (though not exclusively) for *people and communities* facing environmental risks, rather than on doing justice to an external, nonhuman *nature*. Movements are certainly concerned with the inequitable distribution of environmental goods and bads, and the inequitable application of environmental regulations; but they are just as concerned with the lack of recognition given to individuals and communities affected by environmental ills, the functioning of communities and cultures, and with the increased political participation of such disenfranchised groups and communities in the environmental decision-making process. In this chapter, the central question is whether these broader conceptions of justice offered by theorists, and often articulated by environmental justice movements regarding human relations on environmental affairs, can also be applied to human relations with the rest of nature. If they can, as I argue, then we can use a similar, though still diverse, set of concepts and discourses about justice on both issues regarding human relations in environmental matters, and regarding human relations with the rest of the natural world.

The third influence here is the fact, discussed in the previous chapter, that recent theories of ecological justice have focused primarily on distribution; they have not addressed other aspects of justice developed theoretically, or conceptions articulated by movements. The point is not to dismiss these distribution-based theories, but to expand the discussion of ecological justice to include issues raised by recent theories and movements—in particular into areas of recognition, capabilities, and participation. The central claim here is clear, if limited: to demonstrate how we might use theories that claim recognition and capacity as components of justice to examine doing justice to nature. Ultimately, the point is to expand the discourse of environmental and ecological justice, to expose a common language of justice, an overlapping set of discourses, and a shared toolbox, which we can use to address issues of both environmental and ecological justice.

I begin by discussing different ways in which recognition may be granted to nature. One key approach aims to recognize what is similar in humans and nonhuman nature. While the standard objection is that nature does not have what it takes to be a partner in a social contract, the argument here is that the similarities we share with nature—sentience, agency, integrity, capacity, for example—vastly outweigh the key differences. I also discuss a more structural approach to recognizing nature, applying Fraser's concept of a 'status injury' to the natural world in justifying its recognition in a theory of ecological justice. I then turn to the application of Sen and Nussbaum's conceptions of capacity. Here, justice is about sustaining certain capabilities, to enable life to function fully. While Nussbaum has offered a discussion of the application of capability theory to individual animals, the argument here is that there are some limitations to her initial approach, and that the notion can be applied more broadly to the capacities of nature, at the community and system level, in addition to the individual. Finally, understanding that both theories of recognition and capabilities are tied explicitly to political participation in their human application, I note the potential of extending such participation to nonhuman nature.

Recognizing Nature I: Community, Sentience, Agency, and Integrity

Community Approaches

So how are we to apply the conception of recognition to the natural world? What is it, exactly, that we are to recognize in nature as an element of ecological justice? If we are to recognize something other than 'humanity' in others, or (as in distributional approaches) their ability to define the good or to enter into contracts, where do we start? First, we can simply recognize nature as part of our shared community, and include ourselves and the rest of the natural world in an expanded community of justice; this approach is not uncommon in some of the literature that proposes expanding distributional justice to address environmental issues, as discussed in Chapter 5.

Numerous authors, especially in environmental ethics, have examined the concept of the recognition of, or respect for, nature; such an argument is not a new concern, though its application to a theory of justice is less common.[1] Most past discussions of recognition focus on our shared community with nature, or on nature as the necessary context and community in which the human moral community exists. This is one crucial route to ecological justice, and I have discussed it at length in Chapter 5. Leopold's classic (1949) 'land ethic,' for example, extended the idea of the moral community to include the nature we stand on and live with. The staying power of this idea is illustrated by the fact that it is the approach taken in one of the most recent proposed theories of ecological justice; Baxter's central argument (2005) revolves around an extension of the moral community to include living nonhuman nature. 'We must do right by other life-forms, but in a precise kind of way, namely by recognizing their claim to a fair share of the environmental resources which all life-forms need to survive and flourish' (p. 4).

The problem is not with the idea of extending the community of justice to nature; this is a valuable conception, and one used by many environmental discourses and movement groups. Yet, as illustrated by Baxter, many in this field understate both the importance and meaning of *recognition* in this proposal. Respect for other community members, and the larger natural community as well, is central to Leopold's view. Likewise, and referring to Leopold, de-Shalit (1997: 84) argues that environmental theory simply asks for an extension of the essential respect at the heart of liberalism. But theorists of recognition have noted that liberal justice theory simply does not explore the underlying obstacles to, and demands for, such respect. Baxter follows this trend; while he sees the extension of the community of justice in simple enough terms, he does not examine the underlying social, cultural, and political issues around this level of recognition of nature—something absolutely necessary in order to transform such a theory into social practice. The point here is that while various distributional approaches to expanding the community of justice—even the most thorough—ultimately rely on human recognition of nature as a support system, none thoroughly examine the process of, or obstacles to, the recognition necessary for a pragmatic implementation of the theory. In other words, their understanding of the recognition of nature is thoroughly under theorized.

I want to examine two rather straightforward ways authors have used the recognition of the natural world to expand the conception of the community of justice—similarities and status injuries. Both of these approaches push us to thoroughly understand and recognize nature, though in different ways; they are crucial to developing a notion of ecological justice that truly extends the community of justice, and moves beyond a focus on the human use of nonhuman nature.

Recognizing Similarities

Beyond broad attempts to extend the community of justice to the natural world, a number of authors have taken a more finely focused path to the recognition of nonhuman nature. One emphasis is on ways of recognizing particular similarities between human beings and other parts of the natural world. Ultimately, much depends simply on how you choose to define what it is in human beings that differentiates us from nature and makes us unique. While traditional justice theorists argue that nonhuman nature does not understand contracts (probably true) or have a notion of the good (though that is debatable), many authors argue that there is more similarity between humans and parts of nonhuman nature than we usually give credit. They argue for the consideration and recognition of nature because of the multiple commonalities or similarities between humans and their environment. Here the focus is on various *qualities* of *the essence of being* that we share with nonhuman nature: needs, sentience, interests, agency, physical integrity, and the unfolding of potential. We can certainly argue for this type of recognition of nature, based on similarities, without asserting that there is *no* difference between humans and nature. While many of these theories attempt to weaken the distinction between human beings and the rest of nature by recognizing qualities of nature that are important in themselves and worthy of the attention of justice, there is rarely a claim for 'equality'. Rather, the argument is that these similarities should lead us to recognize our shared qualities and, so, include that similar, yet nonhuman, nature in the sphere of justice.

Similar to the approach taken by some in the distributive discussions in Chapter 5, a number of authors have explored the loophole in Rawls's discussion of exceptions to the rule stating that only moral persons could be included in the community of justice. If persons who are *sentient*, yet not fully morally capable persons in Rawls's scheme are extended inclusion in the scheme of justice—for example, the mentally disabled or children—then we should also make room for other sentient creatures that are similar to them. The point here is that liberalism recognizes the category of sentience in special cases, and grants human individuals with this quality the status of subjects, even if their full agency is limited. The extensionist argument is that nonhuman nature can fill the same

133

theoretical space by recognizing the quality of sentience outside the human realm.[2]

This focus on sentience has been central to the arguments for extending liberal standing or rights to nonhuman animals and the natural world. Singer (1975) is perhaps the most famous to bring this shared quality of sentience to bear on the debate, arguing (following Bentham) that as animals can feel pain, we should extend a utilitarian calculus to them and work to reduce their suffering. Stone (1974), the previous year, saw both sentience and consciousness in the natural world, posited that such qualities could exist in entities other than individual animals, and proposed the extension of legal rights to entities such as trees and rivers. In both, it is the recognition of a particular quality that nature shares with human beings that leads to the demand to extend the human framework of rights to that nature.

Sentience, however, is not the only similar quality used in this respect; numerous authors have focused on other qualities, and made the connection to justice in addition to rights. Benton (1993), for example, notes the similarity in the basic *needs* of humans and other parts of nature. Surely, he argues, there is more that connects our basic needs—air, water, sustenance, habitats, health, the biosphere, etc.—than what justice theorists have traditionally used to distinguish us. Likewise, Baxter (2001: 57; 2005) argues that admission to the community of justice should be based on whether candidates for inclusion have *interests*. Taylor (1986) notes that recognition of dignity and authenticity can be applied to the natural world as well as human beings. And in his discussion of extending a form of discursive democracy to nature, Dryzek (2000) relies on the notion of *agency*. Simply put, nature offers a form of communication; we know if something is 'off' in nature through its expression of agency, for example, through floods, fires, ozone holes, climate change, disappearing tigers, and mad cows. Again, the attempt is to extend inclusion in the moral (and in Dryzek's case the discursive) community by breaking down the theoretical barriers—and recognizing some key similarities—between human beings and nonhuman nature. Overall, many in the literature of environmental theory agree that, as Wissenburg (2001: 178) posits, 'some animals deserve to be treated as subjects by virtue of properties like agency and consciousness;' and, in fact, many go beyond animals to see agency, or interests, in nonhuman nature more generally. The practice of moral extensionism, Rodman (1983) argues, is an advance in ecological consciousness beyond earlier conservationism and preservationism; here, we admit that humans have duties to nonhuman nature, based on the recognition of the possession of some similar qualities, such as sentience.

Yet Rodman sees some key problems with the practice. The first difficulty, he argues, is the perpetuation by many of an

atomistic metaphysics...locating intrinsic value only or primarily in individual persons, animals, plants, etc., rather than in communities or ecosystems, since individuals are our paradigmatic entities for thinking, being conscious, and feeling pain. Yet it seems bizarre to try to account wholly for the value of a forest or a swamp by itemizing and adding up the values of all the individual members. (1983: 87)

In discussing Singer, Rodman (1977: 89) specifically points out that his animal rights approach would apply to woodrats, but not to cactus or sagebrush—and to individual woodrats rather than the species. This moral atomism, he argues, 'does not seem well adapted to coping with ecological systems' (Rodman 1977: 89). In other words, we cannot base an ecological ethic of justice solely on the singularity of the liberal model of human beings; such an ethic must address the larger breadth of the communities of the natural world. So the first major problem with the extension of liberal concepts based on shared traits is its association with moral atomism and liberal individualism; used in a limited way, it may preclude a more necessarily communalist or systems approach.

Interestingly, another of the reasons for Rodman's resistance on this point is that such an extension is, in fact, an insult to nature, as we use the loophole of not-fully-rational humans for the rest of nature. In his criticism of both Singer and Stone, he argues that while on the one hand we elevate nonhuman nature by virtue of specific qualities such as sentience or consciousness, on the other,

nonhumans are by the same process degraded to the status of inferior human beings, species-anomalies: imbeciles, the senile, 'human vegetables'—moral half-breeds having rights without obligations (Singer), 'legal incompetents' needing humans to interpret and represent their interests in a perpetual guardian/ward relationship (Stone). Is this, then, the new enlightenment—to see nonhuman animals as imbeciles, wilderness as a human vegetable? (Rodman 1977: 94)

Such an individualistic attempt at extension, rather being new or radical, simply 'perpetuates the basic presuppositions of the conventional modern paradigm, however much it fiddles with the boundaries' (p. 95). It is also an example of the misrecognition of nature itself, which I return to below.

135

More recently, Plumwood (2002*a*) raises a related objection to the similarity approach. She argues that this conception is based on having to see something of ourselves in nature in order to recognize it. Plumwood sees this as the continuation of 'human and rational supremacy' that does not break down the artificial human/nature dualism. However, that does not have to be the case; the similarity approach does not necessarily depend on extending what is purely human (or, in Rodman's case, less than fully human) to nature, but may be a way to understand and recognize what is *natural* and not necessarily unique to humans. Here we can extend the community of justice by basing that community in some type of quality that we *share* with nature. This takes a recognition that we are *like* nature—not as separate or unique as we would like to think—and is something that Plumwood herself desires. This goes back to the argument made by Rodman (1977) that we develop a vocabulary that encompasses humans and nonhuman animals, but that is not based on purely *human* notions.[3] The challenge posed by both Rodman and Plumwood is for us to recognize the distinctiveness of nature, but also the commonalities that we share. The focus, then, is on qualities that human beings have in common with many animals and/or the rest of the larger natural world; they are powerful indicators of what we share more broadly as the essence of being. In other words, there is plenty to recognize as shared by both humanity and the nature in which it operates. In this sense, the theoretical walls built by liberals between these two realms seem limited, artificial, and unnecessary. The central point here is that we can easily find similarities with nature on which we can build a moral community and, through recognition of such similarities, a more inclusive theory of justice.

Recognizing Integrity

There is one particular characteristic shared by the human and nonhuman world that has garnered more attention than others, and possibly for good reason; this is the idea of the integrity of systems. We could base the recognition of both human beings and nonhuman nature on a respect for nature's 'bodily integrity', the recognition of the potential in nature to develop, its autonomy, resilience, or a respect for autopoiesis—the quality of a self-directing, self-regulating, or self-correcting entity or system.[4] Low and Gleeson's first and central principle of ecological justice (1998: 156) focuses on just this quality: 'every natural entity is entitled to enjoy the fullness of its own form of life'.[5] Benton (1993: 212) insists that such a discussion of the conditions necessary for living well or flourishing is applicable not just to various animals, but to plant life as well; we can also extend this to the relationship between the two forms of life in larger ecosystems. Achterberg (1993: 97) argues that nature must have the opportunity to survive, with its integrity intact, in the environment of diversity and autonomy that is characteristic of the biosphere.

Rodman turned to Kant to justify this move, and argued that 'one ought not to treat with disrespect or use as a mere means anything that has a *telos* or end of its own—anything that is autonomous in the basic sense of having a capacity for internal self-direction and self-regulation' (1983: 88).[6] Such autonomy is recognized in humans, though, he argues, it is more properly associated with all living natural systems. While similar to the later arguments for the recognition of autopoiesis noted above, Rodman argues that it is not a form of human extensionism. 'It seems to me an observable fact that thistles, oak trees, and wombats, as well as rainforests and chaparral communities, have their own characteristic structures and potentialities to unfold, and that it is as easy to see this in them as it is in humans, if we will but look' (Rodman 1983: 90). Here Rodman differentiates the approach of Singer and Stone, on the one hand, with that of Leopold, whose position, he argues, is based not on extensionism, but on 'a recognition of an ecological sensibility' (1977: 110). The point here is that it is a recognition of autonomous integrity that is necessary to allow for the unfolding or realization of the potential of nature. This understanding helps us include not only an individualistic notion applied to specific creatures, but a more broad ecological one applicable to habitats and ecosystems. Thus, we develop a recognition of the potential of a landscape or an ecological community to maintain its integrity, and to flourish.

Much of this argument regarding integrity is reflected in what Rodman called ecological sensibility, or what has become known as an ecocentric perspective,[7] but the recognition of nature can come out of a more human-centered concern for integrity. This is exactly the argument that Hayward (1998) makes: respect for nature can come directly out of a respect for our own selves and each other. Hayward claims that an interest in integrity is the most fundamental human interest. This concern with integrity, meaning an integrated, undivided whole, begins with an interest in the integrity of ourselves as organisms, and expands to psychological, cognitive, and moral integrity. Hayward argues that this human interest in self-respect and integrity provides reasons to respect nonhuman beings and their environments. If we have an interest in respecting integrity in ourselves and other people, we do not have a good reason to withhold that respect from the rest of nature. We are part of nature, and it is part of our human interest to integrate ecological concerns. Basically, Hayward argues for a concern for the integrity of nature based on rational and enlightened human self-interest rather than a belief in the intrinsic value of nature.

Hayward notes that the focus on human rights as an element of justice demonstrates an obvious human interest in physical integrity. Honneth (1992: 190–91) makes the same claim in his discussion of recognition: physical abuse is one key form of disrespect, and the absence of physical abuse is one element of recognition and, so, of justice. Clearly, we can expand the notion of the recognition of physical integrity to nature, so that an abuse of that integrity, or a harm to the 'body' of nature, is an element of disrespect and malrecognition. Interestingly, we can also refer to this as a respect for dignity. Honneth's concern for physical integrity refers to the dignity of the party involved—human, in his case. But Sagoff (1990) also uses the term dignity in discussing something that we share with environment; he argues that this helps us define our relations with current and future generations, and with nature itself. Nussbaum has also recently focused on dignity as it applies to animals, and I return to the concept in terms of capabilities below.[8]

Overall, then, it seems there is plenty to recognize in nature. Extending ecological justice into the realm of recognition, we find much to appreciate about the natural world. Recognizing sentience, needs, agency, or integrity in nature gives us avenues to expand our understanding of the community of justice, and of ecological justice specifically. But some theorists of recognition, such as Young and Fraser, do not just focus on the importance of recognition itself; the point is to understand the barriers to such recognition. This brings us the question of status.

Recognizing Nature II: Status Injuries

As discussed in Chapter 2, some theorists of recognition, such as Taylor (1994) and Honneth (1992, 1995), focus on the psychological need for recognition. The central idea for these authors is that self-worth comes from the recognition given by others; hence the need for reciprocal and intersubjective recognition. In applying this conception to the natural world, we risk the criticism that recognition, then, depends on the psychological response of animals and other parts of nature. This concern mirrors, and brings us back to, the conflict in theories of recognition between a focus on the psychological state of the victim and the more general condition of a status of mis- or malrecognition. But even for the most radical animal rights theorists and ecocentrics, such a psychological need cannot be applied to nature, as recognition from humans is not a vital psychological need of nature in terms of its own self-worth.

Fraser's central argument against Honneth is that we need to treat recognition as a question of social *status*—as a *status injury* based in social mis- or malrecognition, not of individual psychological feelings on the part of the victims of injustice. Fraser's insistence on the status of a group or victim makes the application of recognition as an element of ecological justice much easier.[9] The status model is not aimed at valorizing individual or group identity, or at recognizing the psychological plight of individual victims, but instead at overcoming subordination (Fraser 2000: 114). In this, we can dismiss the criticism that recognition of, for example, the agency or integrity of the natural world necessitates an anthropomorphizing or a psychological need for recognition in the nonhuman world. We can see nature injured, its interests ignored, autonomy dismissed, or its integrity damaged without resorting to such psychological language or conceptions.

While he did not use the term 'recognition', Rodman offered a similar status-based defense of including the natural world in the moral schemes of human beings. His thorough critique of moral extensionism was ultimately based on the argument that extending existing notions of human-based ethics simply do not recognize nature for itself.

As a general characterization of nonhuman nature [extensionism] seems patronizing and perverse. It is not so much that natural entities are degraded by being represented in human legal actions, or by not having us attribute to them moral obligations. They are degraded rather by our failure to respect them for having their own existence, their own character and potentialities, their own forms of excellence, their own integrity, their own grandeur. (Rodman 1977: 94)

Ultimately, Rodman sought a form of recognition of nature that took into account the existence of individuals, systems and the relations between them, and a duty to noninterference with the unfolding of natural ways and potentialities.[10] What is particularly impressive with this move by Rodman is that he clearly addressed the recognition of nature in terms of the status we accord the nonhuman world. This goes against the critique that a recognition of the natural world may depend on a subjective, psychological response on the part of nature.[11]

If we understand recognition in a structural sense, as the necessary inclusion in decisions that impact the subject—either sentient and capable of feeling excluded, or not—then there is no inherent or necessary reason to exclude nonhuman nature from representation in a theory and practice of justice. Treating nature as an end, with integrity and/or autonomy, is a way to justify recognition without a need for a psychological state of distress; the focus is on the status, not psyche, of the natural world.

So how, exactly, are we to understand a status-based misrecognition of nature? Fraser identifies three ways in which a lack of recognition, or mis- or malrecognition, degrade the status of individuals or an identity. All of these are applicable to an understanding of the status injury we impose on individual animals, species or communities, and the natural world as a whole. Fraser's three forms of status misrecognition are (a) a general practice of cultural domination, (b) a pattern of nonrecognition, which is the equivalent of being rendered invisible, and (c) disrespect, or being routinely maligned or disparaged in stereotypic public and cultural representations (Fraser 1998: 7). These are structural, social, and symbolic indicators of misrecognition or lack of respect, and they are directly related to the status of the individual or community being maligned. Importantly, none of these factors rely on the psychological interpretation or feelings of the victim. Fraser has developed her concern regarding status injuries with an initial focus on gender, and more broadly with the demands of movements that address issues of identity. But her framework offers us a way to apply misrecognition to the natural world without relying on psychological arguments, and without a focus solely or necessarily on moral extensionism. While extensionist arguments may allow us to consider broader forms of justice, including justice to particular entities in the natural world, a status-injury approach moves beyond the atomistic language of liberal rights and justice and into the realm of the recognition of nature's potential, integrity, and being on a much larger scale.

It is not very difficult to think of cases where we can see nature being maligned and disrespected in any or all of the three ways outlined above. In the causes of, and discussions surrounding, global climate change, for example, we see all forms of status-injurious misrecognition—the domination of nature by extractive industries, the invisibility of nature in political planning (even with warnings beginning decades ago), and the disparaging of the natural world in discussions of the mitigation of impacts on human communities at the expense of nature.

The point is to examine the range of social and cultural values and practices that impede the full recognition of a group as an accepted member of the moral and political community. We focus not simply on the similarity of characteristics of humans and nonhumans, but on the commonality of patterns of oppression and status injuries in political, social, and cultural realms. It is crucial to understand that the question of status injuries and recognition exists not only in the political realm, but in the social and cultural realms as well; I deal with the latter here, and come back to the political in the discussion of procedural justice. In the social and cultural realms, the key to understanding injustice is an understanding of the social norms, language, and mores that mediate relations with those who are denigrated, and so less well-off in the scheme of justice.

Dean's notion of 'accountability' (1996) is very useful in understanding, and responding to, misrecognition in the social and cultural realms. In Dean's framework the focus is on the process of the construction of the status of the misrecognized; she insists we uncover where accountability and responsibility lie for both the construction of problematic notions and the reconstruction of ones based in more authentic recognition. In addressing nature specifically, Bennett (2004: 349) insists on a 'recognition of the agential powers of natural and artifactual things, greater awareness of the dense web of their connections with each other and with human bodies, and, finally, a more cautious, intelligent approach to our interventions in that ecology'. The view here is a Foucauldian one: what nature is, and how it has been treated and misrecognized, is maintained by the construction of the meaning and status of, and relationship with, nature. In this, we are both individually and socially—in addition to politically—complicit. Becoming accountable for that treatment, and recognizing both our own individual role and cultural alternatives to this construction, are important components of recognition—and so, of justice. Still, and importantly, such recognition is based on an understanding of the status injury to nature, and it does not require us to give a psychological subjectivity to that nature.

Here, the conception of justice occupies much space beyond the bounds of the state. Certainly, recognition could be demonstrated by the state—including proxy representation to elements of nature, or even just taking the notion of ecosystems and ecosystem health and integrity seriously enough to place evaluations of human activity within their context. I discuss these institutional remedies below and in a later chapter. But accountability for mis- or malrecognition, and the reversal of the status of nature in everyday life, must also be achieved in the social and cultural realms. In fact, the whole discussion of ecological justice, and of developing a common language for both environmental and ecological justice, is a way to open up public discourse to new ways of thinking about, and interacting with, nature. Status itself is partially based in discourse, and opening ecological justice in these directions may begin to address status-based injuries to nature.

Lash and Featherstone (2001: 14) argue that recognition is the source of modernity's social bond. They are interested in what happens as that bond breaks down, under pressure from the homogenizing forces of globalization and the reality of difference. The concern here is that modernity's recognition never went far enough; while it may have constructed a limited social bond, it never constructed a bond with the natural world that would have enabled a more constructive and sustainable relationship to develop. Instead, the lack of recognition of nature, the exclusion of nature from theories of justice, and the dismissal of parity for nature have led modernity to a crisis of sustainability. Modernity's social bond is unsustainable without a simultaneous recognition of, and bond with, the rest of the natural world. That is a status-based argument for the recognition of nature in a theory of ecological justice.

The Capabilities Approach

Such recognition, and status, can be approached with another discourse of justice as well. The capabilities approach offers an alternative way to look at justice, and, in turn, justice to nature. As discussed in Chapter 2, the capabilities approach, developed both individually and collaboratively by Amartya Sen and Martha Nussbaum, focuses on the variety of activities that humans need in order to fully flourish—from political freedoms to health care to social affiliation. Importantly, capabilities theory moves beyond a sole focus on a utilitarian or goods focus—justice is about more than GDP, for example—and into how individuals translate the goods they have into functioning lives. In addition, the capabilities approach incorporates distributional concerns along with recognition and political inclusion for a fairly comprehensive vision of justice. It is a lack of flourishing that is indicative of injustice, and the absence of specific capabilities that produce flourishing that is to be remedied.

The broad argument here is that this language of capabilities and functioning can also be applied to the natural world in a theory of ecological justice. The capabilities approach is important for ecological justice because flourishing is not an element that relates only to humanity, nor is it an element based in human life that we simply apply to nature along the lines of similarity. Capabilities include what is necessary for functioning and flourishing of human and nonhuman alike; it is an integral aspect of the living process. In this section, I want to discuss how the theory could be applied to nature.

Sen's only forays into the question of the relationship between capabilities and ecological sustainability remain squarely in the future generations approach. Anand and Sen (2000: 2035) argue that 'we can talk of sustainability only in terms of conserving a capacity to produce well-being' for people in the future. 'The moral obligation underlying sustainability is an injunction to preserve the capacity for future people to be as well off as we are' (p. 2038). Likewise, in discussing the preservation of endangered animals (Sen 2004), Sen focuses on what he calls 'sustainable freedoms'—the preservation, and possible expansion, of 'the substantive freedoms of people today "without compromising the ability of future generations" to have similar, or more, freedoms'. He argues for the importance of future generations to have the freedom to enjoy the same environmental benefits—from clean air to rare species—that earlier generations enjoyed.

Nussbaum (2004, 2006a, 2006b), on the other hand, has more thoroughly addressed the application of the approach to nonhuman nature, though her discussion is limited, for the most part, to individual animals. As Nussbaum argues, we share a world with other creatures, we have much in common with them, have many types of relationships with them, and share many of the same features. It is plausible, then, to think that these relationships ought to be regulated by a conception of justice. Put another way, 'the fact that humans act in ways that deny animals a dignified existence appears to be an issue of justice, and an urgent one' (Nussbaum 2006a: 326).

Yet while Nussbaum's expansion of her theory of justice to animals is an important and helpful step, it is limited in many ways. Notions of *functioning* and *capability* could be even more useful than Nussbaum posits, when applied to considering doing justice to the natural world as a whole.[12] There are, however, key challenges to be examined in expanding capabilities theory in this way. The definition of a flourishing life and the list of capabilities necessary for nonhumans to thrive—both individuals and systems—are central to applying this approach to ecological justice.

Nussbaum and Animals

Nussbaum breaks crucial ground by extending the capabilities approach to justice beyond humans, arguing that it is applicable to a wide range of types of animal sentience and dignity, and of corresponding needs for the flourishing of these creatures. She even offers a comprehensive capabilities list for animals based on those central to human capabilities (2004: 314–17, 2006*a*: 392–401). Nussbaum argues that the capabilities approach 'is capable of yielding norms of interspecies justice that are subtle and yet demanding, involving fundamental entitlements for creatures of different types' (2006*a*: 327). While I find much of value in Nussbaum's extension of the approach, my argument is that the notion of capabilities can be applied beyond the individual animals that Nussbaum addresses, into a broader notion of ecological justice.

Nussbaum begins her discussion of justice to animals with a helpful overview of the limitations of both contractarian and utilitarian theories. Kantian social contract theories, which include Rawls, fall short because of their demand for both rationality in the parties and the requirement of a contract between equals; in this, they deny the possibility of a relationship of justice between humans and nonhuman nature. As focused as Kant was on citizens treating other human beings as ends in themselves, he was quite clear that animals, and nature, have only instrumental worth. Rawls (1971: 504ff.), as discussed in Chapter 5, fully agrees that animals do not have the properties that humans do that would necessitate them being treated in accordance with the principles of justice. They would need both a capacity for a conception of the good, and a capacity to understand the conception of justice.[13]

Nussbaum takes on these shortcomings bluntly. The problem with contract theories, and Kant and Rawls specifically, is that they deny that animals are subjects, agents, and ends in themselves. Compassion, where Rawls and most of his followers leave the human responsibility toward animals, does not go nearly far enough; creatures, argues Nussbaum, have an *entitlement* not to be mistreated. 'When I say that the mistreatment of animals is unjust, I mean to say not only that it is wrong *of us* to treat them in that way, but also that they have a right, a moral entitlement, not to be treated in that way. It is unfair *to them*' (Nussbaum 2006*a*: 337). Capabilities theory can treat nonhuman animals as ends, and do this by focusing on the things that limit the flourishing of animal existence. 'The basic moral intuition behind the approach concerns the dignity of a form of life that possesses both deep needs and abilities' (Nussbaum 2004: 305).

After laying out the limitations of contract theory, Nussbaum takes on utilitarianism. Utilitarian theory has been better than contract theory in addressing animal justice, but only to a point. As it is outcome oriented, and is focused on sentience of pleasure or pain rather than rationality, theorists such as Bentham and Singer have been able to apply it beyond human beings. Yet utilitarianism has a number of shortfalls. One is that given its (basic) focus on total pleasure, it is easy to argue that the suffering brought to animals, in, say, medical testing or food production is outweighed by the pleasures of health or an enjoyable meal.[14] A more important problem, to Nussbaum, is that utilitarianism that includes animal pain crosses a liberal line into a substantive view of the good. Capabilities avoid this pitfall by insisting only on a partial conception of the good—a list of basic capabilities for all creatures—while the actual flourishing of animals (or not) is left to whatever religious or secular conception a society pursues (Nussbaum 2006a: 341). This is, in essence, a classic opportunity argument, rather than an outcome argument.

Ultimately, Nussbaum (2006a: 351) argues that

no sentient animal should be cut off from the chance for a flourishing life, a life with the type of dignity relevant to that species, and . . . all sentient animals should enjoy certain positive opportunities to flourish. With due respect for a world that contains many forms of life, we attend with ethical concern to each characteristic type of flourishing, and strive that it not be cut off or fruitless.

This approach involves direct obligations of justice to animals. 'It treats animals as subjects and agents, not just as objects of compassion.' So the basic opening argument posed by Nussbaum is that capabilities is a much better approach to extending justice to nonhuman animals than either contract theory or utilitarianism.

Unfortunately, Nussbaum does not address a whole host of other theories of environmental or ecological justice, such as those that focus on recognition of various qualities of animals or nature described above. Yet Nussbaum focuses on one quality that, she argues, human beings share with other animals—at least sentient ones. The preservation of *dignity* is at the heart of her argument for extending capability theory to nonhumans. 'Each form of life is worthy of respect, and it is a problem of justice when a creature does not have the opportunity to unfold its (valuable) power, to flourish in its own way, and to lead a life with dignity' (Nussbaum 2006b: B7). The respect for dignity is central to capabilities theory; as Nussbaum notes, the reason why 'capabilities are intrinsically connected to equal dignity pertains to ideas of nonhumiliation and reciprocity that seem particularly human; and of course those capabilities in general are important only for humans' (2006a: 382). Yet dignity is also central to her application of capabilities to animals, even if she does not directly equate human and animal dignity; Nussbaum argues that 'there is no respectable way to deny the equal dignity of species across species' (p. 383). A life that preserves dignity requires a particular list of capabilities—a list quite similar to that offered for humans. Nussbaum suggests that a

dignified existence would seem at least to include the following: adequate opportunities for nutrition and physical activity; freedom from pain, squalor, and cruelty; freedom to act in ways that are characteristic of the species...; freedom from fear and opportunities for rewarding interactions with other creatures of the same species, and of different species; a chance to enjoy the light and air in tranquility. (2006a: 326)[15]

Given the above discussion on the difference between psychological and status-based recognition, I am doubtful that dignity is the most appropriate word here. Primarily a psychological term referring to self-respect, it also only fits for the most sentient and self-conscious of species. While Nussbaum refers to 'a life with the type of dignity relevant to that species' (2006a: 351), this begs the question of how dignity differs across species, and opens Nussbaum to the criticism that she reads too much into the psychology of most animals. Misrecognition itself does no direct injury to nature—only the most sentient and self-conscious of nonhuman animals can be harmed by disparaging remarks (though claiming that such a harm is to its dignity is, again, a stretch). But such misrecognition by the human community makes harm to the natural world much more likely; it enables the behavior that threatens the integrity or flourishing of individuals or natural systems. A conception of integrity or of flourishing, as discussed previously, would be better choices than the term dignity; they apply more uniformly across a greater spectrum of nonhuman nature and refer to status rather than any hint of psychology. This does not take much of a shift in the focus of Nussbaum's theory; all of the capabilities in her ultimate list directly apply to the integrity of a life, not just dignity.

But Nussbaum seems quite biased toward sentient and even self-conscious animals—not much of a progression beyond the contractarians she criticizes. I say 'seems' because Nussbaum offers some mixed messages on sentience. On the one hand, she insists that sentience 'is not the only thing that matters for basic justice, but it seems plausible to consider the possession of sentience as a threshold condition for membership in the community of beings who have entitlements based on justice' (2006*a*: 361–2). Yet immediately following this, she moves beyond sentience.

Given the fact that pleasure and pain are not the only things of intrinsic value for the capabilities approach, the approach, strictly speaking, should not say that the capacity to feel pleasure and pain is a necessary condition of moral status. Instead, we should adopt a disjunctive approach: if a creature has *either* the capacity for pleasure and pain *or* the capacity for movement from place to place *or* the capacity for emotion and affiliation *or* the capacity for reasoning and so forth (we might add play, tool use, and others), then that creature has moral standing. (2006*a*: 362)

While this list clearly opens consideration of extending justice beyond sentient animals, Nussbaum immediately bows out of such a discussion, noting that 'we have enough on our plate if we focus for the time being on sentient creatures' (Nussbaum 2006*a*). Fair enough, but Nussbaum, then, leaves the line drawn in a very human-biased way, not very far from the line that contractarians have drawn. Still, the idea of an either/or list of qualities in nature that would make it a subject of justice leaves open the possibility of expanding capabilities beyond sentients in theory, even if it gives us a lot to do.

Animals, Species, Systems, and Capabilities

The much bigger issue is that Nussbaum, unfortunately, focuses only on individual creatures, remaining more in the realm of animal rights than in a broader notion of ecological justice. Nussbaum argues that the capabilities approach, applied to nonhumans, insists 'that no animal should be cut off from the chance at a flourishing life, and that all animals should enjoy certain positive opportunities to flourish' (Nussbaum 2004: 307). Justifying this limited focus on individual animals, Nussbaum argues that 'damage to the species occurs through damage to individuals' (2006*a*: 357). Nussbaum may move away from liberal contractarianism, but she is still tied to a very individualist conception of liberal rights, where individuals, and in this case individual animals, are the only possible agents of justice.[16] Yet damage to species, in fact, occurs mostly through loss of habitat, ecological support systems, symbiotic relationships, and, in a larger sense, damage to ecosystems as a whole. It is the functioning of a system, not an individual, which is at the heart of an ecological problem like species extinctions. Nussbaum simply does not examine the larger question, and, in fact, even conflates the discussion of *species* with that of *ecosystems and biodiversity*, two very different things. Individual members of species can live far apart, in different conditions, and so it is quite difficult to extend a notion of justice to a species as a whole [though Nussbaum discusses how we may have particular capabilities to protect endangered species (2006a: 357–8)]. But almost all individual animals—human and nonhuman—need not just some others of their own species, but a full environment, including nonsentient life and ecosystem relations, as part of their capability set in order to flourish. It is simply not possible to talk about the flourishing of individual animals without reference to the environment in which this flourishing is to occur.[17] Systems are living entities with their own integrity; atomizing nature into isolated animals devalues a form of life, and the way that this form of life flourishes. Nussbaum's individualistic focus, then, unnecessarily limits the reach of a capabilities approach in a system of ecological justice.

If the capabilities approach is about flourishing, and most animals flourish in particular environments, flourishing in this respect means contributing to the set of relationships that make up, and support, the system as a whole. We can use this reasoning to critique Nussbaum's support of modern zoos, which, for example, she praises for replacing antelope predation for tigers with hanging balls on ropes (2004: 311). Such an activity may replace the individual physical actions of predation, and so support that capability, but it is completely out of the context of flourishing in place and in interactions with others, where predation supports not just the individual animal, but also the flourishing of a larger system. Addressing the individual capability of a single animal, or a group of animals in captivity, does nothing to improve the flourishing of the species and its numerous ecological relationships.

The capabilities approach could enrich ecological justice by bringing recognition to the flourishing of *systems* as a whole *as well as* the individual animals Nussbaum includes. Nussbaum recognizes the importance of the social realm in her discussion of the capabilities set for humans—social recognition, for example, is a central capability—but she does not translate that into a concern for the ecological realm of individual animals. Clearly, the focus on capabilities should include the larger systems which contribute to individual capabilities—in the application to both humans and nonhuman systems alike. But further, systems themselves might be considered agents for the work they do in providing the various capacities for their parts to function—that is, purifying water, contributing oxygen, providing nutrition, and sustaining temperature. In this case, the central issue of ecological justice would be the interruption of the capabilities and functioning of a larger living system—what keeps it from transforming primary goods into capabilities, functionings, and the flourishing of the whole system.[18]

Take, for example, a river system.[19] Water, a primary good, is increasingly taken from the river for agricultural and urban use. The effect is a serious impingement on the functionings of the river—to support fish species and native flora, or to supply silt to beaches that support other wildlife on the riverside. We could address the problem in a purely distributive way, say, by simply adding water to the river from the bottom of a dam upstream. This delivers a primary good, water, but it does not necessarily assist the river system (or the flora and fauna within it) in its capability to function. The water may be too cold, or come at the wrong time of year; it may assist in some functioning, for example supporting nonnative trout, but not in others, like supporting native fish species. To bring back the capability of a river system to fully function, we must address those factors that inhibit that capability: our tendency to understand a river as a power source, or as an agricultural aqueduct, and our need to understand the impact of dams and recognize water as something that supports more than agriculture and thirsty cities. Applying Nussbaum's full capabilities list, some of the most salient issues would be in regard to health, integrity, affiliation, relation with other species, and control over the subject's environment.

I do not think such a community or ecosystem approach strays too far from Nussbaum's own discussion. In fact, she understands the role of systems, and drops hints about the possible expansion of her approach beyond sentient animals throughout her own work—though her comments are inconsistent. On the one hand, she recognizes that 'creatures cannot flourish in isolation, and thus for animals as for humans, the existence of suitable groups and communities is an important part of the flourishing of individuals' (Nussbaum 2006a: 357). She also notes that '[e]nhanced attention to habitat and reproductive environment is necessary...in order to continue the way of life that existing individuals are living' (p. 358). Later, Nussbaum admits that '[a]nimals "in the wild" are entitled to an environment that is the sort in which they characteristically flourish: so protecting this capability also means protecting animal environments' (p. 397). Reverting to her liberal contractarian, and legal, roots, Nussbaum also claims that for 'nonhuman animals, the analogue to property rights is respect for the territorial integrity of their habitat, whether domestic or "in the wild"' (p. 400). Why Nussbaum does not follow through on the promise of systems, or at least of moving beyond sentient creatures, may simply have to do with time and focus. At one points she notes that she does not comment on issue of plants or the natural world in general, though she thinks 'that the capabilities approach can be extended to deal with these issues' (p. 447, *n.* 24); she also says that '[b]iodiversity as such may be a good, but what sort of good it is, and what its relation may be to political justice, seem to be questions best left for another inquiry' (p. 357).

So while there is some promise of moving beyond a liberal individualism, the messages are mixed, and there is much going on here that is problematic. While Nussbaum notes the possibility of extending capabilities framework to plants and whole of nature, she immediately goes on to state quite clearly that her 'view, then, is individualistic in making the living creature, not the group or the species, the basic subject of justice'. While there is the possibility of an expansion noted, Nussbaum seems to go out of her way to shut those considerations down. My point is simple: there is no theoretical need to shut them down, as the capabilities approach is applicable to both individual animals and larger systems—as long as we are free to define capabilities differently for each entity under consideration, an issue I return to shortly.

The other attraction of a more systems based approach is that it helps us make sense of many of the arguments used by the environmental community in its attempt to defend nature by using concepts like preservation, restoration, and systems integrity. There the focus on doing justice to nature is on deconstructing the impediments to nature's own capabilities to fully and continually function. Concern is for the integrity of natural processes themselves. Take again, for example, Low and Gleeson's first principle of ecological justice, that 'every natural entity is entitled to enjoy the fullness of its own form of life'. The fullness of its own form of life is, in Sen and Nussbaum's terms, its functioning. This approach helps us flesh out what, exactly, the moment of injustice is in this principle: that point where nature is robbed of the capability to reach its functioning.[20] In understanding the injustice to nature in this way, we focus, then, on the social, cultural, political, and institutional meanings and processes that keep this natural functioning from being realized. This helps us understand some of the criticisms of small nature reserves (the Nature Conservancy approach), or unconnected bits of wilderness (the US wilderness system, which does not feature connecting corridors). Sure, it may make us feel better to leave 'nature cemeteries', as Luke (1997: ch. 3) describes such small-scale preservation. But this does not allow for the full functioning—or the capability to function—of particular ecosystems. These set-asides are nature cemeteries specifically because such methods do not provide nature the *capability* to fully *function* for the well-being of the ongoing integrity of the system. They are not unlike the zoos Nussbaum defends—where support for capabilities is artificial and incomplete.[21]

Harm, Harmony, and Tender Gazelles

This brings me to another critique of Nussbaum's approach—her tendency to sanitize the capabilities and functioning of some animals. Nussbaum argues that she aims to limit the 'harm-causing capabilities' (2006*a*: 369) of animals. She notes that we, as humans, limit our capacity to harm, and curb the flourishing of harmful talents. Yet while we (try to) limit humans' killing as part of our flourishing, this focus causes some particular problems in Nussbaum's account, and illustrates an essential bias toward harmony in nature.[22] Nussbaum insists that the 'capability to kill small animals, defined as such, is not valuable' (p. 370). 'But a lion who is given no exercise for its predatory capacity appears to suffer greatly, and there is no chance that education or acculturation would remove this pain' (p. 370). Her answer is to allow for the capability to exercise a predatory nature, while avoiding the harm done to smaller animals. As noted earlier, Nussbaum claims that zoos that offer tigers large balls on ropes can meet the capability need, and the solution is 'the most ethically sound'. Yet Nussbaum neglects to mention that those same tigers are most likely offered plenty of meat to eat, in order to function. With this the case, why not let them do their own killing? Why separate the capability of predation from its natural end, and function—food? Why sanitize the capability of the tiger simply because it makes humans uncomfortable to see a tiger 'crunch' on a 'tender gazelle', as Nussbaum puts it (p. 370)? Such sanitization keeps us—humans—from fully understanding species-based capabilities. If the question is the simultaneous protection of the tiger's prey—itself most likely a sentient animal—we need to understand and accept that part of the flourishing of animals is to be the protein for other life forms. All flourishing is not a pretty version of harmony; some is not-so-pretty, but nonetheless harmonious. To be food for others is the essence of functioning for some beings. Acorns can become oak trees, or they may become squirrel food; gazelles can breed in social units, or may become tiger food. Either direction represents a particular form of flourishing, as long as one recognizes that flourishing happens in systems, with creatures in relation with one another.

Nussbaum wants to avoid the 'gruesome deaths of animals at the hands of other animals...any nonviolent method of population control (e.g. by sterilization) is to be preferred to a violent method' (pp. 379–80). Perhaps this is why she supports the castration of certain male animals, such as horses, dogs, and cats, in order to decrease the possibility of doing violence to other animals (p. 395). Interestingly, Nussbaum notes that 'it is best for humans not to engage in too much second-guessing of animal capabilities, but to try to observe what each creature actually considers important, on the basis of what it does' (p. 371). But how does our observation of nature bring us to sanitize what we perceive as conflict and violence? It may be the case that, for human beings, we choose a less violent route out of our own perceptions of the good—for example, by preferring birth control to infanticide or starvation—but this should not necessarily be the case for other animals. There is good reason to limit hunting by humans; it is not crucial to our flourishing any longer, and only limits the flourishing of other animals and systems. But the only reason for limiting the hunting and predation for other animals, it seems, is because of the distaste and discomfort of some humans, including Nussbaum. Some animals are aggressive. Tigers hunt, and eat other animals; they only play with balls when deprived of that capability.

Yet we should also understand that the capabilities approach helps us make sense of the argument, often used against (a misunderstood notion of) ecocentrism, that we should simply let nature 'take its course'. Of course, letting nature just take its course, say by letting viruses run unchecked, would impinge on the capability of *other* living beings to function at their fullest. Using the capabilities approach, designs and processes which allow *more* capability to function for living beings and systems would be more just than those that increase or expand functioning at the cost of another. Both Sen and Nussbaum are very careful to focus not on an ultimate guarantee of full functioning, but only on the capabilities necessary for individuals to function as they see fit. We may provide for the capabilities for various parts of nature to function, but still choose the route that denies that functioning to certain parts of nature in order to allow others to flourish. Still, a focus on systems gets us away from dilemmas, such as doing justice to individual animals in a larger ecosystem. While there is no need to prevent wolves from devouring individual lambs, or tigers the tender gazelles, the capabilities approach applied to ecosystems focuses on a balance of each species to retain the capability to function, in order to provide for a systemwide ecological justice.[23]

Defining Capabilities Lists

So if we apply the capabilities approach to justice, how, exactly, are we to define capabilities for various individual animals, species, and systems? This could be a rather difficult question, if, as with one interpretation of capability theory, the task of defining capabilities necessarily lies with the subject of justice, and what he, she, or it wanted to do or be. In order to avoid the criticism that the capabilities approach is paternalistic, Sen (2005, for example) insists that subjects should participate, both individually and collectively, in the definition of capabilities lists. Sen avoids generating any of his own lists, and insists only on broad political freedoms.[24] Such concerns with paternalism, and subject self-definitions of capabilities, are quite valid in the human realm. If this were the only way to define or understand a necessary set of capabilities, we could not apply the theory to a nonsentient, nonreasoning, and noncommunicative nature. There would have to be a way to define not only what an ecosystem, for example, would *need* to flourish, but also that the ecosystem itself would *want* to flourish, and flourish in a particular way.

Thankfully, the capabilities approach does not need the subject of justice to be part of the definition or framing of the principles of justice; that is, as Nussbaum (2006*a*: 349) notes, a contractarian view. There is no need to limit the capabilities-based understanding of justice to subjects that use reason to define their own desires for doing or being. Sen, indeed, focuses on human agents who use reason, but we need not insist that agency be articulated through reason and speech. In applying a capabilities approach to nature, we do not need to have a particular animal or ecosystem express a desire for a particular functioning; rather, we need to recognize a different type of agency—a potential, a process, or a form of life illustrated by its history, ecology, way of being, and nonreason-based forms of communication.

In Nussbaum's argument, the capabilities approach as it applies to animals requires us to seek a 'limited set of political principles focused on enabling or protecting, not a comprehensive conception of good animal lives' (p. 352). Nussbaum notes that it will take study to understand the necessary capabilities of various species, but we do need to develop 'species norms' for each species' capability set, and to judge whether a particular creature has decent opportunities for flourishing.

In short, the species norm (duly evaluated) tells us what the appropriate benchmark is for judging whether a given creature has decent opportunities for flourishing . . . [I]n each case, what is wanted is a species-specific account of central

153

capabilities (which may include particular interspecies relationships . . .) and then a commitment to bring members of that species up to that norm, even if special obstacles lie in the way of that. (p. 365)

We should not automatically use a list of human capabilities to apply to all other animals, or interpret those particular capabilities in the same way as they are applied to other creatures; rather, we should be informed by the way of life of both animals and natural systems in coming to understand the capabilities necessary for them to fully function.

Coming to understand capability lists for all animals will be an incredibly difficult task, and even more so for nonsentients and systems, yet the process will be fruitful in numerous ways. On the one hand, the development of an understanding of capabilities will depend on what Nussbaum calls 'sympathetic imagining' (p. 355). 'Imagining and story-telling remind us in no uncertain terms that animal lives are many and diverse, with multiple activities and ends both within each species and across species.' I assume that in addition to such imagination, ecological science would also be a good resource. 'Part of respect for other species is a willingness to look and study, learning the internal rhythms of an animal community and the sense of value the way of life expresses' (p. 372). Interestingly, this brings us back to the value of recognition, and the importance of observation, as discussed by Rodman. As he noted, while 'we can never get inside a muskrat's head and know exactly what the world looks like from that angle, we can be pretty certain that the view is different from ours. What melts away as we become intrigued with this plurality of perspectives is the assumption that any one of them (e.g., ours) is privileged' (Rodman 1983: 89). This attention to the plurality of capabilities across species is important, and gives us a way to use both science and local knowledge to inform the development of capabilities sets.

Importantly, we remain in Nussbaum's insistence on plurality and flexibility in coming to an overlapping consensus on capabilities sets. Certainly, different participants in the development of such sets would have different views about what flourishing would mean, and what capabilities would be necessary to bring a subject, or a system, there. Still, even given different notions of the good on the part of such participants, an overlapping consensus on capabilities could be drawn around the basics needed to ensure flourishing, even if there are different definitions of that end. At the core in the human realm are the capabilities necessary to be in a position to develop one's own notion of the good—for liberals, the highest end of a human life. For other animals, nonsentients, or ecological systems, the consensus could be developed around the capabilities necessary for that subject to attain its highest possible level of functioning, or to function in a way that acknowledges the integrity and autonomy of the individual or system.

Still, given that it is human beings doing the imagining and the study, such a definition of capabilities is inherently paternalistic. Yet Nussbaum is particularly sensitive to this issue, and argues that while we recognize the inherent paternalism of humans defining the capabilities of nature, we can still respect the autonomy of the natural world 'if we adopt a type of paternalism that is highly sensitive to the different forms of flourishing that different species pursue' (Nussbaum 2006a: 375).

An intelligent, respectful paternalism cultivates spaces for choice. Animals are centers of activity, and no treatment is respectful that does not allow them to initiate activity on their own in some ways and to some degree . . . Consideration of the species norm helps us to craft forms of paternalism that are respectful of animal needs, even when those needs are plural, qualitatively non-homogenous, and not necessarily present to the animal's consciousness. (p. 378)

A human project to define nature's capabilities recognizes that there are a variety of animals, species, and systems. There is 'not a single conception at all, because the plurality of forms of life is very important to the whole idea' (p. 356). It is this recognition of the plurality, in terms of both nature's need and our own representations, that tempers and minimalizes the paternalism inherent in the practice. It is important that fallibility and flexibility in the definition are recognized at outset, as is the usual case with the definition of human capabilities, at least as defined by Nussbaum, as well as Sen (see, in particular, 2005). I return to this point in the following chapters.

Clearly, such a broad exercise in determining various capability sets for different animals was not part of Nussbaum's recent work. She offers only a basic and overarching capabilities list for animals (2006a: 392–401) that is identical to her list for human beings, though rethought for the animal world. Specifically, the list of capabilities applies to animals in the following ways:

- Life: all animals are entitled to continue their lives, though Nussbaum offers numerous caveats, and plausible reasons for killing.

- Bodily health: the entitlement to a healthy life. This entails the institution of laws that ban cruel, neglectful, ill, harsh, and cruel treatment of animals.

- Bodily integrity: 'animals have direct entitlements against violations of their bodily integrity' (p. 395). The difference from bodily health here is the focus on the integrity of the body, so Nussbaum gives the example of the inappropriateness of declawing cats.[25]

- Senses, imagination, and thought: ensuring access to free movement and other sources of pleasure; this would limit the confinement of animals.

- Emotions: Animals are 'entitled to lives in which it is open to them to have attachments to others, to love and care for others' (p. 397).

- Practical reason: This is probably the most difficult capability to transfer from the human list to the animal list, but Nussbaum insists that 'we need to ask to what extent the creature has a capacity to frame goals and projects and to plan its life' (p. 398).

- Affiliation: Nussbaum keeps the two parts of the human capability for animals, an interpersonal and a public part. The first has to do with the opportunity to form attachments, bonds, and relationships. The latter is the entitlement 'to live in a world public culture that respects them and treats them as dignified beings' (p. 398).

- Other species: Like humans, animals should be able to 'live with concern for and in relation to animals, plants, and the world of nature' (p. 398). Here, the capability is identical.

- Play: Again, necessary for all sentient lives, human and nonhuman animal.

- Control over one's environment: As with the human list, this includes both political and material dimensions for animals. In the first, 'the important thing is being part of a political conception that is framed so as to respect them, and is committed to treating them justly' (p. 400). For the latter, in place of property rights for humans, animals should get 'respect for the territorial integrity of their habitat' (p. 400).

Surely, Nussbaum means for such a list to be for guidance only; she is quite clear that capabilities would differ for even different sentient animals. It is also clear that Nussbaum is concerned only with sentient animals in this list, and with a particularly harmonious understanding of their lives. If we are to expand a capabilities list to include nonsentient animals, species, and interactive ecosystems, such categories will take more explanation, some will simply not fit, and others may be necessary. Laying out a *theory* of capabilities as an element of ecological justice is one thing; the details will take much more work—an interdisciplinary project of theorists, ecologists, and a variety of other participants. In essence, the implementation of a capabilities approach requires a concomitant dedication to engagement, plurality, participation, and inclusive procedures as an element of justice. It is to that process that I now turn.

Addressing Recognition and Capabilities: The Role of Procedural Justice

The focus here so far has been on legitimizing and exploring ways of extending recognition and capabilities to nonhuman nature. After discussing how such concepts can be extended to nature in a number of ways, the pragmatic question now is how the *lack* of recognition and capabilities of nature can be addressed. Participation and procedural justice are prerequisites for the implementation of both recognition and capabilities. Both Fraser, in discussing justice based in recognition, and Nussbaum, in her discussion of the capability of 'control over one's environment', point to participation as an integral part of any definition of justice (Fraser 1998, 2000; Nussbaum 2000, 2006a), and this element is the key to ecological justice as well.

Fraser argues that procedural justice is based in political parity. Subordination is to be overcome by establishing the misrecognized party as a full member of society, capable of participating on par with the rest—what Fraser (2001: 27) calls 'participatory parity'. The goal is to establish full status as a partner or peer for those that have been subordinated both culturally and distributionally. Parity in cultural, social, and political institutions would begin to address misrecognition, capabilities, and the underlying—and resultant—inequities in distribution. For many theorists and social justice activists alike, redressing misrecognition means eliminating values and practices that impede participation, making political and social decision-making institutions and practices more inclusive, and broadening the definition of acceptable communication in that decision-making. Recognition itself, then, brings the political parity necessary for participation. Fraser does not address the question of the recognition or participation of nature, but her focus on status and subordination

157

would be applicable to the natural world. Extending this recognition for nature in cultural, social, and political institutions would grant parity—presupposing the moral worth and political status of nonhuman nature.

Illustrating the link between a focus on capabilities and procedural justice, Nussbaum (2006a: 388) hopes that this type of recognition and inclusion, particularly of nonhuman animals, will come to be. Eventually, she posits, a claim for animal justice can be part of an overlapping public consensus; the fact that the claim is for minimal capabilities, rather than full functioning of all animals, should make that easier. The key capability related to participation is that of 'control over one's environment'. As noted above, Nussbaum insists that the most important thing here is a political conception and practice that respects animals, and is committed to treating them with justice. As with Fraser, there is a central connection between recognition and participation. Nussbaum only very briefly describes what she means by political participation for the nonhuman, and it is a very legalistic vision: entitlements that can be defended by human representatives, and property rights to the 'territorial integrity' of habitat.

Participatory parity for nature and political participation of the nonhuman would not strictly mean votes for animals; the goal is more broadly the recognition of the consideration of the natural world in human decision-making. I return to more specific institutional implications of this inclusion in Chapter 8, but the point here is that while theories of ecological justice can be expanded by examining and incorporating theories of recognition and capabilities, ecological justice cannot be achieved without a concomitant expansion of procedural justice.

Conclusion

Ecological justice, then, has distributional, recognitional, capabilities, and participatory components. Each of these concepts can be extended to encompass the nonhuman world. We can recognize the similarities between human beings and the rest of nature, or the injustice of its status in relations with us. Capabilities can be applied to both individual animals, as Nussbaum suggests, and to broader environmental systems. We can extend participatory parity to include the nonhuman natural world in political decision-making. Ecological justice, then, has little reason to limit itself to the distributional realm. Distribution, recognition, capabilities, and participation can be tied together in an enlarged theory of justice that draws from numerous themes—a theory that is applicable in the human realm as well as the realm shared by humans and nonhuman nature. To do justice to nature means attending to issues of social and political recognition, individual and system capabilities, as well as the social and political institutions where exclusion of such concepts can be addressed.

Environmental justice movements that focus on environmental issues within human communities have developed innovative and integrated notions of justice that mirror this theoretical framework. The point here is to extend both that expansive and inclusive theory of justice, and the broad political project, into ecological justice and relations between humans and nonhuman nature as well. Such a project allows us to tackle numerous questions and strategies in the quest to do justice to nature. But, strategically, it also means we can use the same broad discourse of justice in both discussions of environmental problems within human communities and the ecological troubles of the broader natural world. In the realm of environmental justice this comprehensive political project is both theoretically sensible and pragmatically necessary. Yet two important questions remain. First, how can we take into account the need to balance emphases of different notions of justice, and, related, how are we to deal with the plurality of interpretations of recognition or capabilities? Finally, and perhaps most importantly, how can we begin to think of pragmatic implementations of such a theory and practice of environmental and ecological justice?

Notes

1. Past authors in environmental ethics have focused on a recognition or respect for the *intrinsic value* in nature in order to justify an extension of our moral and ethical community to nature. However, none connect this respect to a theory of justice. In fact, environmental ethics as a whole has come under fire for its lack of political relevance. See especially Light and Katz (1996) and de-Shalit (2000).

2. For an early example, see Vandeveer (1979) (discussed in Dobson 1998: 170–1).

3. Still, argues Eckersley (2005), Rodman uses liberal terminology and bases his arguments on the liberal dedication to autonomy. While this may be true, Rodman (1977, 1983) broke key ground early in the history of environmental political thought with both his critique of the individualistic moral atomism at the base of moral extensionism, and his reconstructive notion of an ecological sensibility.

4. On autonomy, see Heyd (2005); on autopeiosis, see Eckersley (1992: 60–1) and McGinnis (1999: 72–5).

5. Though, as discussed in Chapter 5, Low and Gleeson insist that all justice, including environmental justice, is about distribution. They neither acknowledge, nor address, recognition directly.

6. This is Kantian solely in the sense of the focus on ends rather than means. Kant himself did not believe in the intrinsic value of animals, and only preferred kindness over cruelty as it taught humans how to be kind to one another. See the discussion in Nussbaum (2006: 330).

7. On ecocentrism, the citations are numerous, though some are more comprehensive and coherent than others. See the discussion in Eckersley (1992), and the collection of Katz, Light, and Rothenberg (2000).

8. I want to make clear that I am not advocating the application of the psychological side of theories of recognition to nature. I think there is an important line between using 'dignity' as a psychological term focused on self-respect, and 'integrity' which may have psychological component in the human case, but also focuses on the unity or wholeness of a system—individual or more broad—that can apply to both individual humans, individual nonhumans, and larger natural systems. See the discussion below.

9. See Fraser's exchange with Honneth in Fraser and Honneth (2003). It is important to note that Fraser does not address the status of nature; I am simply extending her argument in that direction.

10. While he developed a notion of ecological recognition, his major expression of the notion (Rodman 1983) stopped with it as a form of ecological consciousness, and possibly a guide for action. Rodman went no further into applying such a concept to the implementation of political concepts such as justice, as have later authors.

11. This type of psychological argument is Bell's reasoning (2003) in excluding nature from political debate. In his view, it is not an injustice to exclude nonhuman nature, as exclusion does not harm them. This may be true in a psychological sense, but not in terms of harm to status.

12. Breena Holland (2004) is the only other political theorist I have found who attempts to apply capabilities theory to the natural world, though her work centers on a theory of value, rather than justice. As she argues, capabilities theory provides a theory of value that can be applied to environmental value. Her focus is on environmental conditions that enable human capabilities, but she includes a recognition of the variety of environmental processes, and interactions between humans and the environment, that are necessary for functioning. Her central point is that this relationship dissolves the difference between human value and environmental value, and permits a single and comprehensive theory of value that encompasses individual, social, and environmental aspects of human functioning and well-being.

13. While Nussbaum posits that Rawls may simply be wrong about the intelligence of animals, even if their intelligence is real we would still do not know how to enter into a contract with them. Here, though, I have to disagree with Nussbaum on the possibility of *imagining* such a contract. All social contract theory is imaginary; if we can stretch to imagine a Hobbesian state of nature, or a Rawlsian original position, we can imagine a contract with nonrational animals (or a contract where we may turn out to be nonrational animals after lifting the veil of ignorance). We may develop a contract with human biases, but liberal social contract theory already imagines contracts with thorough cultural biases, and seems not too concerned about it.

14. Actually, this is the specific rationale being offered by a *pro*-animal testing organization in the UK. See Cowell (2006).

15. Nussbaum feels that this insistence on animal dignity may cross a liberal line into a notion of the good, so leaves it as 'a metaphysical question on which citizens may hold different positions while accepting the basic substantive claims about animal entitlement...' (2006a: 383). The fallback is a less sweeping idea, but nonetheless still based in the recognition of the importance of animals in an overall theory of justice.

16. Marx's critique of individualist liberal rights is handy here, though he was, again, only partly right: we are species beings, but we are also *more* than species beings—we are systems beings.

17. Nussbaum also follows those from Aristotle to Bentham to Singer in noting that 'differences of capacity affect entitlements'. More specifically, more 'complex forms of life have more and more complex (good) capabilities to be blighted, so they can suffer more and different types of harm' (2006a: 360). Still, there is nothing here about relations in ecosystems or environments. It may be painless to kill a nonsentient mollusk, but if one harms their environment, and impacts a system, we do damage that impacts all others in that system. A harm to nonsentients that is considered 'trivial' may impact a whole host of individual animals, species, and systems.

18. It should also be noted, in making the connection between environmental and ecological justice, that this type of systems flourishing is articulated by environmental justice movements. There, as discussed in Chapter 3, concerns regarding environmental injustices do not only focus on harm to individuals—e.g. health impacts caused by exposure to toxic chemicals. Environmental justice activists also often focus on the discrimination that leads to such exposure, and the effect of such contamination, on the whole community. So a systems approach to functioning and capabilities applies equally to the environmental justice of communities as well as the ecological justice of ecosystems.

19. This is the particular case of the Colorado River through the Grand Canyon.

20. Low and Gleeson (1998), unfortunately, do not discuss this aspect of Sen's work. Dobson, in the other major work on environmental justice, addresses

Sen's conception of justice, but his interpretation limits the potential promise of the approach. For Dobson (1998: 132), Sen demonstrates that 'concern for human welfare need not necessarily lead to a concern for environmental sustainability....' The problem, as Dobson sees it, is that Sen focuses on capabilities rather than goods; as such, Dobson argues, Sen's approach only appreciates natural capital instrumentally, as it enables the realization of human capabilities. But this interpretation is problematic in two key ways. First, even if Sen has an instrumental view of nature, he has shown a keen interest in sustainability, especially as it is linked to the potential of just development (e.g. Sen 2002, 2004). The capabilities approach allows for consideration of human agency and participation in environmental decision-making, something key in most definitions of sustainable development. But more importantly for this discussion, Dobson misses the opportunity to apply Sen's (and Nussbaum's) language and conception of justice to nature itself.

21. Nussbaum seems to have a particular weak spot for zoos. Tigers are happy swatting balls, and many 'animals will do better in an imaginative and well-maintained zoo than in the wild, at least in present conditions of threat and scarcity' (2006*a*: 375–6). This praise for zoos can only happen if, first, you think in terms of individuals and not the systems in which they live and flourish, and second, if you do not intend to *use* a theory of justice to animals to argue for their protection in their habitats. Taking Nussbaum's position to the extreme, as long as we have a few happy individuals of each species, well-kept in kind zoos, justice is done. Frankly, and obviously, a theory of ecological justice must go further than that in its prescriptions.

22. This is the case even though Nussbaum criticizes (and, actually stereotypes) nature writers for doing the same (p. 367).

23. For those concerned about viruses, however, there is, of course, always the fallback to Nussbaum's and Singer's sentience approach, where more value is given to the functioning and flourishing of the more sentient creatures in a system.

24. I return to this important point in the Chapter 7.

25. Yet, as noted above, Nussbaum approves the castration of certain animals, which would be compatible with their flourishing in nonviolent lives.

Part IV

Plurality, Reflexivity, and Engagement

7

Justice and Plurality

What we have so far are arguments for both environmental justice and ecological justice that incorporate a variety of conceptualizations of justice, including distribution, recognition, participation, and capabilities; they can each be articulated at both the individual and community level. There is, then, a plurality of potential definitions, and they come from both environmental movements and environmental theorists. But examining and theorizing definitions is only part of the effort here; now, two key questions remain. First, how do we reconcile this definitional plurality both theoretically and in terms of a strategy for environmental and ecological justice movements? Second, and perhaps most pragmatically, how are we to implement and attain such notions of environmental and ecological justice? These are the tasks of this chapter and Chapter 8.

My argument, as laid out in the introduction, is that a plurality of discourses of justices is a good thing—it is both theoretically justifiable and pragmatically applicable. First, theoretically, a variety of definitions of justice is not something that has to be feared. Here, I refer to a long tradition of pluralist theory to make the case. Second, the fact that movements articulate justice in a myriad of ways should be an indicator to theorists to examine the value of such plurality. One of the most important shifts in progressive movements over the past couple of decades, including environmental movements and movements for social and environmental justice, is their willingness to accept different discourses in the same movement. Such difference, I understand, cannot simply exist side by side in a static state; plurality demands engagement, and I address this process in these concluding chapters as well.

Universalist Aspirations and Pluralist Realities

I find it quite unfortunate that many attempts to define ecological justice defend a very limited, singular, and universal notion of justice rather than embrace a pluralistic, and so pragmatic, understanding of how justice can be defined and used. As noted in Chapter 5, Low and Gleeson (1998) have a contradictory approach to the question of the relationship between plurality and justice. On the one hand, they are quite attentive to cultural differences in particular, and note that any understanding of justice has to be interpreted through local cultures and institutions (p. 67). Yet their fear of plurality leads them to claim that acceptance of different notions of justice in different contexts would make justice 'meaningless' (p. 197). For Low and Gleeson, it seems that the acknowledgment of difference is only to be valued if it can 'provide a route back to universal principles' (1998: 38)—by which they mean not simply justice, but a particular and distributive understanding of justice.

Likewise, Baxter (2005) begins his examination of ecological justice with a defense of a singular and universal theory of justice against constructivist or contextualist claims. He argues (pp. 62–3) that pluralist theories (such as Warren's 1997 discussion of moral status) can have the appearance of arbitrary selection, and he supports Callicott's insistence (1990) that appealing to more than one ethical theory can lead to inconsistency and self-serving conclusions. Baxter is clearly after a singular universally applicable notion of ecological justice that extends distributive considerations to a large part of the natural world, and sees such a singular approach as the only reasonable and sustainable way to ground such an extension.[1]

In both of these texts, the need for a political ethic of justice is articulated and defended, but only in the singular. Yet why cannot there be a variety of ethics and definitions of justice that come into play on various environmental decisions, in different contexts? In contrast to Low and Gleeson, and to Baxter, on ecological justice, those who write about environmental justice movements, such as those discussed in Chapters 3 and 4, have much less of a problem with multiple or plural conceptions of justice. Many authors see at least a dualistic focus on distribution and participation, and others acknowledge the role of recognition as well. There can be multiple reasons, based in different conceptions of justice, for opposing trash incinerators in minority communities, the bioengineering of food, or snowmaking with wastewater on a sacred mountain. Plurality in definition does not make justice disappear; on the contrary, acceptance of such varied arguments highlights the importance of justice as it is experienced and articulated in numerous ways. It is the insistence on singularity and universalism in a theory and practice of justice that would produce exclusion and the disappearance of multiple articulations, issues, and movements. Pluralism is both empirically real in the expression of justice claims, and pragmatically necessary to avoid the mistakes of exclusion so common to universalism and paternalism.

My goal here is not the development of a universally defensible, singularly defined, and permanent notion of environmental and ecological justice; rather, my aim is to lay out and bring attention to a broad and overlapping set of environmental and ecological justice discourses that exist in practice. Claims for environmental and ecological justice have, can, and will be made in different ways and terms in different places, contexts, and times. Conceptions of justice have, can, and will be articulated using the language of distribution, recognition, participation, and/or capabilities. The point is not to dismiss one or the other conception, or to insist on one or the other approach in the singular, but to find a way to incorporate these disparate claims and notions in a broad, inclusive, and pragmatic understanding of, and movement for, environmental and ecological justice.

Interestingly, Peter Wenz (1988) used this approach in one of the earliest theoretical discussions of environmental justice; it has, unfortunately, since been ignored. For Wenz, such pluralistic notions of justice are quite welcome on a both theoretical and practical level. Environmental justice, he argues, is understood in numerous ways, depending on context. He sees value in the fact that we are 'attracted to using one theory in one kind of situation and a different theory in a different kind of situation'. Wenz argues that we need a pluralistic theory of environmental justice 'that enables us to appeal in a consistent manner to principles featured in a variety of theories, even when those principles can not all be reduced to or derived from a single master principle' (1988: 313). It is simply important to comprehend different peoples' interpretations of justice, as it helps us to understand and tolerate others (p. 2). In this, Wenz illustrates the importance of the relationship between pluralism and justice; I want to explore this connection more thoroughly.

Pluralist Defenses of Multiplicity

While defenses of pluralistic notions of justice may be few in the literature of ecological justice, they have become more common in political theories of justice. Traditional theories of just distribution, such as Rawls's, tend to focus on absolutely universal principles; Rawls's basic principles of justice, the principle of equal liberty and the difference principle, form the basis of many an undergraduate course. Walzer (1983) began a move away from a concern with a singular universal theory of justice in favor of understanding the concept in historical and cultural place; this move has particular resonance in dealing with environmental justice. While still wed to the notion of distribution, Walzer (p. 6) attempts to introduce a language of difference. He argues

that the principles of justice are themselves pluralistic in form; that different social goods ought to be distributed for different reasons, in accordance with different procedures, by different agents; and that all these differences derive from different understandings of the social goods themselves—the inevitable product of historical and cultural particularism.

For Walzer, not only are different things valued differently by different people, but this means that the very criteria for distribution will differ according to how we value things. Social meanings of objects, procedures, and principles are historical and will change over time; hence Walzer introduces a notion of a 'distributive sphere', where conceptions of justice are limited in place and time. Walzer's approach to the discussion of justice in a real, diverse world is more complex and more grounded than Rawls's 'veil of ignorance'. While Walzer remains tied to the concept, and language, of justice purely as a concept of distribution, we can extend his arguments regarding justice and plurality into additional conceptions of justice, in addition to various interpretations of distribution.

Most contemporary justice theorists consider themselves pluralist in a sense, in that they accept a variety of notions of the good (and we can see this in relation to different ways of understanding and relating to both human communities and nature). Some are also 'contextualist' like Walzer, meaning that they see different principles of justice applicable in different sorts of situations. Miller (2003: 350), for example, argues that principles of justice should be developed depending on the social makeup of those making the claim and on the relationship they have with other parties in a justice dispute. Even so, a thorough and critical concept of pluralism has not thoroughly taken root in most writing on justice.

A critical pluralism, I believe, offers us a possible framework for thinking about the validity of plurality in social justice generally, and environmental and ecological justice specifically; with it, we can theorize generally while remaining open to the very real and practical differences that exist in practice. Connolly (2005) argues that pluralism prizes diversity along several dimensions, and actively supports the plural against various drives to singular, unitary, and universal ends. He suggests that such an approach requires a 'bicameral' approach to political life, in which we can accept ambiguity and 'keep a foot on two worlds, straddling two or more perspectives to maintain tension between the two' (p. 4). The starting point for such a point of view is the empirical reality, and pragmatic acceptance, of the reality of difference.

Connolly consciously resurrects a classic notion of pluralistic philosophy, best articulated by William James. James saw the methodology of 'radical empiricism' as the basis of pluralist philosophy; here, 'all we are required to admit as the constitution of reality is what we ourselves find empirically realized in every minimum of finite life' (James [1909] 1977: 145). James argued that as both what is experienced and the consciousness of that experience varies for people, a pluralist universe is empirically and objectively grounded. He was adamant that the pluralistic philosophy captured the actual world better than universalist theories, and that the 'prestige of the absolute has rather crumbled in our hands' (1909 [1977]: 63), as pluralism is realized as more empirically evident than universalism.

James's pluralist approach was not just a validation of the empirical reality of difference, but an insistence on understanding that difference will never come together in to a single coherent unity, as the philosophical absolutists desired. According to James, the pluralist view

is willing to believe that there may ultimately never be an all-form at all, that the substance of reality may never get totally collected, that some of it may remain outside of the largest combination of it ever made, and that a disruptive form of reality, the *each-form* is logically as acceptable and empirically as probable as the all-form commonly acquiesced in as so obviously the self-evident thing. (James [1912] 1976: 14–15)

Connections can be made in the pluralistic universe without recourse to an insistence on singularity or uniformity; the result is what James calls a 'multiverse' rather than a universe. Incommensurability—of values, visions, and reality itself—was central to James's explication of pluralism; he simply wanted philosophy to recognize and embrace the real world of difference and disunity.

Likewise, the tenets of value pluralism and incommensurability were central to Isaiah Berlin's examination of the relationship between political pluralism and liberalism. While Berlin is most well known for his work on liberty, he premises the need for such a focus with an acknowledgment

169

against the universalist, monist view. '[S]ince some values may conflict intrinsically, the very notion that a pattern must in principle be discoverable in which they are all rendered harmonious is founded on a false a priori view of what the world is like' (Berlin 1969: li). Universalism, he argued, reduces every value to the lowest common denominator, and 'drained both lives and ideals of the specific content which alone gave them point' (Berlin 1990: 245). The belief that there is a final, single unity 'rests on the conviction that all the positive values in which men have believed must, in the end, be compatible, and perhaps even entail one another... [but] not all good things are compatible, still less all the ideals of mankind' (Berlin 1969: 167). Berlin, of course, used such a view to justify multiple forms of liberty; but, along with James, we can apply such a pluralist view to justice as well.

By the 1980s, a number of authors began to both resurrect important aspects of pluralism's earlier generation and imagine new paths for pluralist theory. The epistemological foundation of pluralism, born in James's radical empiricism though ignored by seemingly everyone but Berlin in the postwar years, came back to the forefront of pluralist thought in order to justify and validate different ways of seeing and knowing the world. Key to this, as McClure (1992) argues, was the revitalization of feminist epistemology and the radical pluralist potential in the multiple subjectivities suggested by Haraway and other feminist theorists. Haraway's descriptions of situated knowledge and embodied objectivity (1988) were based on a metaphor of vision—that depending on one's experience, context, or view from one's body we can see and understand the same object in multiple ways. In this sense, as with James, only partial perspectives can be considered objective. Similarly, Deleuze and Guattari (1983) inspired postmodern pluralists with their argument to return to a focus on multiplicity. Empirically, they argued, we live in an age of partiality, where we are defined by the many and varied states, situations, and groups through which we pass. These arguments resurrected James's radical empiricism in the postmodern context, and reawakened the pluralist political response to the reality of difference. Mouffe, for example, explicitly claims a pluralist intent—starting political analysis with the recognition of difference, and refusing 'the objective of unanimity and homogeneity which is... based on acts of exclusion (1996: 246). As Hardt and Negri (2000) argue, the move is one from a focus on transcendence to immanence; here, there is a recognition that we can no longer simply use a single, universal, and transcendent standard to evaluate the world (Moore 2006: 6).

As Connolly (2005: 80) explains, James was a theorist who broke from the tradition of theorists reaching for certainty, and yet one who combined a 'vigorous *defense* of his philosophy to *modesty* about its status'. Connolly himself continues this tradition, arguing that

as you come to feel this larger web of loose affinities and uncertain connections, you outgrow the implicit idea that the world was designed for us alone, or that human beings can master it entirely, or that we can in principle know it completely . . . or that we can insulate ourselves from the rest of the world. (p. 92)

Connolly and these other contemporary pluralist theorists illustrate that plurality has once again become the basis of a radical and critical political theorizing, focusing on the reality and political meaning of difference, as well as the potential of relations across that difference, rather than on the dreams of monist or universal definitions of political concepts.[2]

Plurality and Conceptions of Justice

Still, very few of these theorists have directly linked the focus on pluralism with definitions of justice. Lyotard (1984) is the exception here. Lyotard insisted, in his definition of the postmodern condition, that singularity and consensus on theoretical definitions are both outmoded and suspect. Famously, however, he asserted that justice was neither—and argued that we simply need to develop an idea and practice of justice that is not linked to the universalism of consensus (p. 66). The recognition of heterogeneity is central to Lyotard's understanding of the future of justice; here, we must understand individuals as existing in a complex fabric of relations, located at a post through which diverse messages pass (p. 15). The fabric and post metaphors may be mixed, but the point is simple: we are each subject to messages about, and discourses of, justice that are multiple, diverse, and overlapping. The key is to pay attention to empirically extant differences, engage them, and understand them as parts of the whole that make up the broader understanding and discourse of justice.

My point is to combine the recognition of the empirical reality of plurality, and the related dismissal of attempts at singular, monist, unitary definitions of justice, in coming to understand and accept a plural conception and discourse of social, environmental, and ecological justice. There are two ways that plurality is a crucial and vital element of understanding and defining environmental justice.

First, one of the important caveats in discussing the various elements of justice I have discussed is that one is never to be considered a

171

replacement for the others. While recognition or participation may be considered central components of environmental or ecological justice, distributional considerations and/or capabilities must be understood as additional and/or complementary notions. It is absolutely essential to tie together conceptions of misrecognition and social subordination and the denial of capabilities with discussions of maldistribution and, importantly, participation. It is not a question of one or the other as the focus of justice, but of understanding that two or more conceptions can be in play simultaneously, depending on situation and context. Fraser, for example, argues that the remedy for maldistribution must focus on political and economic restructuring; but movements understand that such considerations will only come along, in part, with recognition, where the remedy is in cultural and symbolic changes in how we regard the presently misrecognized. In addition, we often cannot address distribution, and we cannot deal with misrecognition, without a focus on institutional procedures. Fraser's recent work on justice (2000, 2001) is based on the premise that these three central components of justice are integrally linked. Likewise, Nussbaum (2000, 2006a) understands that recognition forms the basis of many items on both human and animal capabilities lists, and includes the important capacity of 'control over one's environment'—including the right of political participation—in capabilities lists for both populations.

The point here is that multiple notions of justice are to be cited and called for, in various combinations and prioritizations, depending on situation and context. We can look at a single instance and see such multiple conceptions. In the case of the use of reclaimed wastewater to make snow at a ski resort on a mountain sacred to local tribes, we can easily see distributional (Native Americans get more environmental bads than others), recognition-based (lack of acknowledgment of tribal cultures), participation-focused (exclusion from decision-making and lack of materials in tribal languages), and capabilities-based (the impact on tribes capability to retain cultural meanings and teachings) notions of environmental justice; we can also see distributional (water moved from one watershed to another), recognition-based (nature's processes ignored), participation-focused (no proxies for impacted species or communities), and capabilities-based (what will water laced with pharmaceuticals do to the reproductive capacity of local animals and plants) notions of ecological justice. All of these exist simultaneously in a single snowmaking proposal.

My argument here is not that all conceptions of justice must be present in *every* case of environmental or ecological justice, as it is in the

snowmaking case, only that we should be open to examining and emphasizing various conceptions of justice—and experiences of injustice—on
different issues. We have numerous components and conceptions of justice, and see that different and multiple theories can apply to various
issues, cases, and contexts. Using the range of theories available to us, and
understanding how they overlap and interact, will illuminate problems
more thoroughly. Such an approach will also bring us to see that what we
may now understand as disparate issues and movements may be brought
together with this shared and overlapping discourse of justice.

Related, the second essential pluralist conception to keep in mind is
not just the importance of the relationship among multiple notions of
justice, but also a resistance to defining any one of those conceptions
in a singular, fixed way. Sen (1992, 2005), for example, argues against
a complete and unique list of the functionings necessary for the good
human life.

My difficulty with accepting [a fixed list] as the *only* route on which to travel arises
partly from the concern that this view of human nature . . . may be tremendously
overspecified. . . . But mostly my intransigence arises, in fact, from the consideration that the use of the capability approach as such does not require taking that
route, and the deliberate incompleteness of my capability approach permits other
routes to be taken that also have some plausibility. (1992: 47)

Sen argues that we can agree on the usability of the capability approach
without specifying any singular agreement on the particular capabilities.
The approach, he argues (2005: 157) 'allows considerable variations in
application'. In contrast to Nussbaum, Sen's 'reluctance to join the search
for such a canonical list arises partly from [the] difficulty in seeing how the
exact lists and weights would be chosen without appropriate specification
of the context of their use' (Sen 2005: 157), which obviously could vary
in different situations. In the above example, the capabilities of the native
tribes would differ from local skiers, and the capabilities important in this
specific case would be different from those listed for other issues, in other
places or times.

Importantly for Sen, any agreement on such a list would not only
violate a notion of plurality and attention to context, but also the crucial
role public discussion should play in any generation of a capabilities
list. 'If reasoned agreement is seen as an important foundational quality
central to political and social ethics, then the case for the pause is not
so hard to understand. The fact that the capability approach is consistent
and combinable with several different substantive theories need not be a

source of embarrassment (1992: 48).' I return to this point in a moment, but it is important here that Sen suggests a level of ambiguity be left in order to allow both plurality and discourse to occur. Against possible arguments that a capabilities approach is either paternalistic or unreasonably fixed, Sen suggests just the opposite—a flexible approach, best left up to public deliberation. 'The richness of the capability perspective broadly interpreted... includes its insistence on the need for open valuational scrutiny for making social judgments, and in this sense it fits in well with the importance of public reasoning' (Sen 2005: 157). To insist on a fixed list of capabilities, he argues, 'would deny the possibility of progress in social understanding, and also go against the productive role of public discussion, social agitation, and open debates' (p. 160). Sen here leaves open differences or changes in the agreed-upon nature of capabilities in various times and places, while emphasizing plurality on a much broader level than the basic proceduralism of Rawlsian and impartialist notions of justice.

Theoretical Plurality and Movement Strategy

A critical pluralism and the engagement it requires, however, makes sense not just theoretically, but in practice as well. Recognizing that justice means multiple things in different places, understanding the variety of conceptions of justice as discourses that can be shared, and bringing that variety of discourses on both environmental and ecological justice into a broad movement, can assist in constructing a movement dedicated to justice, while open to the multiple manifestations and experiences of environmental and ecological in justice. On this, I have to agree wholeheartedly with Connolly: 'Perhaps pluralism is a philosophy for wimps, for those whose beliefs are too saturated with uncertainty and ambivalence to take definitive action. I don't think so' (Connolly 2005: 3). But not everyone agrees.

The context of injustice is central here. The principles of environmental justice articulated by movements come partly out of the claims of particular types of social groups (such as indigenous communities, or victims of environmental impacts) or their relation with states or the international community. It also comes out of political and social relationships—particularly those that include exclusion and a lack of recognition; examples here include groups excluded from corporate decision-making in their communities, or from economic regimes such as the World Bank or

WTO. In practice, various groups and organizations that appeal to notions of environmental justice address differing and multiple, yet integrated, notions of justice. There may be certain principles of justice that apply in different types of situations, or different emphases groups may have in those situations. Such contextualization is broader than self-described justice pluralists (such as Miller or Walzer) have described.[3] Simply put, priorities change according to context; so to, then, do articulations of grievances and strategies.

This may be both a theoretical and a practical reality, but the question then becomes one of strategy. Can such a diverse movement with varied notions of justice, many of which are locally centered, both grow in terms of its discourse and the issues it encompasses, yet retain its cohesion as a movement and accomplish its stated aims? Ultimately, the argument here is that a broad pluralist, yet contextualist, approach works as a movement discourse and strategy; but, again, not everyone agrees.

There are two general, though oddly quite opposite, critiques of plurality as a movement strategy. On the one hand, some argue that movements need to keep themselves finely defined, in order to retain a focus and reach for achievable goals—even if those are quite limited. On the other hand, other critics argue that movements need to let go of their particularity in order to achieve universal ends. Let me address them one at a time.

Getches and Pellow (2002) urge the environmental justice movement to limit itself, and in particular to focus only on 'communities that exhibit traditional characteristics of disadvantage—where high poverty levels, large populations of people of color, or both are concentrated' (p. 5). In essence, Getches and Pellow want to limit the range and application of the environmental justice movement to communities of color, as if environmental injustice cannot happen to other communities. Unfortunately, this simply goes against both the practice of the movement, which is strong in mixed and poor white communities as well, and against a thorough understanding of exactly what the justice of environmental justice is. Race is a central component of a conception of justice as recognition, but it is not the only one; and, as discussed earlier, movements address more than justice as recognition. Getches and Pellow do understand that seeing 'the causes of injustice as intertwined, and environmental injustice as but a symptom among other multiple manifestations of injustice, helps us to understand the interconnection of issues and to form a vision for a better society' (p. 20). Yet they insist on a very limited application and policy focus, to 'what reasonably can be accomplished' (p. 20). This seems entirely too limiting to movements. During the recent Bush administration, for example, the definition of what might be reasonably accomplished has been thoroughly limited. Does that mean that a movement is required to limit its vision and definition depending on the political opportunities of the moment? Why cannot a movement have both a broad definition of environmental justice, and a pragmatic understanding of policy circumstances, simultaneously? While such a prescription may make sense in terms of one vision of movement strategy, it takes away the ability for movement actors to make connections with other movements and to fully address all the aspects of injustice that are tied to environmental injustice.

Pellow and Brulle (2005), however, give the same cautionary and limiting prescription in a more recent piece. While they recognize that environmental justice is based in numerous concerns and movements, they argue that 'there are limits to how much plurality a movement can embrace' and that environmental justice 'activists must bound and limit the purview of their concerns' (pp. 15–16). But there is no guidance given for exactly how such limits are to be articulated, or what comes of the various alliances that have been made across issues and issue groups that are to be trimmed from the definition of the environmental justice movement. The problem might not be the reality of the widespread nature of environmental injustice, which is reflected in this expansion of the movement's concerns. Rather, the problem may be in a framing that cannot encompass this plurality clearly enough. The problem may be that, as Anthony (2005: 92) argues in the same volume, 'the popular understanding of environmental justice is based on too narrow a view of "environment" and too narrow a view of "justice"'. Rather than dismiss the use of a broad environmental justice frame because it applies to so many issues, we should examine what it is about environmental justice that resonates with so many communities on so many issues. We should attempt to broaden our understanding of the frame and discourse. Such a broader discourse could help participants, and the larger public, understand the links among these diverse issues and movement groups; it is a language and discourse that can envelope those diverse movements with the same underlying explanation, critique, and resolution. This is the point of using a term like justice; its meaning is expansive, and broadly applicable to a wide range of social, cultural, political, and environmental issues.

The argument here is that a more thorough definition of justice, one that encompasses the expressed concerns of environmental justice and other groups, can offer a workable frame. Distributional concerns, along with calls for recognition, participation, and the protection of the capabilities and functioning of communities can come together in a frame that can strengthen both the explanatory and mobilizing reach of the movement. This is the essence of Taylor's important discussion of the environmental justice 'frame' (2000). Environmental justice now has a broad enough frame, or discourse, that adherents come from a variety of cultural and collective identities. Many individuals and groups recognize and support other collective identities within an extended framework of environmental justice. This is actually one of the most important internal accomplishments of the US movement, and is exemplified in the way that urban African-Americans, new Asian immigrants, and indigenous nations are all key parts of the environmental justice community. This expansive identity and discourse has already been immensely successful; the argument here is to extend that discourse even further, using a broad, diverse, and plural language of justice that is applicable not only across numerous communities and situations in the struggle for environmental justice, but also into calls for ecological justice to the nonhuman natural world.

David Harvey (1996) also alludes to the importance of recognizing the varied notions of the justice of environmental justice—though, again, not entirely in a positive light. Harvey's critique is quite different from that of Getches, Pellow, and Brulle, but it is also problematic for a pluralistic understanding of environmental justice. Harvey (1996: 388) recognizes the importance of the use of recognition as an element of justice, and approvingly notes the refusal on the part of the US environmental justice movement to cast the discussion in monetary terms alone. Equity may be about costs and benefits, but justice is much broader, and Harvey notes that the US movement demonstrates this. The use of identity-based arguments for recognition, including those of various racial and indigenous groups, is apt under the circumstances, argues Harvey.

Yet while Harvey is one of the rare theorists to bring recognition into an understanding of environmental justice in practice, he sees something amiss in the plurality such an acceptance might bring. Such a diverse movement confronts us 'with a plurality of theories of justice, all equally plausible and all equally lacking in one way or another' (p. 398). Harvey sees the initial justification and necessity of local, contextual, and particular battles with their different readings of justice; but, he argues, they are ultimately contradictory and the movement cannot be successful without pulling together a single universal critique and definition of environmental justice. Harvey (p. 400) wants the movement to 'create a more transcendent and universal politics' which must 'transcend particularity;' he insists on a move from the multiple and particular to the singular and universal. Here, the implication is that the local and contextual must be transcended and replaced by a monist approach.

Harvey's justification for this move is that a notion of, and a movement for, environmental justice must 'confront the realities of global power politics... not simply with dispersed, autonomous, localized, and essentially communitarian solutions', but with a 'more complex politics' and a more 'rational ordering of activities' (p. 400). Harvey here does not examine the possibility that such dispersed and localized notions, taken together, could actually take on both the discourse and power of global capital; rather, he does not see the possibility of such a decentralized— ideologically and physically—movement having such an effect without resorting to a more 'rational' universalism.[4]

I (and I believe many in environmental justice movements) agree with Harvey that the achievement of environmental justice will come only with 'confronting the fundamental underlying processes (and their associated power structures, social relations, institutional configurations, discourses, and belief systems) that generate environmental and social injustices' (p. 401). But such a crucial confrontation need not come at the expense of the localized, particular places where that power and injustice are experienced, known, and resisted. It may be, as Harvey argues, that movement groups can develop such universal discourse and action without fully sacrificing their particularist base; yet such universalism should not be prioritized above the local and plural, as Harvey insists. If Foucault (1978, 1980) taught us anything, it is that power is multiple, and arises everywhere in everyday situations and must be constantly resisted where it is experienced. It is no different with (in)justice. The strength and staying power of movement networks is a strong illustration here.[5]

I am reminded here of the news coverage surrounding the protests at the WTO meeting in Seattle in 1999. There, numerous groups from different contexts (labor, indigenous, environmental, north, and south) and with a variety of critiques (distribution, recognition, participation, and community functioning) came together in organizing large-scale and diverse events. Labor activists marched arm-in-arm with environmental activists dressed as sea turtles. Groups brought to the table, and to the streets, a variety of critiques of the injustices of the WTO specifically, as well as the economic model the organization represented. As I watched these events, my initial reaction was amazement that such diverse groups could plan, organize, teach, and protest together; this was a far cry from the ideological singularity defended by many protest groups in the 1960s and 1970s. And yet, watching the news coverage, commentators (when not blaming protesters for 'rioting') shook their heads and dismissed the protest groups for not having a single and coherent plan for global economic design; if they did not have a better, single, idea, the commentators inferred, their protest was useless and devoid of pragmatic meaning.

There was no recognition, in the mainstream media, of the pluralist accomplishment: labor and environmentalists marching arm-in-arm—recognizing the value of each other's positions and critiques, and understanding the importance of bringing them together in a single event. It was a watershed in global social justice organizing, and yet missed by a media that did not value the pluralistic accomplishment.

What the growth of such pluralistic networks demonstrates is that a large-scale social or environmental justice movement can be unified, but it cannot be uniform. An insistence on uniformity will limit the diversity of stories of injustice, the multiple forms it takes, and the variety of solutions it calls for. The movements demonstrate the power of what Mary Parker Follett (1918) long ago called a 'unity without uniformity' as they illustrate justice and environmental justice on so many dimensions simultaneously. Follett's conception is pretty straightforward, and brings some substance to the idea of 'unity in diversity.' She discussed a form of unity that would have people recognize differences rather than dismiss them by differentiating quite clearly the terms unity and uniformity. 'Unity, not uniformity, must be our aim. We attain unity only through variety. Differences must be integrated, not annihilated, nor absorbed.' Uniformity, she argued, was absorptive, rather than inclusive. Follett's is a salad bowl metaphor, rather than a melting pot; she used 'good words' like compound and harmonize, as opposed to 'bad words' like fuse and melt (p. 29).[6] There is no contradiction, in this form of unity, between unity and differentiation; in fact, Follett argued, heterogeneity is the only way to construct unity (p. 40).

Environmental justice movements demonstrate the power of a unity without uniformity as they illustrate environmental justice on so many dimensions simultaneously. The issues that the transnational movements address, regarding, for example, resistance to environmentally harmful forms of economic development, the globalization of food production, and the continued disregard for indigenous rights illustrate *both* the diverse ways issues such as equity, recognition, participation, and capabilities are articulated *and* the possibility for unity across this diversity. As demonstrated by these battles, environmental justice movements have been successful in bringing together such disparate issues and experiences of injustice behind a unified, but not uniform, banner. An insistence on uniformity behind that banner, to an identity, critique, or singular program, is not only counter to the movement itself, but also a violation of justice as based in recognition and democratic process. It is also a denial of the plural and contextualist understanding of justice.

It is also important that environmental justice organizing—USA or global—has never been about establishing a major, single NGO based in DC or London or anywhere. Nor has it ever been about developing a singular and universal notion of justice; rather, its principles are inherently plural.[7] Environmental justice organizing has always been network-based, and those networks have recognition and democratic process at their core. Nor has environmental justice ever been about one issue, outlook, critique, demand, or strategy. Unity comes with the recognition of both similarities and differences, and an understanding of how different contexts define various groups.[8]

Now the fact that activists tend to accept ambiguity and plurality more often and thoroughly than theorists is not necessarily a reason to construct a theory that way. Political and social theory must still criticize, refine, and expand the articulations and conceptions of movements. But theorists must engage activists who articulate their struggles and goals with terms used in the academy, and philosophers have to listen to such activists and learn something from them. Academics should not be afraid of adopting an approach that has been articulated by movements, especially when their approach has made such activism, and the issues involved, more engaging in the eyes of the public.

That said, the adoption of plurality in the conception of justice, and the development of flexible networks, remains mostly in the realm of environmental justice. The main challenge, as I see it, is to expand this plural approach so that it includes not only environmental justice, but ecological justice as well. A critical engagement, and an institutionalized ecological reflexivity, may be the way to accomplish this.

Plurality and Engagement

The concept that links plurality in theory and in movement strategy with the next important step—the institutionalization and implementation of justice—is engagement. Pluralism, from its origins, has always gone beyond the recognition of plurality to a central concern with how such difference is to be communicated and engaged. Values and identities can be shared, or at least understood, across differences. As a pluralist approach negates the prominence of a singular or universal view, the task is to examine what each perspective provides, how to adjudicate among them, and how to reconcile conflicting perspectives in democratic practice. The job for the pluralist critic is 'to relate various perspectives to each other in acts of criticism within reflective practices that articulate and adjudicate such conflicts' (Bohman 2001: 90). Importantly, conflicts are to be resolved 'practically in ongoing and reflective practices'. Simply put, pluralism demands engagement.

Berlin, for example, noted the importance of what we learn from others across difference. He calls on us to try to understand 'the standards of others . . . to grasp what we are told' by them. Their difference does not preclude us from 'sharing common assumptions, sufficient for some communication with them, for some degree of understanding and being understood' (1969: 103). Galston (2002: 90–1) argues that, ideally, pluralist participants see others not as ignorant, short-sighted, or blinded by passion, but rather as fellow citizens who happen to see things differently, and whose positions might be right, add to the larger picture, or at least have some value. Tully (1995: 25) notes that the 'ability to change perspectives—to see and understand aspectivally—is acquired through participation in the intercultural dialogue itself'. Connolly's 'bicameral' orientation to political life requires both a 'presumptive receptivity toward others' and the ability to understand competing perspectives (2005: 4). Sen (2005: 161) notes that any discussion on capabilities has to include, even for domestic notions of justice, 'views from "a certain distance"'.

This focus on active pluralist engagement is especially necessary as cultures mix and individuals find themselves in more than one cultural world simultaneously—traditional Native Americans in environmental organizations, developers learning about indigenous cosmology, European activists networking with organizations in Africa, urban dwellers coming to know and interact with nonhuman animals that surround them.

James embraced the need to see alternatives and imagine other states of mind (1978: 4). Follett called for an inclusive, integrative resolution of differences, brought about 'by the reciprocal adaptings of the reactions of individuals, and this reciprocal adapting is based on both agreement and difference' (1918: 35). She was concerned that addressing conflict not lead to the dismissal of diversity. 'What people often mean by getting rid of conflict is getting rid of diversity, and it is of the utmost importance that these should not be considered the same...' (1924: 300). Key to both James and Follett was a process open to difference and yet focused on making connections across that difference.

A number of contemporary pluralist theorists pick up on this process, and the need for both engagement, and an ethic of agonistic respect, across difference. For Tully, intercultural dialogue is the central task of pluralist politics, and in order for negotiation to occur across difference, an ethic of mutual respect and recognition will 'enhance a critical attitude to one's own culture and a tolerant and critical attitude towards others' (1995: 207). Taylor (1994: 34) notes that identity is never worked out in isolation; 'but that I negotiate it through dialogue, partly overt, partly internal, with others.... My own identity crucially depends on my dialogical relations with others.' Connolly, however, is the key theorist who espouses such an ethos within a critical pluralist frame. The response to a pluralizing society that is continually and agonistically overlapping, interacting, and negotiating needs to be an ethos of what Connolly calls critical responsiveness, the 'indispensable lubricant of political pluralization' (1995: xvi). Such an 'ethical connection... flowing across fugitive experiences of *intrasubjective* and *intersubjective* difference opens up relational possibilities of agonistic respect, studied indifference, critical responsiveness, and selective collaboration between interdependent, contending identities...' (xvii). Connolly's ethos is crucial to a viable process of engagement across difference.

Central to pluralist engagement is the attitude that conflict across difference is to be welcomed, and certainly not avoided. The key claim of those supporting agonistic encounters is that moral conflict and engagement across differences is a valuable and indispensable part of social and political life. Such conflict is good for the body politic, and both groups and individuals within it. Honig (1993) points out that too much political theory has been about avoiding conflict and eliminating dissonance, resistance, and struggle—the displacement of politics. While she looks to Nietzsche and Arendt as examples of those who do not displace rivalrous encounters, both first generation and more recent pluralist theorists embrace such agonistic engagement.

Now, most of this literature on pluralist engagement assumes a public, or set of participants in the engagement exercise, that is widely diverse—antiabortion and prochoicers discussing sex education in schools, Muslims and Christians on US foreign policy, developers and environmentalists on growth planning. As a result, much of the debate is to be full of agonistic conflict. Some pluralist authors claim that such agonistic relations disrupting hegemonic ideas and producing stable agreement is simply unfounded; Deveaux (1999) argues that agonism could actually lead to the entrenchment of existing ideas and identities and 'make it more difficult for diverse cultural communities to see that they do share at least some social and moral views, norms and interests in common with others' (p. 15).

My argument here is that the ideals of pluralist engagement and agreement should be attainable within and across the communities dedicated to a particular end—environmental and ecological justice. While there may be something critical to be said about the idealism of an agonistic pluralism in an entrenched and divisive society, if such pluralistic aims are to be realized anywhere, they should be attainable by a diverse community that still has key conceptions and ends in common. In other words, if pluralist engagement cannot bring a form of recognition of others' positions, validation of their reasonableness, and the effort necessary to ally and network where there is a preexisting common ground, around both environmental sustainability and the conception and attainment of justice, then it simply cannot happen anywhere. Movements for environmental and ecological justice, then, can be an important testbed for pluralist ideals, engagement, and practice.

I believe Wenz's early work on environmental justice, again, can be helpful there. Wenz (1988: 2) argues that it is important to understand different peoples' interpretation or principles of justice—this helps us to understand others. The plurality argument is the key, but it then necessitates engagement across these differences. Getting others to understand your experience and framework, and vice versa, is how pluralistic notions are learned, understood, recognized, and accepted. This is the difference between a pluralism based in simple acceptance and toleration and a critical pluralism based in more thorough recognition and mutual engagement. Such engagement is related to the necessity of combining recognition with participation in actions to achieve environmental and ecological justice.

Wenz noted an important limitation to the process of engagement—distance. In response, he developed what he calls a 'concentric circle' theory of environmental justice, where we give moral priority to those closer to us—family for example—and less priority for those further away—foreigners, or other species (Wenz 1988: ch. 14). This makes sense because we engage more with those closest to us. The problem with such a theory is that it is difficult to identify with and argue for justice for those away from the center of our own circles.

I want to argue that the actions of many in both environmental and ecological justice movements actively counter this distance. The point of communicating diverse battles, even those emanating from continents away, or in the depths of rainforests, is to give those far from, or different from, ourselves a voice and to acknowledge their situation. The explosion of diverse discourses of injustice, the availability of these discourses via the Web, alternative media, or mainstream media, and the attention brought to the diversity of environmental injustices through the actions of international civil society, forges empathy, recognition, and unity—even across great distances. This was one of the key lessons of the first major WTO protests in Seattle, and continues in a variety of movement networks. Diverse people come with different stories of injustice, with varying emphases on equity, recognition, capabilities, and/or participation. It is common to see those with different experiences of environmental injustice sharing stories. Through participation and recognition—two key elements of justice itself—those who are distant and many circles away (using Wenz's analogy) become much closer.[9] This reflexive engagement—ecological and otherwise—is what has brought unity, without uniformity, to many of the diverse groups attached to national and global networks. Such networks are underpinned with 'a conceptualization of protest and struggle that respects difference, rather than attempting to develop universalistic and centralizing solutions that deny the diversity of interests and identities' of participants (Routledge 2003: 335). These networks and organizations provide what Routledge (2003, 2005) calls a 'convergence space', where pluralistic engagement leads to a 'heterogeneous affinity' (2003: 345). Insisting on 'transcending' those particular experiences and knowledges would surely be one way to destroy the tentative unity without uniformity developed in various protests and networks for social, environmental, and ecological justice.

The trick, of course, is developing ways to institutionalize such engagement, in both the political and public spheres.

Notes

1. Callicott has been taken to task for this position by colleagues in environmental ethics more sympathetic to the pluralist and pragmatist approach; see, e.g. the response by Light (2003).

2. This resurgence of theory based on one form or another of James's radical empiricism was not always expressly pluralist. Theorists such as Fred Dallmayr, Carol Gould, Will Kymlicka, Anne Philips, and Iris Young revisited pluralist questions—and imagined new responses—within discourses of difference, multiculturalism, and constitutionalism. Others, such as William Connolly, John Gray, and Chantal Mouffe, have attempted an explicit resurrection of the term along with the key concerns of pluralization.

3. An argument for this type of contextualization in environmental political theory is made by Hunold and Dryzek (2002), though their focus is on movement strategies in the context of different types of states.

4. The ultimate goal of environmental justice, for Harvey, is the reclamation of 'a noncoopted and nonperverted version of the thesis of ecological modernization' (p. 401). But he seems to have left out the important elements of local 'subpolitics' and 'reflexive modernization' which Beck (1992)—and many others—includes in such a model. That said, the Harvey work I am criticizing came before the strength of networks, especially at the global level, became obvious.

5. See, e.g. numerous works that focus on the power of civil society and networks, including Donatella and Tarrow (2005), Keck and Sikkink (1998), Klein (2002), Routledge (2003, 2005), Schlosberg (1999a), Wapner (1996).

6. I am not sure what it is about pluralists and food. Follett uses the salad metaphor. James's ideal was of a sort of banquet, 'where all the qualities of being respect one another's personal sacredness, yet sit at the common table of space and time' ([1896] 1979: 201. And Connolly (2005: 9) notes that a 'majority assemblage in a culture of multidimensional pluralism is more analogous to a potluck supper than a formal dinner'. Maybe it is the populism within pluralism that leads these authors to focus on something we can all share....

7. See, e.g. Climate Justice Declaration (2004), Environmental Justice and Climate Change Initiative (2002), International Climate Justice Network (2002), and Madison, Miller, and Lee (1992).

8. For more on critical pluralism and its relationship to environmental justice in practice, see Schlosberg (1999a, 1999b).

9. It is crucial to note here that identity politics is rarely about identity itself, and especially not about elevating an identity or way of knowing above others (except for supremacist movements, which can be differentiated and critiqued on this very notion). Rather, identity-based movements are about bringing attention to the relationship between identity and various forms of oppression and injustice. Identity politics seeks acknowledgment, recognition, and 'player' status in a world of heterogeneity; they are about communicating with others, bringing others knowledge, and insisting on accountability in the construction of identity, inequality and injustices (see Dean 1996: 52 on that last point).

8

Ecological Reflexivity, Engagement, and Institutions: Implementing Environmental and Ecological Justice

At this point, we have a broad set of definitions of environmental and ecological justice, as well as a justification for accepting and embracing the plurality of those definitions and the movements behind them. But, of course, that is not enough. The pluralistic processes I discussed in the previous chapter, from the recognition of a variety of understandings of justice to citizen engagement within and across them, must, at some point, be formalized into practice if we are to attain, and not simply define, environmental and ecological justice.

The key remaining question is how we institutionalize the engagement necessary for multiple conceptions and practices of environmental and ecological justice to be shared, deliberated, understood, and implemented. A number of authors have approached the question of institutionalization much more directly and thoroughly than I plan to, and the list just within green political theory is long and rich.[1] This specific concern with institutionalizing engagement across difference is addressed in both the pluralist literature and the deliberative democratic approach to political practice; an environmental angle adds additional concerns. My interest is at the confluence of these three areas, and there are five key conceptions and practices at the heart of this confluence.

First, a form of reflexive modernization—citizen-directed policy informed by broad inclusion, ecological reflection, and social learning—is the key in both the political and public spheres. Second, in order to attain both environmental and ecological justice, we must be sure that views from the margins, the remote, and the natural world are recognized and represented, either directly or through proxies; the role of science—in particular in providing the material for ecological reflexivity—is a crucial part of this representation. Third, any institutions of engagement could not exist solely at the state level; the focus must be at multiple levels— including both the state political realm and the transnational level. And for both state and transnational levels, engagement needs to happen in both the state political and the public sphere or cultural realm. Deveaux (2000), who thoroughly addresses the interface of pluralism and delibera- tive democracy, argues that macro-level democracy alone cannot secure adequate respect and recognition for cultural minorities; this requires more democratic practices down to the micro-level of society.

Forth, though related to both the previous and the next, the institu- tional engagement of environmental issues must always remain flexible. Some environmental issues are local, some regional, some specifically located yet crossing borders, and others global. A pluralistic and deliber- ative view associated with environmental institutions must recognize the flexibility necessary to deal with the multiple levels of engagement neces- sary for different issues and events. Finally, pluralists eschew the idea that any result of an agonistic engagement is ever permanent. Institutionally, this means an ever-adaptive management—policies are developed and implemented, but constantly revised with input from feedback, additional knowledge, and ongoing discourse. Pluralism—the engagement, the ago- nism, the understanding, and the resolution—is always in the making. From James to Connolly, pluralists have cited the influence of Bergson's notion of creative evolution and the continuously creative nature of our engagements; the process is one of becoming, rather than finishing. It gives us a permanent and always contingent politics, affirming the importance of ongoing engagement.[2]

Institutionalizing Reflexive Engagement and Ecological Reflexivity

Let me address some of these issues in some depth, beginning with the first and core concern: a practice of reflexivity and social learning. Connolly, from the pluralist perspective, argues that the civic virtues at the heart of crucial pluralist engagement 'must become embedded in numerous institutional practices for a positive ethos of pluralism to be' (2005: 65). Like many participatory democrats before him (from Rousseau to Pateman 1970), Connolly insists that the ethics and values necessary for engaged citizen practice can be learned through this practice, and reinforce themselves like a 'pluralist resonance machine' (Connolly 2005: 67). Eckersley (2004) makes a similar set of arguments in her call for a new type of green state; expanded opportunities for citizen engagement can bring learning about others, and others' conceptions of environmental issues, to the forefront of state—and global—decision-making. Such learning helps us attain both better ongoing practice and better social and environmental outcomes. Similarly, Dryzek (2006) focuses on practices of reflexive engagement and intelligence, and examines a variety of institutional forms of deliberative engagement; importantly, Dryzek expands this discussion beyond just local and state practice to suggest forms of engagement at the transnational level as well. Dryzek also insists that such forms of engagement should work not only in formal governmental institutions, but, crucially, in extra-governmental forms based in the public sphere.

At the core of any form of institutionalization of engagement is the idea of citizen learning and reflection. Connolly (2005: 122–3) sees pluralist engagement being based in two key civic virtues. First is an understanding of agonistic respect, where citizens can understand and respect the positions and reasoning of others while remaining of a different mind on an issue. Second is an ethos of critical responsiveness, or '*careful listening and presumptive generosity* to constituencies struggling to move from an obscure or degraded subsistence below the field of recognition, justice, obligations, rights, or legitimacy to a place on one or more of those registers' (p. 126). As noted earlier, Connolly conceives of this as a type of internal bicameralism, where a participant is both in one's own position, but willing to see others from outside that perspective and willing to have others look at one's own position from another perspective. For Eckersley (2004), such processes are a form of social learning, where participants come in to a dialogue to enlarge their thinking and have their preferences transformed.

Of course, from the perspective of environmental and ecological justice, the necessity is a form of citizen deliberation that is inclusive of environmental and ecological points of view, positions, and interests that are traditionally excluded. At a minimum, I want to argue that such participation requires an opening in democratic decision-making for communication from environmental and ecological perspectives—a type of democratic and *ecological reflexivity*. This refers to a form of reflexive modernization that brings attention specifically to the problematic effects of modernity on the nonhuman world. One of the ways that Beck (1997, 1998) describes reflexive modernization is in terms of being more reflective, as in a population coming to terms with both the effects of the modern world and a more critical response to them. Beck (1997: 15) argues that

reflexive modernization is the attempt to regain a voice and thus the ability to act, the attempt to regain reality in view of developments that are the consequences of the successes of modernization. These developments call the concepts and formulas of classical industrial society fundamentally into question from the inside, not from crisis, disintegration, revolution or conspiracy, but from the repercussions of the very ordinary 'progress' on its own foundations.

And, importantly, they are also called into question by the responses to such repercussions of social movements like the environmental justice movement and various ecological movements. As Beck notes, there are 'a variety of new insecurities, and loss of faith in progress, science, and experts' (p. 12).

In this reflection on the impacts of modernization, however, we should remember that voices in response to contemporary environmental ills should not be limited to those based on the human experience. Diverse human participation, while essential, is not the only focus of a dedication to just procedures. Ecological justice requires the inclusion of the rest of the natural world in a thoroughly developed practice of ecological reflexivity. Social, cultural, political, and specifically institutional participation could, in a sense, be extended to a natural world experiencing an infringement of recognition, physical integrity, potential, and/or capabilities. As Latour (2004: 58) argues, political theory 'abruptly finds itself confronted with the obligation to *internalize* the environment that it had viewed up to now as another world.' This is the key challenge of ecological justice and ecological democracy.

It is the remoteness from not just physical inclusion, but also from the perceptions of participants, that underlies environmental and ecological injustice. Plumwood has argued that the bad news from below, in particular from the socio-economically less well-off and the natural world itself, is rarely heard in current political and economic systems. Privileged groups are likely to be epistemically remote and distanced from the impacts of their actions on both other humans and the nonhuman natural world.

There is clearly a serious problem about the ecological rationality of any system that allows those who have most access to political voice and decision-making power to be also those most relatively remote from the ecological degradation it fosters, and those who tend to be least remote from ecological degradation and who have to bear the worst ecological consequences and risks to have the last access to voice and decision power (Plumwood 2002b: 4).

Latour (2004: 63) argues that we need to modify the meaning of the word 'discussion' in a future ecological tradition—one that moves beyond the political norm of reasoned speech devoid of the natural realm. Deliberation, argue many in the environmental field, 'is the process by which we *learn* of our dependence on others (and the environment) and the process by which we learn to recognize and respect differently situated others (including nonhuman others and future generations)' (Eckersley 2004: 115). Discourse allows an engagement not just of different notions of nature, but also provides a forum for deliberation around a variety of justice claims (Bowersox 2002: 48). Ecological reflexivity and deliberation bring engagement across difference.

Dryzek (1995, 2000) has developed a very helpful notion of ecological communication, and in this context it we can use it as not just an element of ecological democracy and reflexivity, but of ecological justice as well. In the past decade Dryzek has argued for the recognition of agency in nature; he suggests extending communication to entities that can act as agents even though they lack subjectivity and rationality.[3] If we accept nature as an agent, one that has its physical integrity and 'bodily' processes respected, we should also listen to its 'speech'. Again, Latour (2004: 65) argues that 'speech is no longer a specifically human property, or at least humans are no longer its sole masters'. Bickford (1996) notes that we silence others in political processes simply by refusing to listen to them; this is why any theory and institutionalization of deliberative democracy must begin with attention to the practice of listening. Following Bickford, Dryzek argues that '[r]ecognition of agency in nature therefore means that we should listen to signals emanating from the natural world with the same sort of respect we accord communication emanating from human subjects, and as requiring equally careful interpretation' (Dryzek 2000: 149). Noting that there is much too human communication beyond speech—body language, facial displays, etc.—Dryzek insists that listening to nonverbal communication from nature is a very rational process not unlike listening to other people. He calls on us to simply hear the signals from nature, and in learning to hear and communicate them, become ecological citizens as well as social beings.[4]

Dryzek is not suggesting the actual presence of nature in democratic conversations—cats in congress or penguins in parliament; the call is, instead, for an expansion of the politics of ideas, brought about by institutional openness. The point is the recognition and inclusion of nature in an egalitarian democratic politics dedicated to transcending and helping to breakdown the boundary between human beings and nonhuman nature (Dryzek 2000: 153). Equality in the capacity to be represented in the polity is at the heart of an expanded democratic politics; in particular the discursive democracy that Dryzek proposes.[5] Eckersley (1999, 2004) has discussed this type of representation of nonhuman nature as a form of Arendt's 'representative thinking' or an example of an 'enlarged mentality'. The nonhuman can become 'imaginary partners in conversation', while human representatives anticipate and assume the position of others to examine proposed norms (or policies) from a variety of perceived perspectives (Eckersley 1999: 27). Nussbaum discusses such a process as 'sympathetic imagining' (2006a: 355). The idea is simple: to include either excluded or silenced others, in particular the natural world, in democratic deliberations. The point is not just to get folks to imagine such differences internally, but to also be confronted or educated by numerous others' imaginings of their own perspectives, from a variety of positions and assumptions.

Of course, this leaves us with some key questions. What, exactly, are the 'signals' that our 'enlarged mentality' should hear from the natural world? Who may bring such representations, and how are they to be brought into the democratic process?

As for the first, disruptions to the physical integrity of nature, especially, should catch our attention—things such as climate change, species extinction, droughts, mad cows and flu-ridden birds, and so on. And each of these disruptions is communicated to us through a variety of signals. Climate change, for example, is demonstrated not just in atmospheric studies, but also by a slew of individual signals—songbirds returning earlier, butterfly species moving north, insect eggs hatching earlier, glaciers and other ice-bound water melting, oceans warming, and weather-related issues such as increased rainfall in certain areas and drought in others. All of these individual global 'warnings' add up to global climate change.

But it is not as simple as developing a talent for ecological reflexivity, learning from others and making informed, reflexive decisions that all are happy with. Conceptions differ and conflict, and if coming to agreement on environmental impacts to *human* interests is a complex and contentious affair, engagement with ecological reflexivity is that much more difficult, given the multiple, ambiguous, and variable meanings of nature across different cultures and times.[6] I agree with Eckersley (2004: 123) that we need to avoid simplistic and naive realist understandings of nature, and to understand the way knowledge of nature is produced, often dismissive of cultural differences and local knowledge. The goal of an ecological reflexivity is to include a variety of knowledge claims, and various interpretations of nature, in a political discourse. The point of such discourse, for Eckersley and other critical theorists and discursive democrats, is a pluralistic and intersubjective understanding among those involved—even if such *understanding* does not lead to *agreement* with the ideas those put forth. Again, the goal of engagement is to bring more broad understanding of positions and impacts of various policy proposals and, so, much more informed decisions.

Yet the goal is also, at the same time, bigger than this. As Barry (1999: 22) has argued, the argument for the inclusion of the interests of non-humans (and, I would add, excluded humans) 'is a reflection of the failure of these interests to be reflected within the interests of citizens. In other words, the creation of democratic institutions to represent non-human interest arises partly from the lack of "green citizenship" and a wider ecological culture'. So the expansion of parties and interests in reflexive democratic decision-making on environmental and ecological issues is not just to represent those interests, experiences, and points of view, but also to expand the environmental learning, and so more broad environmental citizenship and ecological reflexivity, in the social and political realm more broadly. Light (2002: 160) points out that by bringing a local population into an issue native to a place, of local importance, that population can form a 'culture of nature' or a version of environmental and ecological citizenship. Such an informed culture of nature, or ecological citizenship, can help a citizenry practice and demonstrate an informed ecological reflexivity.

Inclusion and Proxies

How are we to institutionalize such inclusion and reflexivity? As worthwhile a process of inclusion of the local public is, that local community may only learn the perceptions of those that participate, and not those excluded from the process. Of course, one of the original demands of environmental justice movement is that 'we speak for ourselves' (Alston 1991); but for those outside the range of the decision-making arena, or for those incapable of speaking for themselves, the central way to bring in such views is through proxies. Proxies represent those who cannot represent themselves in instances where nonparticipants are impacted;

they also often represent conflicting interests (Smith 2003: 115). As Baxter (2000b: 55) clearly puts it, 'the inarticulate need proxies'. The use of proxies is a clear way to bring in the 'remote' others that Plumwood refers to; it also allows participants to get a better understanding of those that may be more 'distant' from our own valuation of interests, as Wenz sees it. Proxies include both these distant others, as well as nonhuman nature and future generations of both humans and nonhumans.

Eckersley (2004, especially chapter 5) provides the most recent thorough description and defense of the use of proxies in environmental institutions, in particular for nonhumans. She insists that even if nonhuman others are not capable of giving approval or consent, we should still proceed as if they could. Eckersley wants us to reconceptualize and expand the territory of decision-making, based on risks that a community is exposed to. The community at risk for a dam, for example, would include all ecological communities in a watershed. For a nuclear reactor, the community might be half the hemisphere; for genetically modified organisms, the community to be included and represented would be even bigger, encompassing the globe. Eckersley (2004: 114) uses the concept of 'political trusteeship: persons and groups within the polity speaking on behalf of the interests of those living outside the polity, for future generations and for nonhuman species'. Following Goodin (1996) and Dobson (1996), Eckersley recognizes that if the first best solution of the affected speaking for them is impossible, the next best solution requires that those interests be represented. Without such a simple recognition, the interests of many of those impacted by policy decisions are excluded, which for Eckersley, and anyone interested in recognition and participation as elements of environmental justice, is simply unacceptable. Such exclusion negates the possibility of a thorough practice of reflection and engagement. As Eckersley notes (2004: 125–6), 'finding an approximate form of representation is better than providing none at all'. The point is to expand the range of views and information, along with the possibilities of ecological reflexivity, for any possible impacts on the widest constituency affected.

There are numerous ways to tap into an ecological reflexivity to bring the nonhuman world into political deliberations via a proxy. Speaking as a proxy for nature, for example, has become a growing tactic in environmental movements. Such representation of nonhuman nature can be based in science, storytelling, or traditional knowledge. People can 'represent' animals or nonhuman nature, imagination and storytelling can play a role, and traditional and/or cultural knowledge can be called on—all are forms of knowledge informed by openness to the signals from nature.

Proxies are already commonly used in liberal decision-making, such as those that act on behalf of children's or prisoner's rights. Even existing generations—the young, but not yet 'communicatively competent'—are taken into consideration through the proxy of interest groups. Future generations, which cannot even send 'signals' as nature can, may 'participate' by having proxies take their concerns into present discourse; we can make the same argument for nature. I often site the example of a citizen at a public hearing who dressed and spoke as an endangered butterfly, explaining to the officials listening (uncomfortably) what a proposed factory would do to her habitat and everyday life. Activists at the 1999 WTO meeting in Seattle marched in sea turtle costumes to illustrate the impact of WTO decisions on turtle populations. In another example, a group of 'grandparents for the future' were arrested protesting a proposed dump in upstate New York. Arrested and asked their names, they all replied 'Allegany County'—their home (DeLuca 1999: 189). The point of proxies is not to insist on the interests of the represented all being considered equal—simply that these interests are taken into account in a democratic deliberative process (Baxter 2005: 123).

Eckersley suggests a variety of ways that proxy knowledge can enhance particular institutional mechanisms of environmental decision-making: require mandatory environmental reporting, include comprehensive and cumulative environmental impact assessments, and/or combine scientific findings with local knowledge and field experience. This would be in addition to a specialized form of environmental advocacy, or a form of proxy representation; Eckersley (2004: 135) suggests an 'independent environmental defenders office, staffed by a multidisciplinary team and charged with the responsibility of environmental monitoring, political advocacy, and legal representation. . . . ' States could bring mandatory attention to ecological feedback gathered through such monitoring, and could extend such studies into the realm of ecological space and ecological footprints (as discussed in Chapter 5). The bottom line, though, is that

as a matter of environmental justice, special procedural measures or due process for disadvantaged minorities, nonhuman others, and future generations are necessary to counteract the systematic biases against the interests of this neglected constituency by those existing political actors who might otherwise pursue more short-term, self-regarding economic interests at the expense of these more diffuse and unrepresented interests (Eckersley 2004: 126).

In other words, do not look for the perfect system of representation before acting on the already obvious imperfect and biased system we have, and to bring a form of presence to those regularly left out of the decision-making process. Again, these arguments are not new, and have been central to many arguments within green political theory; the point here is that such institutionalized representation is not just in accord with a green notion of democracy, but of human, environmental, and ecological justice as well.

While Eckersley briefly mentions the role of science in proxy representation of nonhuman interests, the relationship between scientific information and a plural deliberative process is not really explored much in the environmental theory literature. As nature has multiple and ambiguous meanings, Eckersley praises the critical theory approach to exploring knowledge claims through the inclusion of diverse discourses, including those from scientific communities (2004: 122–3). Latour (2004), as well, focuses on innovative ways science can be brought in, and engaged, in a model of environmental democracy. My point here is that deliberation allows us to engage both the diversity of human discourses about nature, and the multiple attempts to interpret them. We simultaneously speak for a nature that we constitute, but also see specific changes that are empirically grounded and obvious—species extinctions, changing climate patterns and ocean temperatures, male frogs with eggs in their testes, increases in cases of childhood asthma, etc. We have both empirical scientific evidence, and various interpretations of that evidence, to bring to the discursive table.

Sarawitz (2004) has recently addressed the role of science in democratic discourse in a provocative piece entitled 'How Science Makes Environmental Controversies Worse', and his (and others') concerns have brought a keen awareness to the environmental sciences of the importance of how science is communicated in the public and political realms. Sarawitz argues that scientific evidence and findings are diverse, and can be used to support any number of positions. In particular, Sarawitz argues that science supplies facts that are used by various parties to legitimate their preexisting normative positions and interests, that competing scientific disciplinary positions may be tied to particular political positions, and that scientific uncertainty should not be understood as a lack of scientific understanding, but instead as a result of the various political, cultural, and institutional contexts in which science is produced. His main point is that as science can be used to back up any number of positions on issues, the ideology and influences on science should be on the table, and examined politically before scientific evidence can be effectively applied. We should not use science as 'proof' which is not to be debated, but instead understand it simply as evidence from a particular location; as with all put forth in a deliberative process, it is to be taken as uncertain and inherently biased—though grounded in a combination of evidence and discourse. While this position is not likely to be widely accepted in the scientific community, it fits well with discussions of plurality and engagement, and deliberative processes.[7] In this, Sarawitz simply adds scientific discourses as another set of positions to be engaged in environmental decision-making.

Let me give an example of one participatory process that encompasses both an awareness of this role of science and an understanding of the importance of empirical support for stakeholder and proxy positions in an institutionalized deliberative process. ForestERA (Forest Ecosystem Restoration Analysis)[8] is a project based out of Northern Arizona University, run by ecologist Tom Sisk, which brings public participation, ecosystem science, and powerful GIS tools together to develop priorities and treatment plans for forest restoration at a landscape scale. Basically, in order to develop agreement among diverse stakeholders, ForestERA begins with a needs assessment, to understand what it is that stakeholders say they are most concerned with, and what data they need to inform any decisions. The ForestERA team then collects data from stakeholders and others, and contributes its own research, in developing GIS-based maps that address and illustrate stakeholder needs on various issues of forest management. Forest conditions and physiographic characteristics of the landscape, data layers on fire potential, watershed, and wildlife habitat, and a variety of additional layers from multiple sources, such as land ownership, weather data, and so on are brought together and offered to stakeholders. Finally, ForestERA hosts workshops to assist stakeholders in developing priorities and treatment plans. Stakeholders see data related to their own requests, and can use that data to illustrate their positions and values as they work with other stakeholders with varied interests.

Importantly here, participants can illustrate their values and interests, including the interests of nonhuman nature, with the same tools as all other participants; they can represent their own interests, and also be proxies for other interests not at the table. Stakeholders learn not only what the interests of other participant are, but also how those interests translate into recommendations, policies, and potential outcomes in the forest under consideration. For example, those interested in preserving viable habitat for a particular species can prioritize those needs—over, say, the economic desire for cutting large diameter trees—in their own assessment of treatment plans for the forest. In this process, ForestERA includes both participatory science and a participatory deliberative process in the development of restoration plans; it also allows stakeholders to see how science can be used in various ways to support diverse interests and values. Stakeholders clearly see themselves as both informing and being informed by the process. The ForestERA process serves as a model for institutionalizing broad inclusion and the engagement of multiple discourses, including scientific ones; it requires reflexivity and social learning on the part of participants—all integral to the type of ecological citizenship necessary for environmental and ecological justice.

One of the important accomplishments of a process like ForestERA is that it allows for the expression and inclusion of local and traditional knowledges. In opening to ecological reflexivity, we cannot rely solely on a singular view of supposed scientific expertise. One of the key demands of indigenous activists in the environmental justice movement is for cultural knowledge, or traditional ecological knowledge (TEK) to be accepted as a valid form of knowledge in public hearings, along with the usual legal and scientific knowledge.[9] TEK is generally defined as the knowledge, practices, or beliefs about the relationship between human communities and their natural environment, which is held by people in societies that are relatively nontechnological and directly dependent on local resources (Berkes 1999; Kimmerer 2002). Its acceptance is growing in the ecological sciences, not least because of recognition that traditional knowledge is based on the same process as modern science: systematic observation of the natural world, leading to predictive abilities. TEK basically calls for us to reconstruct the term 'expert' to include alternative forms of knowledge (Gauna 1998: 36). The demand for the recognition and inclusion of TEK has been taken up not only by indigenous activists, but also by scientific entities such as the Ecological Society of America, the World Conservation Union, and the political muscle of the United Nations (UNESCO 2005). The point here is the necessity of engagement with differing, and currently silenced or remote others who provide a unique, and grounded, knowledge of human–nonhuman relations (Plumwood 2002a, 2002b). Expanded participation, through the recognition of the necessity of including the natural world and its signals and proxies into democratic discussion, brings an extension or reconstruction of expertise beyond modern scientific knowledge, to include traditional, cultural, and alternative forms of knowledge and representations of nature.

In all of these extensions of ecological participation, we must pay attention to a broad representation of the interpretations of effects on nature; there can be no single privileged voice. Such discourse allows for the presentation—and intersubjective recognition—of different points of view and interpretations of nature. Just as children or others unable to speak for themselves have numerous proxies in the form of interest groups, so should nature be represented with multiple voices. With apologies to Dr. Seuss (1971), there is never a single 'Lorax' speaking for the trees. Through listening to signals from nature, empowering proxies, and including a variety of types of communication and knowledge, we bring a multiplicity of positions to bear in ecological reflexivity and environmental decision-making.

State-based Approaches

ForestERA, however, is a process that, for now, only provides recommendations to agencies like the Forest Service or Bureau of Land Management on the issue of forest management—recommendations they can freely ignore. The process exists in the realm of civil society, with no formal link, beyond the advisory, between recommendations and the adopted policies and practices of the state agencies. One of the key issues in discussing and designing the institutionalization of inclusion and engagement is the difference between an emphasis on forms of engagement in the public or cultural sphere and the same practices in state-based institutions.

The central problem with contemporary liberal states, of course, is that there is very little reflexivity of the type we are discussing in existing institutions. State policymaking processes are most often inherently unreflexive (Eckersley 2004: 86); in the case of the contemporary USA, the state is often *anti*-reflexive—cutting funding for environmental science, or explicitly ignoring it in decision-making (see, e.g. Mooney 2005), and listening only to homogeneous voices in a bubble. While this has led some to focus on the potential for reflexive engagement either in the public sphere or in international institutions, at levels from the local to the transnational, many insist that we not give up on the role the state can play.

As both Eckersley (2004) on the greening of the state in general, and Baxter (2005), on its role in institutionalizing ecological justice in particular, note, the state is the unit we are going to have to deal with in the near future, at the very least. While there is a long and rich history in environmental political thought that focuses on anarchistic, nonhierarchical, bioregional, communitarian, anti-statist, and networked societies, 'there are still few social institutions that can match the same degree of capacity and potential legitimacy that states have to address ecological problems' (Eckersley 2004: 7). States, claims Eckersley in her defense of their use, can curb the excesses of capital, are amenable to forms of democratization, and can embody the public values necessary for environmental justice to be achieved. While one can accuse Eckersley of being optimistic, we could also see this approach as thoroughly pragmatic, compared to other proposals coming out of green political theory. Eckersley forcefully and thoroughly points out the democratic, and so deliberative and reflexive, potential of the state.

A number of authors in the environmental politics literature have noted the high levels of democratic involvement in environmental policymaking. 'One of the most distinctive features of modern U.S. environmental protection policy', writes Andrews (1999: 240), is the 'broad right of access to the regulatory process, which extends not only to affected businesses but to citizens advocating environmental protection.' Paehlke (1989) argues that the environmental arena has led all others in the scope and extent of innovations in public participation, including public inquiries, right-to-know legislation, alternative dispute resolution, advisory committees, and policy dialogues. Eckersley (2004: 15) sees 'right-to-know legislation, community environmental monitoring and reporting, third-party litigation rights, environmental and technology impact assessment, statutory policy advisory committees, citizens' juries, consensus conferences, and public inquiries' as evidence of the development of engaging discursive designs within the framework of the state. In other words, there are already a number of formal mechanisms for an ecological reflexivity to be brought into the political process; states could institute more thorough incorporation of such information into actual policy processes. The point of all of these, of course, is to bring in a variety of viewpoints, including from the little-heard yet affected, and even, possibly, from proxies for the nonhuman world. Hence the leading edge of democratic public participation, and future potential, according to these authors, is in the way states can engage environmental issues and policy. Eckersley (p. 137) explicitly ties such state institutions with the attainment of environmental justice.

Some push in a direction other than deliberative institutions, into the realm of establishing environmental rights within liberal democratic states. Hayward (2005b) makes the best and most comprehensive statement here. The central claim is that 'a right of every individual to an environment adequate for their health and well-being should receive express provision in the constitution of any modern democratic state' (p. 1). There is a key link between such state-based rights and both environmental justice and democratic participation, as Hayward recognizes. States remain key sites of legitimate power, and it may be that the defense of sovereign rights may be a way for states, especially poorer states, to protect their peoples' interests and environment (p. 21). In addition, such rights can 'foster citizen involvement in environmental protection measures' (p. 7); their existence can play a role in the cultural and educational discourse of a country. But Hayward avoids an argument for the rights of animals or nature, as a thorough notion of ecological justice would require. On the one hand, he argues, a weak form of anthropocentrism recognizes the link between human interests and the good of nonhuman constituents; with a human right to an adequate environment, we might anticipate a 'fortuitous spill-over effect to non-humans' (Redgwell 1996: 87). On the other, such environmental rights do 'not preclude the taking of other, complementary, approaches to environmental and ecological problems. It might also serve in many ways to support them and to enhance their potential for success' (Hayward 2005b: 35). Baxter (2005: 161) goes a step further, and concludes his work on ecological justice citing the potential of a constitutional approach for animals and non-human nature; he insists on combining the recognition of the moral status of nonhumans with a species-oriented approach of conservation legislation, and embedding them in constitutional protections for animals, as Germany has done (Connolly 2002). My concern with such constitutional proposals is what the approach lacks; as good as the instrumental outcome of a set law may be for environmental and/or ecological justice, such an approach lacks the necessary engagement, reflexivity, and citizen learning necessary for environmental and ecological justice to flourish.

In addition, while all of these proposals for an emphasis on state-based approaches to implementing aspects of environmental and ecological justice are genuine and well-grounded, environmental justice activists have good reason to be suspicious, if not cynical, about such an emphasis on the state. In the USA, the environmental justice movement attempted to work directly on state-based tactics to attain its ends, and met with very little success. Such approaches were limited in their conception of justice, and, frankly, were often little more than exercises in inauthentic cooptation.

Not surprisingly, early responses to calls for environmental justice on the part of the state in the USA were primarily distributional in tone. The first major legislative proposal in the USA on environmental justice, sponsored by then-Senator Al Gore and Representative John Lewis in 1992, was solely distributive in its analysis and proposed solutions (though it was never passed by the then-Democratic Congress). Likewise, the EPA's first attempt to come to grips with the environmental justice issue focused exclusively on the distribution of environmental risks. Its very name, *Environmental Equity: Reducing Risk for All Communities* (USEPA 1992), demonstrated the state's limited focus. Both of these policy moves were criticized by many in the US environmental justice community for not taking into account racial discrimination (the issue of cultural recognition and disparagement, as well as community functioning) and for not including the input of many academics and activists who had been working on the environmental justice issue for years (issues of both recognition and, more directly, participation). Even the highpoint of national policy on environmental justice, the Executive Order signed by President Clinton in 1994, was focused almost entirely on distributional issues; it required federal agencies to identify and address the disproportional impact on health and/or environment on people of color and low-income communities.

The few responses on the part of the state that did attempt to address other aspects of environmental justice often fell short as well. Environmental justice activists have been less than satisfied with participation offered them by, for example, the EPA in its advisory committees on environmental justice. The National Environmental Justice Advisory Committee (NEJAC) began as the EPA named environmental justice as a top priority early in the Clinton administration. Composed of stakeholders, many of whom had traditionally been ignored by the EPA, the NEJAC listened to hundreds of community members around the country give testimony on local environments. They passed numerous resolutions and gave the EPA much advice—but it was only an advisory body, and could not make policy. While many local and individual problems have been addressed via the NEJAC, numerous members have questioned its influence. One major participant called the NEJAC 'a kind of federally sanctioned, formal mechanism for offering advice to EPA, which they generally don't pay attention to'. This inauthenticity does not go unnoticed. A 'place at the table' will be welcomed, but will be seriously questioned if that participation does not result in a real change in the level and quality of community recognition in the development of environmental policy. Just because one is given some sort of 'voice' does not mean that they will be satisfied with a process that continues to deny them real results. Many environmental justice activists have criticized inauthentic participation in state-based mechanisms; this type of false inclusion, or attempted cooptation, results in disempowerment and increased cynicism regarding government generally.[10]

Policymakers and agencies need to understand that simply providing one element of justice—some studies of distributional inequity, some recognition of activists and communities by validating their issues, some limited notion of participation by including communities in policy discussions—will ultimately be unsatisfactory. Arguments arise that the policymakers or agencies are merely engaging in inauthentic strategies to buy time and distract the movement; a more strongly worded critique would be that these political entities are giving a certain level of (ultimately inauthentic) recognition and/or inclusion in order to defuse the movement and, ultimately, deny them distributional equity, real recognition, actual community functioning, and/or real participation.

The problem, of course, is that states are structurally constrained, and this limits the impact movements can have (Dryzek, Hunold, and Schlosberg 2002; Schlosberg and Dryzek 2002; Dryzek et al. 2003). Environmental initiatives usually run head-on into the imperative of states to support economic growth. In the USA, for example, every time environmental initiatives are perceived to harm economic growth, they are defeated and/or dismissed. One of the key goals of a broad discourse of environmental and ecological justice is to tap into both public and governmental discourses of economic stability, security, and legitimacy. Many argue that the concept of ecological modernization can be used to overcome the usual impasse by arguing that good environmental policy can both protect communities and nature and add to the economic bottom line (Barry 2003). But this argument has not influenced the US state to date; the Bush Jr. administration, as exemplified by its energy, transportation, environmental, defense, and foreign policies, only thinks of the environment–economy interface in zero-sum terms. Outside the USA, however, such a discourse that appeals to the imperatives of the state—not just economic growth, but security and legitimacy as well (which all have environmental justice components)—may have more traction.

Engagement and Reflexivity in the Public Sphere

Given the existing constraints on states, and the slow move to embrace a green tint to state imperatives, many argue that movements should focus attention not only on the state, but also on mechanisms in civil society and in the public sphere in order to achieve some of the benefits of engagement and reflexivity. Torgerson's work in this field (1999, 2000) both broke new theoretical ground and more thoroughly legitimated the political choice of movements to focus on the public sphere; Dryzek's most recent work (2006) makes the same argument for the transnational sphere as well. The goal of such work is the justification, and development, of a robust green public sphere where the public engages environmental issues. This would assist in enabling the enlarged thinking and reflexive public learning necessary for participatory justice, and help develop the avenues and talent for proxy representation.

Eckersley (2004: 147) ties together theoretical arguments from Habermas (1997), Cohen and Arato (1992), and Torgerson on the value of the public sphere. That sphere embodies a dual politics that is aimed both at the state and its policies, as well as the knowledge and identities in the public sphere itself. Torgerson has been the most articulate and effusive advocate of such a role of the green public sphere, arguing that the idea of this public sphere is more important, and useful, than the idea of a movement. Likewise, Dobson (2004) insists on the development of an environmental citizenship that includes diverse forms of engagement. Dialogue should be an end in itself, and not just focused on instrumental gains. As Torgerson puts it, 'the green public sphere has a necessary commitment to debate; its inclination is not simply tolerance, but a cultivation and provocation of disagreements that will stimulate an exchange and development of differing opinions' (Torgerson 2000: 16). The public sphere, then, is where movements can challenge existing political systems, orthodoxy, and practices, and where the pluralism of environmental values and positions can be articulated (Smith 2003: 125). As Habermas has long claimed, the public sphere, then, would be a source of critical and reflexive reasoning, and offer a realm of politics beyond the basic instrumentalism of implementing policy. This is also the ideal of pluralist, reflexive citizenship that follows Connolly's insistence (2005: 7) that pluralism is marked by 'the periodic eruption of new constituencies seeking a place on the register of legitimacy. It is also defined by multiple *sites* of potential citizen action, within and above the state'. As discussed in Chapter 7, such sites serve as places for engagement for movement activists. Networking outside the state and the pressures of interest group policymaking gives groups the space for deliberation and the development of broadly defined, yet unifying discourses on social, environmental, and ecological justice. Finally, though, the point is, ultimately, to have an impact, instrumentally, on political outcomes; critical engagement of a variety of discourses in the public sphere produces and impacts broader public opinion, which can in turn influence collective decision-making (Dryzek 2000, 2006).

Many of the discussions of the role the public sphere can play in cultivating and embodying engagement focuses on the national level, but both Eckersley (2004) and, especially, Dryzek (2006) emphasize the role a transnational public sphere can play. Dryzek presents a picture of transnational discursive democratic practice that is fully consistent with the reflexivity of a critical pluralism; engagement across difference is promoted by transnational deliberation in the public sphere. A number of theorists of international politics (Lipschutz 1992; Wapner 1996; Cochran 2002; Routledge 2003) have discussed the role of an international public sphere—activists and movement groups that coordinate across national boundaries, engage in communicative and discursive practices, and focus on global issues. As Dryzek argues (2006), such transnational resistance groups are a manifestation of reflexive modernization at the international level. They are not simply disruptive, as they constitute global public spheres that can affect the content and relative weight of global discourses and, so, the outcomes of international politics. These activists and groups fully intend to keep their political action in the public sphere, and while they ask for voice and participation in both the public and private realms, do not seek formal power in the institutions of national governments or international governance.

Evidence of such influence is rather simple to see. Before the anti-WTO protests in Seattle in 1999, the practices of the WTO specifically, and the ideology of the so-called Washington consensus on neoliberal globalization more generally, were questioned by critics in small pockets of resistance. After Seattle, such discourse has become global, ubiquitous, and ongoing. The power of global civil society was seen in the massive coordinated protests against the start of the Iraq war; at that time, some began to call global public opinion the 'new' or 'second' superpower (Moore 2003; Tyler 2003), even though it failed to prevent the war. But, again, the point is not always instrumental policy ends; rather, the effectiveness of such transnational movements can be measured in terms of their success in bringing a critical reflexiveness to bear on such policy decisions. Certainly, over the years since the start of the war, we have seen this level of success in civil society, in both the USA and transnationally. As discussed in Chapter 4, we can see numerous movement groups—organizing around neoliberal globalization, food autonomy and security, indigenous rights, and on global climate change and climate justice—working in various public spheres to have an impact, and to achieve elements of environmental and ecological justice. Most recently, we can see such broad, diverse, and discursive efforts in the public sphere impacting the global, and especially the USA, discourse on climate change (Gore 2006; Kluger 2006).

Crossing Borders with Innovative Designs

The point here is not to go into the specifics of any particular institutional forms necessary for environmental and ecological justice; I am more interested in laying out the specific transformations in participation and practice necessary in *any* institutional, or extrainstitutional, design that aims to achieve environmental and/or ecological justice. There, plurality, inclusion, participation, engagement, and reflexivity are central—whether within a state-based institution or in the more fluid public realm, from the local to the transnational. There are, however, a number of institutional experiments that have the potential to embody these characteristics. Many have discussed the potential of deliberative democratic processes in particular (especially Dryzek 2000, 2006; Smith 2003). Deliberative institutions do not guarantee green or just outcomes, but we do not have that guarantee now; the key attraction of such processes is that they embody the characteristics necessary to embrace and achieve environmental justice. As Smith (2003: 80) notes, the characteristics to look for in such designs include inclusiveness, unconstrained dialogue, a sensitivity to environmental values and conditions, and, ultimately, a just decision; I would add the engagement, recognition, and social learning noted above.

Smith's overview of deliberative democracy and environmental concerns examines three models of deliberative designs: mediation, referendums and initiatives, and various types of citizen forums. There are a variety of problems with each type—mediation, for example, depends much on the skills of trained and active mediators—is susceptible to the influence of financial and power imbalances, and is often just a one-time event, while environmental issues need more long-term management (Smith 2003: 82–5; see also Amy 1987; O'Leary and Bingham 2003). Initiative and referendum allow new issues on the agenda, and often bypass the imperative and institutional constraints faced by the state, and can lead to a debate of often excluded issues in the public realm (Smith 2003: 94–6). But they also suffer from a number of problems, including financial inequalities, mediation of the discussion by elites and the media, and the tendency of the public to reject things they do not understand. Finally, Smith notes the popularity of citizen forums, such as deliberative opinion polls, citizen juries, and consensus conferences; in addition to providing a participatory venue for discussion of policies, there is evidence that participants in such forums may continue to be more civic minded and active after the process is over (Fishkin 1997; Smith 2003: 88). While such forums are best for unconstrained dialogue (except for deliberative polls), they are also open to strategic abuses. The other major problem with such forums is that they are rarely attached to actual policymaking; so while they may expand opportunities for dialogue, bring in those participants and ideas often excluded, and generally bring discussion of issues into the public realm, they are often simply detached from institutional politics. Smith (2003: 102) concludes in a sensible way, as he must, by noting that there is no single best design, and that different models of deliberative decision-making work better in different circumstances.

I agree, but want to offer a short discussion of three additional models that not only bring the strengths of deliberation, inclusion, engagement, and reflexivity to bear on environmental decision-making, but that also assist in crossing the boundary between state institutions and the public sphere. Collaborative decision-making, public sphere oversight, and Web-based deliberation and participation are all growing forms of public sphere access to institutionalized decision-making.

In the USA, experiments in broader discursive environmental decision-making have been increasing, due in part to the demands of environmental and environmental justice movements. Collaborative decision-making is one main focus, especially in natural resource and forestry decisions. Central to these deliberative and, sometimes, policy-implementing processes is a connection to community and place. Recognition, of both communities and the land itself, is the basis of the process. As the editors of one of the few academic overviews of the practice put it, collaboration 'emphasizes the importance of local participation, sustainable natural and human communities, [and] inclusion of disempowered voices' (Brick, Snow, and van de Wetering 2001: 2). Numerous collaborative processes, especially in the US west, have brought together various perspectives from the community and put them in a room with representatives from government agencies, industry, and the scientific community. The idea is to get beyond the adversarial model that has left so many disenchanted with the standard process of environmental decision-making in the USA. While the reviews remain mixed, and differ, again, depending on the particular case and context, such experiments have brought inclusion and reflection to policymaking and implementation that has traditionally been captured by the resource interests. And there is support for the process from within the environmental justice community (Lee 2005). Collaborative projects do have the potential to be an avenue for implementing recognition and participation, and for taking distribution, capabilities, and individual and community functioning seriously in developing environmental policy.

Bringing interests together from the public sphere and the state has also been attempted in another innovative way. In more urban settings, the environmental justice movement often focuses on the institutionalization of public oversight of particularly controversial facilities. Many states require a local advisory committee when a facility is initially licensed or when it comes up for renewal of a permit, and EJ activists have insisted on thorough and authentic public participation in these processes. These committees 'offer the opportunity for a qualitatively deliberative process, one that creates an opportunity for lay and technical people to work together, have a dialogue, and reach consensus' (Cole and Foster 2001: 112). Some communities have gone a step further, and have brought permanent status to such advisory committees. In Eugene, Oregon, for example, a local 'Toxics Board' was established to oversee the reporting of toxic substances in larger production facilities. The board has representatives from the environmental community and industry, and is central to both the oversight of toxics management and the distribution of information to the public. Such institutions provide an ongoing center for participation, discourse across difference, and, importantly, the information necessary to make environmental decisions in the community.

As plausible the potential is in these experiments in community collaboration or advisory groups, they are few and far between. They are also only workable on local, or at most regional, issues. It is quite difficult to get a national collaborative board, or a reasonable representation of the public sphere at the national or international level. With this limitation, the most broad, and possibly promising, current arena for diverse recognition and public participation is in the development of electronic or Web-based participation by citizens in state or international decision-making.

Research into the practice and potential of online deliberation covers a broad array of activities.[11] One of the problems with this research is that there are so many avenues for such participation—websites, usenets, bulletin boards, chats, blogs, and podcasts—making it difficult to systematically track and measure the impact of online deliberation. As Froomkin

(2003: 777) notes, 'the Internet can be seen as a giant electronic talkfest, a medium that is discourse-mad'.

In the USA, online public participation in the public comment process of rulemaking in government agencies has grown in the past decade—in particular on environmental rules. Numerous federal agencies, such as the Department of Transportation, Department of Agriculture, and Environmental Protection Agency, are moving ahead with the implementation of Internet-based public participation as a way of meeting the required public comment process in regulatory rulemaking.

The development of rulemaking technologies appears to embody a democratic direction. Many agencies now use open electronic dockets, which allow citizens to review and comment on the rules proposed by agencies, supporting documentation, and the comments of other citizens. On these sites, the public can offer comments on both proposed rules and on others' comments on those rules. The result is often an interesting discourse far more broad and open than the current public comment process, which is dominated by industry. Electronic rulemaking systems are also highly structured, hence quite different from other Web-based discourse that is one-way, isolated, or homogeneous. Sunstein (2001) argues that the Internet enables people to pay attention to other, like-minded people, and ignore those who are unlike them or disagree with their positions on issues. The Web, for Sunstein, diminishes exposure to heterogeneity and is far from the ideal of a real public forum. Yet the structure of e-rulemaking, in particular the open docket system, enables citizens to engage the positions of others, including those with whom they disagree. In other words, the open docket architecture of e-rulemaking may mitigate some of the antideliberative dangers engendered by the Web.

Web-based participation in rulemaking also goes somewhere; simply put, the process frequently leads to actual changes of agency-enforced rules. Here, a focus on rulemaking differs from other examinations of Web-based discourse. A common critique of online deliberative polling, cyberjuries, or Web-based policy discussions is that the deliberative work often produces few if any tangible or pragmatic results. People spend time and energy working toward consensus, only to see it ignored or rejected politically. This problem of implementation deficit can deplete citizen energy devoted to discourse. Rulemaking requires agencies to respond to substantive public comments. It may be the only form of online deliberation that regularly ends in actual policy implementation. There are dangers, of course; agencies may insist on one-way submission of comments, rather than discourse. They may also limit what counts as acceptable discourse by paying attention to only legal and scientific commentary. But the potential of online deliberation is still there.[12] In focus groups for a related project (Schlosberg, Shulman, and Zavestoski 2006), various environmental agency officials in the USA were highly supportive of citizen engagement in the rulemaking process. They saw it as a way to both bring in more citizen views and expertise and as a way to challenge and counterbalance the political pressure to side with the administration and industry against environmental outcomes.

I do not want to conclude with a blanket endorsement of online deliberation as the chosen form of institutionalized inclusion with which to achieve environmental justice, but it is an area that is currently understudied. Such e-deliberation can be not only state-based, but we can also imagine global e-forums with broad participation as a method of encouraging inclusion, engagement, and social learning. As a number of recent studies claim (Smith 2003; Kahn and Kellner 2004), the Web may be used in a democratic manner to construct new social and political relations, and use those virtual communities to add pressure to political entities; in this, the Web may be used as a base, and a communicative node, for a worldwide social justice movement. Numerous social and environmental justice networks already use the Web for these purposes.[13]

Final Words

The first step in the development of environmental and ecological justice is more reflective, critical, and engaged individuals, communities, and movements; there is some evidence that such practices are growing, in particular in the environmental and ecological justice movements explored earlier. But the more reconstructive moment of a reflexive modernization requires such diverse and critical knowledges regarding nature and environments be brought into more socially, environmentally, and ecologically reflexive institutions. Beck argues that modernization demands this step; ecological democrats argue that democracy demands it. My argument here is that a broad understanding of environmental and ecological justice requires it as well. The ecological public sphere and the potential ecological state, in order to address environmental and ecological justice—and to provide distributional equity, recognition, participation, and the capabilities and functioning necessary for a good life—must continue to reflexively evolve the crucial role of participatory and discursive institutional structures in achieving just ends. A broad discourse of environmental and ecological justice, converging and congealing in movements and networks from the local to the global, is one way to provide the pressure necessary to implement such change.

Notes

1. See, most recently, Baxter (2005), Dobson (2004), Dryzek (2006), Eckersley (2004), Hayward (2005*b*), and Smith (2003).
2. This is an especially crucial lesson for movement groups that enter the state political realm, and that risk falling into a passive, limited, and potentially coopted form of inclusion. For a discussion of this danger, see Dryzek et al. (2003).
3. Both are a requirement for entry into, e.g. Habermas's notion of communicative action.
4. This certainly gets away from the presumed rationalistic prejudice of deliberative democracy to other forms of communication (hence Dryzek's insistence on 'discursive' rather than 'deliberative'). Just as Young (1996) wants to expand such discourse to include forms of communication other than the blatantly purposive/argumentative, Dryzek goes beyond this Habermasian bias to accept other forms of communication in 'signals' from nature.
5. Dryzek is certainly not alone in this attempt to bring representation of the natural world into democratic, and in particular deliberative democratic, practice. See also Goodin (1996), Eckersley (2000), and Smith (2003).
6. On the ambiguity involved in understanding nature, see Bennett (2004), Cronon (1996), Macnaghten and Urry (1998), or Soper (1995).
7. Such an understanding is also a growing part of graduate programs in the environmental sciences that are stressing the role of the environmental scientist in the political process.
8. See information about the project, and publications, at www.forestera.nau. edu. I have been involved in a social science analysis of a ForestERA project in northern New Mexico; this project has a wide diversity of participants, including government agencies, environmental groups, Native American pueblo communities, and Spanish land-grant communities (many of which have been in conflict with one another for many years). The goal is to assess the social learning of the process, including the level of recognition of the positions of others.
9. For guidance on including traditional cultural knowledge in decision-making, see USEPA (1996), NEJAC (2000, 2004), and UNESCO (2005). For an overview of the use of indigenous knowledge in development strategies, see Briggs (2005).
10. Say what one will about the Bush Jr. administration and its environmental policies; at least it is comparatively honest about its exclusion of the

environmental community. The NEJAC had twenty-five meetings, roundtables, and public dialogues during the Clinton administration; only four have been held during the Bush administration.

11. See, e.g. Beierle (2004), Coglianese (2004), Schlosberg, Shulman, and Zavestoski (2005), Shane (2004), Shulman (2004), and Witschge (2004).

12. The best example of diverse online discourse with an impact in US rulemaking is that of 50,000-plus public comments in an open forum leading to the development of rules on organic food. The online pressure helped defeat agriculture's attempt to include things like irradiation, sewage sludge fertilizers, and genetic engineering in the definition of organic. See Shulman (2003).

13. That said, as with all other modes of institutionalizing engagement and, so, the possibility of environmental and ecological justice, we must acknowledge the obvious: that the digital divide continues to exclude a huge portion of the population of the world from this particular institutional possibility.

References

Achterberg, Wouter (1993). 'Can Liberal Democracy Survive the Environmental Crisis? Sustainability, Liberal Neutrality and Overlapping Consensus', in Andrew Dobson and Paul Lucardie (eds.), *The Politics of Nature: Explorations in Green Political Theory*. London: Routledge.

Adamson, Joni, Evans, Mei Mei, and Stein, Rachel (2002). *The Environmental Justice Reader: Politics, Poetics, and Pedagogy*. Tucson, AZ: University of Arizona Press.

Adeola, Francis O. (2000). 'Cross-National Environmental Injustice and Human Rights Issues: a Review of Evidence in the Developing World', *American Behavioral Scientist*, 43(4): 696–706.

Agyeman, Julian (2005). *Sustainable Communities and the Challenge of Environmental Justice*. New York: New York University Press.

—— Bullard, Robert D., and Evans, Bob (eds.) (2003). *Just Sustainabilities: Development in an Unequal World*. Cambridge, MA: MIT Press.

Alston, Dana (ed.) (1991). *We Speak for Ourselves: Social Justice, Race, and Environment*. Washington DC: The Panos Institute.

—— (1992). 'Moving Beyond the Barriers', in Charles Lee (ed.), *Proceeding: The First National People of Color Environmental Leadership Summit*. New York: United Church of Christ Commission for Racial Justice.

Amazon Watch (n.d.). *Camisea Natural Gas Project*. Retrieved October 9, 2005, from http://www.amazonwatch.org/amazon/PE/camisea/

Amy, Douglas (1987). *The Politics of Environmental Mediation*. New York: Columbia University Press.

Anand, Sudhir and Sen, Amartya (2000). 'Human Development and Economic Sustainability', *World Development*, 28(12): 2029–49.

Andrews, Richard N. L. (1999). *Managing the Environment, Managing Ourselves: A History of American Environmental Policy*. New Haven, CT: Yale.

Anthony, Carl (2005). 'The Environmental Justice Movement: An Activist's Perspective', in David N. Pellow and Robert J. Brulle (eds.), *Power, Justice, and the Environment: A Critical Appraisal of the Environmental Justice Movement*. Cambridge, MA: MIT Press.

—— Chavis, Ben, Moore, Richard, Li, Vivien, Douglas, Scott, and LaDuke, Winona (1993). 'A Place at the Table: A Sierra Roundtable on Race, Justice, and the Environment', *Sierra*, 78(3): 50–61.

References

Aristotle (1980). *The Nichomachean Ethics*. Oxford: Oxford University Press.
Attfield, Robin (1999). *The Ethics of the Global Environment*. West Lafayette, IN: Purdue University Press.
—— (2001). 'Sustainability, Global Warming, Population Policies and Liberal Democracy', in John Barry and Marcel Wissenburg (eds.), *Sustaining Liberal Democracy: Ecological Challenges and Opportunities*. Basingstoke, UK: Palgrave.
Austin, Regina and Schill, Michael (1991). 'Black, Brown, Poor, and Poisoned: Minority Grassroots Environmentalism and the Quest for Eco-Justice', *The Kansas Journal of Law and Public Policy*, 1(1): 69–82.
Bakker, Isabella and Gill, Stephen (eds.) (2003). *Power, Production and Social Reproduction*. London: Macmillan-Palgrave.
Barry, Brian (1995). *Justice as Impartiality*. Oxford: Oxford University Press.
—— (1999). 'Sustainable and Intergenerational Justice', in Andrew Dobson (ed.), *Fairness and Futurity: Essays on Environmental Sustainability and Social Justice*. Oxford: Oxford University Press.
—— (2001). *Culture and Equality*. Cambridge: Polity.
—— (2005). *Why Social Justice Matters*. Cambridge: Polity.
Barry, John (1999). *Rethinking Green Politics*. London: Sage.
—— (2003). 'Ecological Modernization', in E. Page and J. Proops (eds.), *Environmental Thought*. Cheltenham, UK: Edward Elgar.
Baxter, Brian (2000*a*). *Ecologism: An Introduction*. Washington, DC: Georgetown University Press.
—— (2000*b*). 'Ecological Justice and Justice as Impartiality', *Environmental Politics*, 9(3): 43–64.
—— (2005). *A Theory of Ecological Justice*. London: Routledge.
Beck, Ulrich (1992). *Risk Society: Toward a New Modernity*. London: Sage.
—— (1997). *The Reinvention of Politics: Rethinking Modernity in the Global Social Order*. Cambridge: Polity.
—— (1998). *Democracy without Enemies*. Cambridge: Polity.
Beierle, Thomas C. (2004). 'Digital Deliberation: Engaging the Public Through Online Policy Dialogues', in Peter Shane (ed.), *Democracy Online: The Prospects for Political Renewal Through the Internet*. New York: Routledge.
Bell, Derek (2002). 'How Can Political Liberals be Environmentalists?' *Political Studies*, 50: 703–24.
—— (2003). 'Political Liberalism and Ecological Justice', Presented in a panel on 'Environmental and Ecological Justice', European Consortium for Political Research General Conference, Marburg, Germany.
Bennett, Jane (2004). 'The Force of Things: Steps toward an Ecology of Matter', *Political Theory*, 32(3): 347–72.
Benton, Ted (1993). *Natural Relations: Ecology, Animal Rights and Social Justice*. London: Verso.
Berkes, Fikret (1999). *Sacred Ecology: Traditional Ecological Knowledge*. Philadelphia, PA: Taylor & Francis.

Berlin, Isaiah (1969). *Four Essays on Liberty*. London: Oxford.

—— (1990). *The Crooked Timber of Humanity*. London: John Murray.

Bernstein, Richard J. (1988). *Beyond Objectivism and Relativism*. Philadelpia, PA: University of Pennsylvania Press.

Bickford, Susan (1996). *The Dissonance of Democracy: Listening, Conflict, and Citizenship*. Ithaca, NY: Cornell University Press.

Boerner, Christopher and Thomas Lambert (2000). 'Environmental Injustice: Industrial and Waste Facilities Must Consider the Human Factor', in Theodore Goldfarb (ed.), *Taking Sides: Clashing Views on Controversial Environmental Issues*. New York: McGraw-Hill.

Bohman, James (2001). 'Participants, Observers, and Critics: Practical Knowledge, Social Perspectives, and Critical Pluralism', in William Rehg and James Bohman (eds.), *Pluralism and the Pragmatic Turn: The Transformation of Critical Theory*. Cambridge, MA: MIT Press.

Borrows, John (1997). 'Living Between Water and Rocks: First Nations, Environmental Planning and Democracy', *University of Toronto Law Journal*, 47: 417–68.

Bowen, William M. (2001). *Environmental Justice through Research-Based Decision-Making*. New York: Garland.

—— and Wells, Michael V. (2002). 'The Politics and Reality of Environmental Justice: A History and Considerations for Public Administration and Policy Makers', *Public Administration Review*, 62(6): 688–98.

Bowersox, Joe (2002). 'Environmental Justice: Private Preference or Public Necessity?', in John Martin Gillroy and Joe Bowersox (eds.), *The Moral Austerity of Environmental Decision Making: Sustainability, Democracy, and Normative Argument in Policy and Law*. Durham, NC: Duke University Press.

Boyce, James K., Klemer, Andrewe R., Templet, Paul H., and Willis, Cleve E. (1999). 'Power Distribution, the Environment, and Public Health: A State-Level Analysis', *Ecological Economics*, 29(1): 127–40.

Bretting, John and Prindeville, Diane-Michele (1998). 'Environmental Justice and the Role of Indigenous Women Organizing Their Communities', in David Camacho (ed.), *Environmental Injustices, Political Struggles: Race, Class, and the Environment*. Durham, NC: Duke University Press.

Brick, Philip, Snow, Donald, and van de Wetering, Sarah (eds.) (2001). *Across the Great Divide: Explorations in Collaborative Conservation and the American West*. Washington, DC: Island Press.

Briggs, John (2005). 'The Use of Indigenous Knowledge in Development: Problems and Challenges', *Progress in Development Studies*, 5(2): 99–114.

Brighouse, Harry (2004). *Justice*. Cambridge: Polity.

Brown, Phil (1992). 'Popular Epidemiology and Toxic Waste Contamination: Lay and Professional Ways of Knowing', *Journal of Health and Social Behavior*, 33(3): 267–81.

—— and Mikkelsen, Edwin (1990). *No Safe Place: Toxic Waste, Leukemia, and Community Action*. Berkeley, CA: University of California Press.

References

Brown, Phil, Mayer, Brian, Zavestoski, Stephen, Luebke, Theo, Mandelbaum, Joshua, and McCormick, Sabrina (2005). 'The Health Politics of Asthma: Environmental Justice and Collective Illness Experience', in David N. Pellow and Robert J. Brulle (eds.), *Power, Justice, and the Environment: A Critical Appraisal of the Environmental Justice Movement*. Cambridge, MA: MIT Press.

Brulle, Robert J. and Essoka, Jonathan (2005). 'Whose Environmental Justice? An Analysis of the Governance Structure of Environmental Justice Organizations in the United States', in David Naguib Pellow and Robert J. Brulle (eds.), *Power, Justice, and the Environment: A Critical Appraisal of the Environmental Justice Movement*. Cambridge, MA: MIT Press.

Bryant, Bunyan (1995). *Environmental Justice: Issues, Policies, and Solutions*. Covelo, CA: Island Press.

⸻ and Mohai, Paul (eds.) (1992). *Race and the Incidence of Environmental Hazards: A Time for Discourse*. Boulder, CO: Westview Press.

Bryner, Gary C . (2002). 'Assessing Claims of Environmental Justice: Conceptual Frameworks', in Kathryn M. Mutz, Gary C. Bryner, and Douglans S. Kenney (eds.), *Justice and Natural Resources: Concepts Strategies, and Applications*. Washington, DC: Island Press.

Bullard, Robert (1990). *Dumping in Dixie: Race, Class, and Environmental Quality*. Boulder, CO: Westview Press.

⸻ (ed.) (1993). *Confronting Environmental Racism: Voices from the Grassroots*. Boston, MA: South End Press.

⸻ (ed.) (1994a). *Unequal Protection: Environmental Justice and Communities of Color*. San Francisco, CA: Sierra Club Books.

⸻ (ed.) (1994b). *People of Color Environmental Groups 1994–95 Directory*. Atlanta, GA: Environmental Justice Resource Center.

⸻ (ed.) (2005). *The Quest for Environmental Justice: Human Rights and the Politics of Pollution*. San Francisco, CA: Sierra Club Books.

Burke, Edmund ([1790] 1999). *Reflections on the Revolution in France*. New York: Oxford University Press.

Byrne, John, Martinez, Cecilia, and Glover, Leigh (eds.) (2002). *Environmental justice: Discourses in international political economy: Energy and Environmental Policy*, Vol. 8. New Brunswick, NJ: Transaction Publishers.

Cable, Sherry, Mix, Tamara, and Hastings, Donald (2005). 'Mission Impossible? Environmental Justice Activists' Collaborations with Professional Environmentalists and with Academics', in David Naguib Pellow and Robert J. Brulle (eds.), *Power, Justice, and the Environment: A Critical Appraisal of the Environmental Justice Movement*. Cambridge, MA: MIT Press.

Callicott, J. Baird (1990). 'The Case Against Moral Pluralism', *Environmental Ethics*, 12: 99–124.

Camacho, David (ed.) (1998). *Environmental Injustices, Political Struggles: Race, Class, and the Environment*. Durham, NC: Duke University Press.

Campesina, Via (2002). *Proposals of Via Campesina for Sustainable, Farmer Based Agricultural Production*. Retrieved January 8, 2006, from http://viacampesina.org/en/index.php?option=com_content&task=view&id=229&Itemid=135

—— (2005). *La Via Campesina Discusses Damage Done by WTO*. Retrieved January 10, 2006, from http://qc.indymedia.org/news/2005/12/5530.php

Capek, Sheila (1993). 'The "Environmental Justice" Frame: A Conceptual Discussion and an Application', *Social Problems*, 40(1): 5–24.

Carruthers, David (forthcoming 2008). 'Environmental Justice and the Politics of Energy on the US-Mexico Border', *Environmental Politics*.

Carson, Rachel (1962). *Silent Spring*. Boston, MA: Houghton Mifflin.

Chavis, Rev. Benjamin F. Jr. (1993). 'Forward', in Robert D. Bullard (ed.), *Confronting Environmental Racism: Voices from the Grassroots*. Boston, MA: South End Press.

Climate Justice Declaration (2004). *The Climate Justice Declaration*. Retrieved January 4, 2006, from http://www.umich.edu/~snre492/cgi-data/ejcc_principles.html

Cochran, Molly (2002). 'A Democratic Critique of Cosmopolitan Democracy: Pragmatism from the Bottom Up', *European Journal of International Relations*, 8: 517–48.

Coglianese, Cary (2004). 'E-Rulemaking: Information Technology and Regulatory Policy', *Regulatory Policy Program Report No. RPP-05*.

Cohen, Jean L. and Arato, Andrew (1992). *Civil Society and Political Theory*. Cambridge, MA: MIT Press.

Cole, Luke W. and Foster, Sheila R. (2001). *From the Ground Up: Environmental Racism and the Rise of the Environmental Justice Movement*. New York: New York University Press.

Collins, Patricia Hill (1998). *Fighting Words: Black Women and the Search for Justice*. Minneapolis, MN: University of Minnesota Press.

Conca, Ken and Dabelko, Geoffrey D. (eds.) (1998). *Green Planet Blues: Environmental Politics from Stockholm to Kyoto*, 2nd edn. Boulder, CO: Westview Press.

Connolly, Kate (2002). 'German Animals Given Legal Rights', *Guardian*, June 22. Retrieved May 22, 2006 from http://www.guardian.co.uk/animalrights/story/0,,741856,00.html

Connolly, William (1993). *Political Theory and Modernity*, 2nd edn. Ithaca, NY: Cornell University Press.

—— (1995). *The Ethos of Pluralization*. Minneapolis, MN: University of Minnesota Press.

—— (2005). *Pluralism*. Durham NC: Duke University Press.

Cooper, David E. and Palmer, Joy A. (1995). *Just Environments: Intergenerational, International, and Interspecies Issues*. London: Routledge.

Council of the Haida Nation (n.d.). *People who look after the Forest*. Retrieved October 9, 2005, from http://haidanation.ca/index.php

References

Cowell, Alan (2006, April 1). 'A Geek, Sure, but No Patsy When It's About Research', *New York Times*. Retrieved May 13, 2006, from http://www.nytimes.com/2006/04/01/world/europe/01pycroft.html

Cronon, William (ed.) (1996). *Uncommon Ground: Rethinking the Human Place in Nature*. New York: Norton.

Dean, Jodi (1996). *Solidarity of Strangers: Feminism after Identity Politics*. Berkeley, CA: University of California.

Deleuze, Gilles, and Guattari, Felix (1983). *Anti-Oedipus: Capitalism and Schizophrenia*. Minneapolis, MN: University of Minnesota Press.

DeLuca, Kevin Michael (1999). 'The Possibilities of Nature in the Postmodern Age: The Rhetorical Tactics of Environmental Justice Groups', *Communication Theory*, 9(2): 189–215.

Deneulin, Séverine (2002). 'Perfection, Paternalism and Liberalism in Sen and Nussbaum's Capability Approach', *Review of Political Economy*, 14(4): 497–518.

de-Shalit, Avner (1995). *Why Posterity Matters*. London: Routledge.

____ (1997). 'Is Liberalism Environment-Friendly?', in Roger S. Gottlieb (ed.), *The Ecological Community*. London: Routledge.

____ (2000). *The Environment: Between Theory and Practice*. Oxford: Oxford University Press.

Deveaux, Monique (1999). 'Agonism and Pluralism', *Philosophy and Social Criticism*, 25(4): 1–22.

____ (2000). *Cultural Pluralism and Dilemmas of Justice*. Ithaca, NY: Cornell University Press.

Di Chiro, Giovanna (1992). 'Defining Environmental Justice: Women's Voices and Grassroots Politics', *Socialist Review*, 22(4): 93–131.

____ (2008, forthcoming). 'Living Environmentalism: Coalition Politics, Social Reproduction, and Environmental Justice', *Environmental Politics*, 17 (2).

Dobson, Andrew (1996). 'Representative Democracy and the Environment', in William Lafferty and James Meadowcroft (eds.), *Democracy and the Environment: Problems and Prospects*. Cheltenham, UK: Edward Elgar.

____ (1998). *Justice and the Environment: Conceptions of Environmental Sustainability and Dimensions of Social Justice*. Oxford: Oxford University Press.

____ (ed.) (1999). *Fairness and Futurity: Essays on Environmental Sustainability and Social Justice*. Oxford: Oxford University Press.

____ (2003). 'Social Justice and Environmental Sustainability: Ne'er the Twain Shall Meet?', in Julian Agyeman, Robert D. Bullard, and Bob Evans (eds.), *Just Sustainabilities: Development in an Unequal World*. Cambridge, MA: MIT Press.

____ (2004). *Citizenship and the Environment*. Oxford: Oxford University Press.

Donatella, Della Porta, and Tarrow, Sidney (2005). *Transnational Protest and Global Activism: People, Passions, and Power*. Lanham, MD: Rowman and Littlefield.

Dowie, Mark (1995). *Losing Ground: American Environmentalism at the Close of the Twentieth Century*. Cambridge, MA: MIT Press.

Dryzek, John (1987). *Rational Ecology: Environment and Political Economy*. Oxford: Blackwell.

—— (1995) 'Political and Ecological Communication', *Environmental Politics*, 4(4): 13–30.

—— (2000). *Deliberative Democracy and Beyond: Liberals, Critics, Contestation*. Oxford: Oxford University Press.

—— (2006). *Deliberative Global Politics: Discourse and Democracy in a Divided World*. Cambridge, UK: Polity Press.

—— and Schlosberg, David (eds.) (2005). *Debating the Earth: The Environmental Politics Reader*, 2nd edn. Oxford: Oxford University Press.

—— Hunold, Christian, and Schlosberg, David (2002). 'Environmental Transformation of the State: A Study of the United States, Norway, Germany, and the United Kingdom', *Political Studies*, 50(4): 659–82.

—— Downes, David, Hunold, Christian, and Schlosberg, David (2003). *Green States and Social Movements: Environmentalism in the United States, United Kingdom, Germany, and Norway*. Oxford: Oxford University Press.

Dumm, Thomas (1994). 'Strangers and Liberals', *Political Theory*, 22(1): 167–76.

Eckersley, Robyn (1992). *Environmentalism and Political Theory*, Albany, NY: SUNY Press.

—— (1996). 'Greening Liberal Democracy: the Rights Discourse Revisited', in Brian Doherty and Marius de Geus (eds.), *Democracy and Green Political Thought*, London: Routledge.

—— (1999). 'The Discourse Ethic and the Problem of Representing Nature', *Environmental Politics*, 8(2): 24–49.

—— (2004). *The Green State: Rethinking Democracy and Sovereignty*. Cambridge, MA: MIT Press.

—— (2005). 'Ecocentric Discourses: Problems and Prospects for Nature Advocacy', in John Dryzek and David Schlosberg (eds.), *Debating the Earth: The Environmental Politics Reader*, 2nd edn. Oxford: Oxford University Press.

Edwards, Bob (1995). 'With Liberty and Environmental Justice for All: The Emergence and Challenge of Grassroots Environmentalism in the United States', in Bron Taylor (ed.), *Ecological Resistance Movements*, Albany, NY: SUNY Press.

Environmental Justice and Climate Change Initiative (2002). *10 Principles for Just Climate Change Policies in the U.S.* Retrieved January 4, 2006, from http://www.ejcc.org/ejcc10short_usa.pdf

Epstein, Barbara (1997). 'The Environmental Justice/Toxics Movement: Politics of Race and Gender', *Capitalism, Nature, Socialism*, 8(3): 63–87.

Faber, Daniel (ed.) (1998). *The Struggle for Ecological Democracy: Environmental Justice Movements in the United States*. New York: Guilford Press.

—— and McCarthy, Debra (2003). 'Neo-Liberalism, Globalization, and the Struggle for Ecological Democracy: Linking Sustainability and Environmental Justice', in Julian Agyeman, Robert D. Bullard, and Bob Evans (eds.), *Just Sustainabilities: Development in an Unequal World*. Cambridge, MA: MIT Press.

Figueroa, Robert M. (2003). 'Bivalent Environmental Justice and the Culture of Poverty', *Rutgers University Journal of Law and Urban Policy*, 1(1).

―― (2004). 'A Cross-Cultural Analysis of Distribution, Recognition, and Environmental Heritage', Paper given at a conference on *Environmental Justice Abroad*, Rutgers University, October 2004.

Fishkin, James S. (1997). *The Voice of the People*. New Haven, CT: Yale University Press.

Follett, Mary Parker (1918). *The New State: Group Organization and the Solution of Popular Government*. New York: Longmans, Green and Co.

―― (1924). *Creative Experience*. New York: Longmans, Green and Co.

Foucault, Michel (1978). *The History of Sexuality. Vol. 1, An Introduction*. New York: Random House.

―― (1980). *Power/Knowledge*. New York: Pantheon Books.

Fraser, Nancy (1997). *Justice Interruptus: Critical Reflections on the 'Postsocialist' Condition*. New York: Routledge.

―― (1998). 'Social Justice in the Age of Identity Politics: Redistribution, Recognition, and Participation', in Grethe B. Peterson (ed.), *The Tanner Lectures on Human Values*, Vol. 19. Salt Lake City, UT: University of Utah Press.

―― (2000). 'Rethinking Recognition', *New Left Review*, 3(May–June): 107–20.

―― (2001). 'Recognition without Ethics?', *Theory, Culture, and Society*, 18: 21–42.

―― and Honneth, Axel (2003). *Redistribution or Recognition? A Political–Philosophical Exchange*. London: Verso.

Freudenberg, Nicholas and Carol Steinsapir (1992). 'Not in Our Backyards: The Grassroots Environmental Movement', in Riley E. Dunlap and Angela G. Mertig (eds.), *American Environmentalism: The U.S. Environmental Movement, 1970–1990*. Philadelphia, PA: Taylor & Francis.

Friends of the Earth (FOE) (n.d.). *Greening Trade*. Retrieved January 3, 2006, from http://www.foe.org/camps/intl/greentrade/index.html

Froomkin, A. Michael (2003). 'Habermas@Discourse.Net: Toward a Critical Theory of Cyberspace', *Harvard Law Review*, 116 (3): 751–873.

Galston, William A. (2002). *Liberal Pluralism: The Implications of Value Pluralism for Political Theory and Practice*. Cambridge: Cambridge University Press.

Gauna, Eileen (1998). 'The Environmental Justice Misfit: Public Participation and the Paradigm Paradox', *Stanford Environmental Law Journal*, 17: 3–72.

Gertz, Emily (July 26, 2005). 'The Snow Must Go On: Inuit Fight Climate Change with Human-Rights Claim against U.S.', *Grist*. Retrieved May 13, 2006, from http://grist.org/news/maindish/2005/07/26/gertz-inuit/index.html

Getches, David H. and Pellow, David N. (2002). 'Beyond "Traditional" Environmental Justice', in Kathryn M. Mutz, Gary C. Bryner, and Douglas S. Kenney (eds.), *Justice and Natural Resources: Concepts Strategies, and Applications*. Washington, DC: Island Press.

Gibbs, Lois (1982). *Love Canal: My Story*. Albany, NY: SUNY Press.

Global Exchange (2000*a*). 'Top Ten Reasons to Oppose the IMF', Retrieved January 15, 2004, from http://www.globalexchange.org/campaigns/wbimf/TopTenIMF.html

—— (2000*b*). 'World Bank/IMF Questions and Answers', Retrieved January 15, 2004, from http://www.globalexchange.org/campaigns/wbimf/faq.html

Global Response (2005) *Stop 'Certified' Logging/Sarawak, Malaysia*. Retrieved January 3, 2006, from http://www.globalresponse.org/gra.php?i=3/05

Goldman, Benjamin A. (1996). 'What is the Future of Environmental Justice?', *Antipode*, 28(2): 122–41.

Goldtooth, Tom (March 25, 2005). 'We Only Have One Mother Earth', *Indian Country Today*. Retrieved January 4, 2006, from http://www.indiancountry.com/content.cfm?id=1096410622

Goodin, Robert (1996). 'Enfranchising the Earth, and Its Alternatives', *Political Studies*, 44: 835–49.

Gore, Al (2006). *An Inconvenient Truth*. Emmaus, PA: Rodale Press.

Gottlieb, Robert (1993, 2nd edn 2005). *Forcing the Spring: The Transformation of the American Environmental Movement*. Washington, DC: Island Press.

Gould, Carol (1996). 'Diversity and Democracy: Representing Differences', in Seyla Benhabib (ed.), *Democracy and Difference*. Princeton, NJ: Princeton University Press.

Gould, Kenneth, Schnaiberg, Allan, and Weinberg, Adam (1996). *Local Environmental Struggles: Citizen Activism in the Treadmill of Production*. Cambridge: Cambridge University Press.

Greenpeace (n.d.). *Impacts*. Retrieved January 3, 2006, from http://www.greenpeace.org/international/campaigns/climate-change/impacts

Greider, William (1996). *One World Ready or Not: The Manic Logic of Global Capitalism*. New York: Simon & Schuster.

Group of Nineteen (2005). *Porto Alegre Manifesto*. Retrieved January 3, 2006, from http://www.zmag.org/sustainers/content/2005-02/20group_of_nineteen.cfm

Guha, Ramachandra and Alier, Juan Martinez (1997). *Varieties of Environmentalism*. London: Earthscan.

Habermas, Jurgen (1981). 'New Social Movements', *Telos*, 49: 33–7.

—— (1997). *Between Facts and Norms*. Cambridge, MA: MIT Press.

Hamilton, Cynthia (1993). 'Coping with Industrial Exploitation', in Robert Bullard (ed.), *Confronting Environmental Racism: Voices from the Grassroots*. Boston, MA: South End Press.

—— (1994). 'Concerned Citizens of South Central Los Angeles', in Robert Bullard (ed.), *Unequal Protection: Environmental Justice and Communities of Color*. San Francisco, CA: Sierra Club Books.

Hampton, Greg (1999). 'Environmental Equity and Public Participation', *Policy Sciences*, 32(2): 163–74.

Haraway, Donna (1988). 'Situated Knowledges: The Science Question in Feminism as a Site of Discourse on the Privilege of Partial Perspective', *Feminist Studies*, 14(3): 575–99.

Hardt, Michael, and Negri, Antonio (2000). *Empire*. Cambridge, MA: Harvard University Press.

Harvey, David (1996). *Justice, Nature, and the Geography of Difference*. Oxford: Blackwell.

Hayward, Tim (1998). *Political Theory and Ecological Values*. Cambridge: Polity.

—— (2005*a*). 'Thomas Pogge's Global Resources Dividend: A Critique and an Alternative', *Journal of Moral Philosophy*, 2(3): 317–32.

—— (2005*b*). *Constitutional Environmental Rights*. Oxford: Oxford University Press.

Hegel, G. W. F. (1967). *Hegel's Philosophy of Right*. Oxford: Oxford University Press.

Heyd, Thomas (ed.) (2005). *Recognizing the Autonomy of Nature: Theory and Practice*. New York: Columbia University Press.

Hofrichter, Richard (ed.), (1993). *Toxic Struggles: The Theory and Practice of Environmental Justice*. Philadelphia, PA: New Society.

Holland, Breena (2004). 'Capabilities Theory and Environmental Value: Linking Human Capacity to Environment Capacity', Paper given at the Western Political Science Association Annual Conference, Portland, OR.

Honig, Bonnie (1993). *Political Theory and the Displacement of Politics*. Ithaca, NY: Cornell University Press.

Honneth, Axel (1992). 'Integrity and Disrespect: Principles of Morality Based on the Theory of Recognition', *Political Theory*, 20(2): 187–201.

—— (1995). *The Struggle for Recognition: The Moral Grammar of Social Conflicts*. Cambridge, MA: MIT Press.

—— (2001). 'Recognition or Redistribution? Changing Perspectives on the Moral Order of Society', *Theory, Culture, and Society*, 18(2–3): 43–55.

Humphrey, Mathew (2003). 'Nonbasic Environmental Goods and Social Justice', in Daniel Bell and Avner de-Shalit (eds.), *Forms of Justice*. New York: Rowman and Littlefield

Hunold, Christian and Young, Iris Marion (1998). 'Justice, Democracy, and Hazardous Siting', *Political Studies*, 46(1): 82–95.

—— and John Dryzek (2002). 'Green Political Theory and the State: Context is Everything', *Global Environmental Politics*, 2(3): 17–39.

Indigenous Environmental Network (2001). *Statement on Energy and Climate Change*. Retrieved January 3, 2006, from http://www.justenergy.org/news/ienstatement.pdf

—— (n.d.). *Globalization*. Retrieved January 3, 2006, from http://www.ienearth.org/globalization.html

—— (n.d.). *EJ and Environmental Racism on an International Level*. Retrieved January 4, 2006, from http://www.ienearth.org/ienej_enviro.html

International Climate Justice Network (2002). *Bali Principles of Climate Justice*. Retrieved January 4, 2006, from http://www.corpwatch.org/article.php?id=3748

International Indigenous Peoples' Forum on Climate Change (2003). *Milan Declaration*. Retrieved January 4, 2006, from http://www.ienearth.org/climate_docs.html

James, William ([1909] 1977). *A Pluralistic Universe*, Cambridge, MA: Harvard University Press.

—— ([1896] 1979). *The Will to Believe and Other Essays in Popular Philosophy*, Cambridge, MA: Harvard University Press.

—— ([1912] 1976). *Essays in Radical Empiricism*, Cambridge, MA: Harvard University Press.

Johnson, Trebbe (1993). 'Native Intelligence', *Amicus Journal*, 14(4): 11–13.

Kahn, Richard and Kellner, Douglas (2004). 'New Media and Internet Activism: From the "Battle of Seattle" to Blogging', *New Media and Society*, 6(1): 87–95.

Katz, Cindi (2001). 'Vagabond Capitalism and the Necessity of Social Reproduction', *Antipode*, 33(4): 708–27.

Katz, Eric, Light, Andrew, and Rothenberg, David (2000). *Beneath the Surface: Critical Essays in the Philosophy of Deep Ecology*. Cambridge, MA: MIT Press.

Keck, Margaret E. and Sikkink, Kathryn (1998). *Activists Beyond Borders: Advocacy Networks in International Politics*. Ithaca, NY: Cornell University Press.

Kiefer, Chris and Benjamin, Medea (1993). 'Solidarity with the Third World: Building an International Environmental Justice Movement', in Richard Hofrichter (ed.), *Toxic Struggles: The Theory and Practice of Environmental Justice*, Philadelphia, PA: New Society.

Kimmerer, Robin Wall (2002). 'Weaving Traditional Ecological Knowledge Into Biological Education: A Call to Action', *BioScience*, 52(5): 432–8.

Klein, Naomi (2002). *Fences and Windows: Dispatches from the Front Lines of the Globalization Debate*. New York: Picador.

Kluger, Jeffrey (2006). 'Polar Ice Caps Are Melting Faster Than Ever . . . More And More Land Is Being Devastated By Drought . . . Rising Waters Are Drowning Low-Lying Communities . . . By Any Measure, Earth Is At . . . The Tipping Point', *Time* Cover Story, April 3.

Krauss, Celene (1994). 'Women of Color on the Front Line', in Robert Bullard (ed.), *Unequal Protection: Environmental Justice and Communities of Color*. San Francisco, CA: Sierra Club Books.

Kuletz, Valerie (1998). *The Tainted Desert: Environmental and Social Ruin in the American West*. London: Routledge.

Kymlicka, Will (1989). *Liberalism, Community, and Culture*. Oxford: Oxford University Press.

—— (1995). *Multicultural Citizenship*. Oxford: Oxford University Press.

—— (2001). *Politics in the Vernacular*. Oxford: Oxford University Press.

LaDuke, Winona (2002). *The Winona LaDuke Reader*. Stillwater, MN: Voyageur Press.

Lake, Robert W. (1996). 'Volunteers, Nimbys, and Environmental Justice: Dilemmas of Democratic Practice', *Antipode*, 28(2): 160–74.

Lash, Scott and Featherstone, Mike (2001). 'Recognition and difference: Politics, Identity, Multiculture', *Theory, Culture, and Society*, 18(2–3): 1–19.

Latour, Bruno (2004). *Politics of Nature: How to Bring the Sciences Into Democracy*. Cambridge, MA: Harvard University Press.

Lavelle, Marianne and Coyle, Marcia (1992). 'Unequal Protection: The Racial Divide in Environmental Law', *The National Law Journal*, 15(3): S2.

Lee, Charles (ed.) (1992). *Proceedings: The First National People of Color Environmental Leadership Summit*. New York: United Church of Christ Commission for Racial Justice.

____ (1993). 'Beyond Toxic Wastes and Race', in Robert Bullard (ed.), *Confronting Environmental Racism: Voices from the Grassroots*. Boston, MA: South End Press.

____ (2005). 'Collaborative Models to Achieve Environmental Justice and Healthy Communities', in David N. Pellow and Robert J. Brulle (eds.), *Power, Justice, and the Environment: A Critical Appraisal of the Environmental Justice Movement*. Cambridge, MA: MIT Press.

Leopold, Aldo (1949). *A Sand County Almanac*. Oxford: Oxford University Press.

Lester, James, and Allen, David (1999). 'Environmental Justice in the U.S.: Myths and Realities', Paper given at the Western Political Science Association annual meeting, Seattle, WA.

Light, Andrew (2002). 'Restoring Ecological Citizenship', in Ben A. Minteer and Bob Pepperman Taylor (eds.), *Democracy and the Claims of Nature*. Lanham, MD: Rowman and Littlefield.

____ (2003). 'The Case for a Practical Pluralism', in Andrew Light and Holmes Rolston III (eds.), *Environmental Ethics: An Anthology*. Oxford: Blackwell.

____ and Katz, Eric (1996). *Environmental Pragmatism*. New York: Routledge.

Lipschutz, Ronnie (1992). 'Restructuring World Politics: The Emergence of Global Civil Society', *Millennium*, 21(3).

Low, Nicholas and Gleeson, Brendan (1998). *Justice, Society and Nature: An Exploration of Political Ecology*. London: Routledge.

Luke, Timothy (1997). *Ecocritique: Contesting the Politics of Nature, Economy, and Culture*, Minneapolis, MN: University of Minnesota Press.

Lyotard, Jean-François (1984). *The Postmodern Condition: A Report on Knowledge*. Minneapolis, MN: University of Minnesota Press.

McClure, Kirstie (1992). 'On the Subject of Rights: Pluralism, Plurality, and Political Identity', in Chantal Mouffe (ed.), *Dimensions of Radical Democracy*. London: Verso.

McGinnis, Michael V. (1999) 'Boundary Creatures and Bounded Spaces', in Michael V. McGinnis (ed.), *Bioregionalism*. New York: Routledge.

McKinley Jr., James C. (January 6, 2006). 'The Zapatista's Return: A Masked Marxist on the Stump', *New York Times*, p. A4.

Macnaghten, Phil and Urry, John (1998). *Contested Natures*. London: Sage.

Madison, Isaiah, Miller, Vernice, and Lee, Charles (1992). 'The Principles of Environmental Justice: Formation and Meaning', in Charles Lee (ed.), *Proceedings: The First National People of Color Environmental Leadership Summit.* New York: United Church of Christ Commission for Racial Justice.

Mander, Jerry and Goldsmith, Edward (eds.) (1996). *The Case Against the Global Economy, And For a Turn Toward the Local.* San Francisco, CA: Sierra Club Books.

Melluci, Alberto (1989). *Nomads of the Present.* Philadelphia, PA: Temple University Press.

Melosi, Martin V. (2004). *Garbage in the Cities: Refuse, Reform, and the Environment.* Pittsburgh, PA: University of Pittsburgh Press.

Michael DeLuca, Kevin (1999). 'The Possibilities of Nature in the Postmodern Age: The Rhetorical Tactics of Environmental Justice Groups', *Communication Theory,* 9(2): 189–215.

Miller, Ansje and Sisco, Cody (2002). 'Ten Actions of Climate Justice Policies', *Second National People of Color Environmental Leadership Summit—Summit II Resource Paper Series.* Environmental Justice and Climate Change Initiative. Retrieved June 1, 2006, from http://www.ejrc.cau.edu/summit2/SummIIClimateJustice%20.pdf

Miller, David (1999a). *Principles of Social Justice.* Cambridge, MA: Harvard University Press.

—— (1999b). 'Social Justice and Environmental Goods', in Andrew Dobson (ed.), *Fairness and Futurity: Essays on Environmental Sustainability and Social Justice.* Oxford: Oxford University Press.

—— (2003). 'A Response', in Daniel A. Bell and Avner de-Shalit (eds.), *Forms of Justice: Critical Perspectives on David Miller's Political Philosophy.* Lanham, MD: Rowman and Littlefield.

Mooney, Chris (2005). *The Republican War on Science.* New York: Basic Books.

Moore, James F. (2003). 'The Second Superpower Rears its Beautiful Head', Retrieved May 23, 2006 from http://cyber.law.harvard.edu/people/jmoore/secondsuperpower.html

Moore, Michael J. (2006). 'Why Immanence Makes Me Itch', Paper presented at the Western Political Association Meeting, Albuquerque, NM.

Mouffe, Chantal (1996). 'Democracy, Power, and the "Political",' in Seyla Benhabib (ed.), *Democracy and Difference: Contesting the Boundaries of the Political.* Princeton, NJ: Princeton University Press.

National Environmental Justice Advisory Committee, Indigenous Peoples Subcommittee (2000). *Guide on Consultation and Collaboration with Indian Tribal Governments and the Public Participation of Indigenous Groups and Tribal Members in Environmental Decision Making.* Retrieved December 27, 2005, from http://www.epa.gov/compliance/resources/publications/ej/nejac/ips_consultation_guide.pdf

—— (2004). *Meaningful Involvement and Fair Treatment by Tribal Environmental Regulatory Programs.* Retrieved December 27, 2005, from http://www.epa.gov/compliance/resources/publications/ej/nejac/ips-final-report.pdf

Norton, Bryan (1999). 'Ecology and Opportunity: Intergenerational Equity and Sustainability Options', in Andrew Dobson (ed.), *Fairness and Futurity: Essays on Environmental Sustainability and Social Justice*. Oxford: Oxford University Press.

Novotny, Patrick (1995). 'Where We Live, Work and Play: Reframing the Cultural Landscape of Environmentalism in the Environmental Justice Movement', *New Political Science*, 17(2): 61–79.

Nussbaum, Martha C. (2000). *Women and Human Development: The Capabilities Approach*. Oxford: Oxford University Press.

—— (2004). 'Beyond "Compassion and Humanity": Justice for Nonhuman Animals', in Cass R. Sunstein and Martha C. Nussbaum (eds.), *Animal Rights: Current Debates and New Directions*. Oxford: Oxford University Press.

—— (2006a). *Frontiers of Justice: Disability, Nationality, Species Membership*. Cambridge, MA: Harvard University Press.

—— (2006b). 'The Moral Status of Animals', *The Chronicle of Higher Education*, 52(22): B6–B8.

—— and Sen, Amartya (1992). *The Quality of Life*. Oxford: Oxford University Press.

Obiora, L. Amede (1999). 'Symbolic Episodes in the Quest for Environmental Justice', *Human Rights Quarterly*, 21(2): 464–512.

O'Leary, Rosemary and Bingham, Lisa B. (eds.) (2003). *The Promise and Performance of Environmental Conflict Resolution*. Washington, DC: Resources for the Future Press.

Oliver, Patsy Ruth (1994). 'Living on a Superfund Site in Texarkana', in Robert Bullard (ed.), *Unequal Protection: Environmental Justice and Communities of Color*. San Francisco, CA: Sierra Club Books.

Olson, Kevin (2001). 'Distributive Justice and the Politics of Difference', *Critical Horizons*, 2(1): 5–32.

Orton, Liz (2003). 'GM crops—going against the grain', *Southern African Regional Poverty Network*. Retrieved October 9, 2005, from http://www.sarpn.org.za/documents/d0000364/index.php

Oxfam, America (2005). *Rodolfo Pocop: An Indigenous Perspective on Mining in Guatemala*. Retrieved January 4, 2006, from http://www.oxfamamerica.org/whatwedo/where_we_work/camexca/news_publications/feature_story.2005-09-15.1253640764

Pace, David (2005). 'AP: More Blacks Live with Pollution', *Associated Press*, December 14. Retrieved May 13, 2006, from http://www.sfgate.com/cgi-bin/article.cgi?f=/n/a/2005/12/13/national/a093744S97.DTL&type=health

Paehlke, Robert (1989). *Environmentalism and the Future of Progressive Politics*. New Haven, CT: Yale University Press.

Page, Edward (2006). *Climate Change, Justice, and Future Generations*. Cheltenham: Edward Elgar.

Pardo, Mary (1990). 'Mexican American Women Grassroots Community Activists: "Mothers of East Los Angeles"' *Frontiers*, 11(1): 1–7.

Pasternak (2006, November 19–22). 'Blighted Homeland', *Los Angeles Times*. Retrieved 2 January 2006, from http://www.latimes.com/news/nationworld/nation/la-na-navajo-series,0,4515615.special

Pateman, Carole (1970). *Participation and Democratic Theory*. Cambridge: Cambridge University Press.

Pellow, David N. (2000). 'Environmental Inequality Formation: Toward a Theory of Environmental Injustice', *American Behavioral Scientist*, 43(4): 581–601.

_____ and Brulle, Robert J. (eds.) (2005). *Power, Justice, and the Environment: A Critical Appraisal of the Environmental Justice Movement*. Cambridge, MA: MIT Press.

Peña, Devon (ed.) (1998). *Chicano Culture, Ecology, Politics: Subversive Kin*. Tucson, AZ: University of Arizona Press.

_____ (1999). 'Nos Encercaron: A Theoretical Exegesis on the Politics of Place in the Intermountain West', Paper given at the New West Conference, Flagstaff, AZ, 1999.

_____ (2002). 'Endangered Landscapes and Disappearing Peoples? Identity, Place, and Community in Ecological Politics', in Joni Adamson, Mei Mei Evans, and Rachel Stein (eds.), *The Environmental Justice Reader: Politics, Poetics, and Pedagogy*. Tucson, AZ: University of Arizona Press.

_____ (2003). 'Identity, Place and Communities of Resistance', in Julian Agyeman, Robert D. Bullard, and Bob Evans (eds.), *Just Sustainabilities: Development in an Unequal World*. Cambridge, MA: MIT Press.

_____ (2005). 'Autonomy, Equity, and Environmental Justice', in David N. Pellow and Robert J. Brulle (eds.), *Power, Justice, and the Environment: A Critical Appraisal of the Environmental Justice Movement*. Cambridge, MA: MIT Press.

Peoples Global Action (1999). 'Draft Declaration of Indian People Against the WTO'. Retrieved 3 January 2006, from http://www.nadir.org/nadir/initiativ/agp/en/pgainfos/980516india.html

_____ (2005). *Call for Action against the Hong Kong WTO Ministerial Conference*. Retrieved January 4, 2006, from http://www.nadir.org/nadir/initiativ/agp/free/wto/hongkong2005/index.htm

Plumwood, Val (2002a). *Environmental Culture: The Ecological Crisis of Reason*. London: Routledge.

_____ (2002b). 'Environmental Justice', in *Encyclopedia of Life Support Systems* (EOLSS). Oxford: EOLSS.

Pogge, Thomas (2002). *World Poverty and Human Rights*. Cambridge: Polity Press.

Pressman, Steven and Gale, Summerfield (2002). 'Sen and Capabilities', *Review of Political Economy*, 14(4): 429–34.

Prindeville, Diane-Michele (2004). 'The Role of Gender, Race/Ethnicity, and Class in Activists' Perceptions of Environmental Justice', in Rachel Stein (ed.), *New Perspectives on Environmental Justice: Gender, Sexuality, and Activism*. New Brunswick, NJ: Rutgers University Press.

Public Citizen's Global Trade Watch (1999). 'Statement From Members of International Civil Society Opposing a Millennium Round or a New Round of Comprehensive Trade Negotiations', in *Mobilization Against Corporate Globalization: A Guide to Civil Society's Activities Surrounding the Seattle WTO Ministerial November 29–December 3, 1999,* Washington, DC: Public Citizen.

Pulido, Laura (1996). *Environmentalism and Social Justice: Two Chicano Struggles in the Southwest.* Tucson, AZ: University of Arizona Press.

Rawls, John (1971). *A Theory of Justice.* Oxford: Oxford University Press.

—— (1993). *Political Liberalism.* New York: Columbia University Press.

Raz, Joseph (1994). *Ethics in the Public Domain.* Oxford. Clarendon Press.

Redefining Progress (n.d.). *Projects: Ecological Footprint Analysis.* Retrieved March 2, 2006, from http://redefiningprogress.org/newprojects/ecolFoot.shtml

Redgwell, Catherine (1996). 'Life, the Universe, and Everything: A Critique of Anthropocentric Rights', in Alan E. Boyle and Michael R. Anderson (eds.), *Human Rights Approaches to Environmental Protection.* Oxford: Clarendon Press.

Regan, Tom (1983). *The Case for Animal Rights.* Berkeley, CA: University of California Press.

Reily, Sean Patrick (June 6, 2004). 'Gathering Clouds: Arizona's Navajo and Hopi Tribes Have Won a Water-Rights Battle against the Coal Company That Has Sustained Their Fragile Economies. But on the Threshold of Impending Victory, a Sobering Question: Now What?', *Los Angeles Time,* p. A1.

Rising Tide (2002). *Political Statement: Rising Tide coalition for Climate Justice.* Retrieved January 4, 2006, from http://www.risingtide.nl/statement/statement_english.html

—— (n.d.). *What is Rising Tide?* Retrieved January 4, 2006 http://risingtide.org.uk/about

—— and Thanos, Nikki Demetria (2003). *Trouble in Paradise: Globalization and Environmental Crisis in Latin America.* New York: Routledge.

Roberts, J. Timmons, and Toffolon-Weiss, Melissa M. (2001). *Chronicles from the Environmental Justice Frontline.* Cambridge: Cambridge University Press.

Robeyns, Ingrid (2003). 'Is Nancy Fraser's Critique of Theories of Justice Justified?', *Constellations,* 10(4): 538–53.

Rodman, John (1977). 'The Liberation of Nature?', *Inquiry,* 20(1): 83–145.

—— (1983). 'Four Forms of Ecological Consciousness Reconsidered', in Donald Scherer and Thomas Attig (eds.), *Ethics and the Environment.* Englewood Cliffs, NJ: Prentice-Hall.

Romero, Simon (October 14, 2003). 'It's Gas vs. Heritage in Navajo Country', *New York Times,* p. C1.

Routledge, Paul (2003). 'Convergence Space: Process Geographies of Grassroots Globalisation Networks', *Transactions of the Institute of British Geographers,* 28(3): 333–49.

—— (2005). 'Grassrooting the Imaginary: Acting within the Convergence', *Ephemera,* 5(4): 615–28.

Sagoff, Mark (1990). *Economy of the Earth: Philosophy, Law and the Environment.* Cambridge: Cambridge University Press.

_____ (1993) 'Animal Liberation, Environmental Ethics: Bad Marriage, Quick Divorce', in Michael Zimmerman (ed.), *Environmental Philosophy: From Animal Rights to Radical Ecology*. Englewood Cliffs, NJ: Prentice-Hall.

Sarawitz, Daniel (2004). 'How Science Makes Environmental Controversies Worse', *Environmental Science and Policy*, 7(5): 385–403.

Schlosberg, David (1997). 'Challenging Pluralism: Environmental Justice and the Evolution of Pluralist Practice', in Roger Gottlieb (ed.), *The Ecological Community: Environmental Challenges for Philosophy, Politics, and Morality*. London: Routledge.

_____ (1999a). 'Networks and Mobile Arrangements: Organizational Innovation in the U.S. Environmental Justice Movement', *Environmental Politics*, 6(1): 122–48.

_____ (1999b). *Environmental Justice and the New Pluralism: The Challenge of Difference for Environmentalism*. Oxford: Oxford University Press.

_____ (2003). 'The Justice of Environmental Justice: Reconciling Equity, Recognition, and Participation in a Political Movement', in Andrew Light and Avner de-Shalit (eds.), *Moral and Political Reasoning in Environmental Practice*. Cambridge, MA: MIT Press.

_____ (2004). 'Reconceiving Environmental Justice: Global Movements and Political Theories', *Environmental Politics*, 13(3): 517–40.

_____ and Dryzek, John (2002). 'Political Strategies of American Environmentalism: Inclusion and Beyond', *Society and Natural Resources*, 15(9): 787–804.

_____ Shulman, Stuart W. and Zavestoski, Stephen (2005). 'Virtual Environmental Citizenship: Web-Based Public Participation on Environmental Rulemaking in the U.S.', in Andy Dobson and Derek Bell (eds.), *Environmental Citizenship: Getting from Here to There*. Cambridge, MA: MIT Press.

_____ Shulman, Stuart and Zavestoski, Stephen (forthcoming, 2006). 'Deliberation in E-Rulemaking? The Problem of Mass Participation', in Todd Davies and Beth Noveck (eds.), *Online Deliberation*. Chicago, IL: Chicago University Press.

Sen, Amartya (1985). 'Well-Being, Agency and Freedom: The Dewey Lectures 1984', *The Journal of Philosophy*, 82(4): 169–221.

_____ (1992). 'Capability and Well-Being', in Martha Nussbaum and Amartya Sen (eds.), *The Quality of Life*. Oxford: Clarendon Press.

_____ (1999a). *Commodities and Capabilities*. Oxford: Oxford University Press.

_____ (1999b). *Development as Freedom*. New York: Anchor.

_____ (August 15, 2002) 'What Can Johannesburg Achieve?', *New York Times*.

_____ (2004). 'Why We Should Preserve the Spotted Owl', *London Review of Books*, 26(3) (February 5). Accessed online at http://www.lrb.o.uk/v26/n03/print/sen_01_.html

_____ (2005). 'Human Rights and Capabilities', *Journal of Human Development*, 6(2): 151–66.

Seuss, Dr. (Theodor Geisel) (1971). *The Lorax*. New York: Random House.

Shane, Peter (ed.) (2004). *Democracy Online: The Prospects for Political Renewal Through the Internet*. New York: Routledge.

Shepard, Peggy M., Northridge, Mary E., Prakash, Swati, and Stover, Gabriel (2002). 'Advancing Environmental Justice Through Community-Based Participatory Research', *Environmental Health Perspectives Supplements*, 110(S2): 139–40.

Shiva, Vandana (1997). *Biopiracy: The Plunder of Nature and Knowledge*. Boston, MA: South End Press.

—— (2000). *Stolen Harvest: The Hijacking of the Global Food Supply*. Boston, MA: South End Press.

Shrader-Frechette, Kristin (2002). *Environmental Justice: Creating Equality, Reclaiming Democracy*. Oxford: Oxford University Press.

Shulman, Stuart W. (2003). 'An Experiment in Digital Government at the United States National Organic Program', *Agriculture and Human Values*, 20(3): 253–65.

—— (2004). 'Whither Deliberation? Mass e-Mail Campaigns and U.S. Regulatory Rulemaking', http://erulemaking.ucsur.pitt.edu/doc/papers/Smarttape12.04.pdf [last accessed April 11, 2005.]

Singer, Peter (1975). *Animal Liberation*. New York: Random House.

Smith, Graham (2003). *Deliberative Democracy and the Environment*. London: Routledge.

Smith, Roy (2003). 'Place and Chips: Virtual Communities, Governance, and the Environment', *Global Environmental Politics*, 3(2): 88–102.

Soper, Kate (1995). *What Is Nature?* Oxford: Blackwell.

Southwest Organizing Project (SWOP) (1995). *Intel Inside New Mexico: A Case Study of Environmental and Economic Injustice*. Albuquerque: SWOP.

Starkey, Deb (1994). 'Environmental Justice', *State Legislature*, 20(3): 27–31.

Stein, Rachel (ed.) (2004). *New Perspectives on Environmental Justice: Gender, Sexuality, and Activism*. New Brunswick, NJ: Rutgers University Press.

Stewart, Frances (2005). 'Groups and Capabilities', *Journal of Human Development*, 6(2):185–204.

Stone, Christopher (1974). *Should Trees Have Standing? Towards Legal Rights for Natural Objects*. Los Altos, CA: Kaufman.

Sunstein, Cass R. (2001). *Republic.com*. Princeton, NJ: Princeton University Press.

Szasz, Andrew (1994). *EcoPopulism: Toxic Waste and the Movement for Environmental Justice*. Minneapolis, MN: University of Minnesota Press.

—— and Meuser, Michael (1997). 'Environmental Inequalities: Literature Review and Proposals for New Directions in Research and Theory', *Current Sociology*, 45(3): 99–120.

Sze, Julie (2004). 'Gender, Asthma Politics, and Urban Environmental Justice Activism', in Rachel Stein (ed.), *New Perspectives on Environmental Justice*. New Brunswick, NJ: Rutgers University Press.

Talshir, Gayil (2001). 'Ecological Sustainability: A Private Case of Social Justice?', in John Barry and Marcel Wissenburg (eds.), *Sustaining Liberal Democracy: Ecological Challenges and Opportunities*. New York: Palgrave.

Taylor, Charles (1994). *Multiculturalism*. Amy Gutman (ed.), Princeton, NJ: Princeton University Press.

Taylor, Dorceta (1993). 'Environmentalism and the Politics of Exclusion', in Robert Bullard (ed.), *Confronting Environmental Racism: Voices from the Grassroots*, Boston, MA: South End Press.

—— (2000). 'The Rise of the Environmental Justice Paradigm: Injustice Framing and the Social Construction of Environmental Discourses', *American Behavioral Scientist*, 43(4): 508–80.

Taylor, Paul (1986). *Respect for Nature: A Theory of Environmental Ethics*. Princeton, NJ: Princeton University Press.

Tesh, Sylvia and Williams, Bruce (1996). 'Identity Politics, Disinterested Politics, and Environmental Justice', *Polity*, 18(3): 285–305.

Torgerson, Douglas (1999). *The Promise of Green Politics: Environmentalism and the Public Sphere*. Durham, NC: Duke University Press.

—— (2000). 'Farewell to the Green Movement? Political Action and the Green Public Sphere', *Environmental Politics*, 9(4): 1–19.

Tully, James (1995). *Strange Multiplicity: Constitutionalism in an Age of Diversity*. Cambridge: Cambridge University Press.

Tyler, Patrick E. (2003). 'Threats and Responses: News Analysis: A New Power in the Streets', *New York Times*, February 17: 1.

United Church of Christ Commission for Racial Justice (1987). *Toxic Wastes and Race in the United States: A National Report on the Racial and Socio-Economic Characteristics of Communities with Hazardous Waste Sites*. New York: United Church of Christ.

United Nations Development Programme (UNDP) (2005). *Human Development Report 2005*. Retrieved June 1, 2006, from http://hdr.undp.org/reports/global/2005/

UNESCO (2005). *Local & Indigenous Knowledge of the Natural World: An Overview of Programmes and Projects*. Retrieved May 13, 2006, from http://www.un.org/esa/socdev/unpfii/documents/TK_Paper_UNESCO_English.pdf

United States Environmental Protection Agency (1992). *Environmental Equity: Reducing Risk for All Communities*. Washington, DC: Government Printing Office.

—— (1996). *The Model Plan for Public Participation*, Washington, DC: EPA Office of Environmental Justice EPA-300-K-96-003.

—— (2000*a*). *Environmental Justice in the Permitting Process*. Washington, DC: EPA Office of Environmental Justice. EPA-300-R-00-004.

—— (2000*b*). *The Model Plan for Public Participation*, Washington, DC: EPA Office of Environmental Justice EPA-300-K-00-001.

United States General Accounting Office (1983). *Siting of Hazardous Waste Landfills and Their Correlation with Racial and Economic Status of Surrounding Communities*. Washington, DC: Government Printing Office.

US Network for Global Economic Justice (n.d.). *Network Platform and Demands to the IMF and World Bank*. Retrieved January 3, 2006, from http://www.50years.org/about

van de Veer, Donald (1979). 'Of Beasts, Persons, and the Original Position', *The Monist*, 62(3): 368–77.

Wackernagel, Mathis and Rees, William (1996). *Our Ecological Footprint*. Philadelphia, PA: New Society.

Walzer, Michael (1983). *Spheres of Justice*. Oxford: Blackwell.

Wapner, Paul (1996). *Environmental Activism and World Civic Politics*. Albany, NY: SUNY Press.

Warren, Mary Anne (1997). *Moral Status: Obligations to Persons and Other Living Things*. Oxford: Oxford University Press.

WCED (1987). *Our Common Future*. Oxford: Oxford University Press.

Weaver, Jace (ed.) (1996). *Defending Mother Earth: Native American Perspectives on Environmental Justice*. Maryknoll, NY: Orbis Books.

Wenz, Peter S. (1988). *Environmental Justice*. Albany, NY: SUNY Press.

Westra, Laura and Bill E. Lawson (2001). *Faces of Environmental Racism: Confronting Issues of Global Justice*. New York: Rowman and Littlefield.

Willett, Cynthia (ed.) (1998). *Theorizing Multiculturalism: A Guide to the Current Debate*. Oxford: Blackwell.

Wissenburg, Marcel (1993). 'The Idea of Nature and the Nature of Distributive Justice', in Andrew Dobson and Paul Lucardie (eds.), *The Politics of Nature: Explorations in Green Political Theory*. London: Routledge.

—— (1998). *Green Liberalism: The Free and Green Society*. London: UCL Press.

—— (2001). 'Sustainability and the Limits of Liberalism', in John Barry and Marcel Wissenburg (eds.), *Sustaining Liberal Democracy: Ecological Challenges and Opportunities*. New York: Palgrave.

Witschge, Tamara (2004). 'Online Deliberation: Possibilities of the Internet for Deliberative Democracy', in Peter Shane (ed.), *Democracy Online: The Prospects for Political Renewal Through the Internet*. New York: Routledge.

Wright, Beverly (1995). 'Environmental Equity Justice Centers: A Response to Inequity', in Bunyan Bryant (ed.), *Environmental Justice: Issues, Policies, Solutions*. Washington, DC: Island Press.

Young, Iris (1990). *Justice and the Politics of Difference*. Princeton, NJ: Princeton University Press.

—— (1996). 'Communication and the Other', in Seyla Benhabib (ed.), *Democracy and Difference: Contesting the Boundaries of the Political*. Princeton, NJ: Princeton University Press.

—— (2000). *Inclusion and Democracy*. Oxford: Oxford University Press.

Index

233